Staining and Wood Polishing

Charles H. Hayward

A Drake Publication
Sterling Publishing Co., Inc. New York

Published in 1979 by
Sterling Publishing Co., Inc.
Two Park Avenue
New York, N.Y. 10016

Printed in U.S.A.
ISBN: 0-8069-8684-0

Previously
ISBN: 87749-0007-4

CONTENTS

v

HOW TO USE THIS BOOK

WHEN you have completed a piece of work you have to decide on the kind of finish you propose to give it: whether it is to be stained or left natural colour; whether the grain is to be filled in, and what sort of polish is to be applied. Chapter 1 will help you to decide on what is most suitable for it, and you may have your own ideas about what you want. Possibly you want to match the finish of some existing piece of furniture, or maybe you have seen a finish which you have liked and want to reproduce.

Turn to the Chapter which most nearly meets your case. It may be a case of looking under the wood of which the work is made, or referring to the special finish you have in mind. Here you will find the treatment described briefly, this telling you what stains to use, whether or not to fill in the grain, the most suitable kind of polish, and any special details to be introduced. You then pass to the relevant parts of the general Chapters on *Staining, Filling in the Grain,* and *Polishing* where these processes are described in detail.

As an example, suppose you have made a walnut cabinet and wish it to be a fairly dark tone with a perfectly flat surface, fully french polished. Turn to the Chapter on polishing walnut and you will see what stain to use, the filler to use, the polish recommended, and any special details that may be peculiar to walnut. Then by reading through the general Chapters on staining and polishing you can embody the special notes in the full description there given.

The same principle applies to, say, a job to be ebonised. Turn to the Chapter on the special treatment required for the work and you will find the materials required and the process described in brief. When you afterwards read the general Chapters on staining and polishing it is merely a matter of adapting the instructions to suit the ebonising process.

The point is that the general principles of polishing hold good for all woods and finishes. It is only in detail that they vary. The preparation of the wood is the same in all cases (except that sometimes oak is not glasspapered; see notes under oak).

A word of warning. If you have never done any french polishing before, do not make a start on your best piece of work.

This book will tell you what to do, but it is only personal experience that will enable you to make a success of your work. In other words, you have to acquire the knack. Take some oddments of wood and experiment on these. Prepare them properly and go through all the stages outlined in these pages. It may seem unnecessary at the time, but it may save much heart-burning later on.

STAINING AND POLISHING

CHAPTER I: FINISHES FOR FURNITURE

THERE are many ways of finishing furniture and other woodwork, and choice is partly a matter of selection in accordance with the characteristics of the work, partly a case of personal preference, and partly it is governed by your own skill and the facilities available. The four chief finishes to-day are :

WAXING, FRENCH POLISHING, CELLULOSING, VARNISHING

Each has its own special advantages and limitations, and these should be considered before a choice is made. There are other finishes occasionally used, such as oil polishing; and there are special treatments such as ebonising, liming, and so on, but these are really nothing more than variations of one of the chief finishes already mentioned. In the same way certain woods may call for special treatment, but this is just a matter of detail, the general procedure of polishing being much the same in all cases. In this book, therefore, we have adopted the plan of giving each main process in its various stages, and then following with its application for certain woods and special finishes.

So far as the preparation of the work is concerned, this applies no matter what finish is to be given. The same thing is largely true of staining (though occasionally certain precautions are necessary, as will be seen). The instructions given under these two headings can therefore be followed in all cases. Where there are any variations they are noted.

Let us now consider briefly the four finishes mentioned.

Waxing. Originally this was a widely used finish, but fell into disfavour when french polish was introduced during the nineteenth century, though it was still retained as a household polish. To-day its use has been revived considerably, probably as a reaction against the overdone use of french polish. It has the effect of slightly darkening the wood, but, apart from this, there is no objectional tinge given to the wood. It gives a most attractive eggshell gloss, and it is very simple to apply. Furthermore, the polish can be renewed at any time. The more often it is rubbed the better the shine. On the other hand it does not keep out dirt specially well, so that a surface which comes in for considerable handling is liable to become marked rapidly.

French polishing. This is still a most popular finish, especially amongst home craftsmen, though in the trade it has been largely superseded by cellulosing. It seals the grain and is thus of considerable value in preventing movement due to moisture absorption; it wears well; and it keeps out the dirt. The latter cannot work into the grain because this is filled in. A wipe with a damp rag usually removes any surface dirt. It will take on an extremely high lustre in the hands of a capable man, and a perfectly satisfactory gloss can be obtained by a less experienced worker.

As against this it is considerably more difficult to apply than wax— in fact, a sound piece of woodwork can be completely ruined by unskilled french polishing. Then, again, a false and objectionable tone can be imparted to the work as a result of the use of the wrong kind of polish. Consider the bird's-eye maple furniture so popular during the Victorian period. How many people realise that the natural colour of this beautiful wood is very light—almost white? Yet when it left the hands of the Victorian polisher it was a dark yellow tone, and it is with this colour that nearly everyone associates bird's-eye maple. This is perhaps an extreme case. French polish can, of course, be perfectly successful as a finish.

Cellulosing. It is only in recent years that this has been applied to furniture. It is capable of a wide variety of effects, from a super-gloss to an eggshell finish; and it is durable. It keeps out dirt, and is highly resistant to water and heat, so that it is ideal for parts liable to be exposed to these. At the same time it calls for a certain amount of apparatus. For the most part it has to be sprayed and few home craftsmen have either the apparatus or the facilities for this. In the trade, of course, it is widely used because it is applied more quickly, does not call for so high a standard of skill, and gives a hard-wearing, durable finish.

Varnishing. This is more usually associated with the woodwork of the house—fitments, etc., than with furniture. Given a high-quality varnish, however, and a skilled worker, a fine result can be obtained. Some men regard it as superior to french polish. It seals the grain well, keeps out dirt, and wears well, and, providing a suitable kind is used, will not discolour the wood. Between this first-class finish and the treacly, sticky effort of the inexperienced are a whole series of finishes, ranging from one extreme to the other; and it is to be admitted that, if varnish really well applied is attractive, there is nothing more deplorable than a badly varnished surface. It is probably for this reason that it is generally restricted to fitments so far as the home craftsman is concerned.

Oil polishing. This is not included in the finishes listed above because it is so seldom used nowadays. It is mentioned here, however, because it has the great advantage of being mark-proof against hot plates and water, and this means that it is of great value for table tops and similar parts. It is easy to apply, but it takes a long time to build up a shine, and it is probably this that has caused it to drop into disfavour. It gives a bright eggshell finish which is quite permanent, and can be renewed at any time.

Catalyst finishes. These are the latest addition to the range of wood finishes, and consist of a liquid plastic to which a catalyst or hardener is added immediately before use. Once the catalyst is added the polish remains usable for only a limited time, after which it hardens and becomes useless. Advantages claimed for it are that it is heat and spirit proof, making it specially suitable for table tops. Several proprietary makes are available.

Staining. It will be realised from the foregoing that a piece of work may be either stained or left unstained regardless of the polish to be applied. Also that the grain may or may not be filled in according to circumstances. It follows then that the main colouring is given by the stain (or its absence), the polish having the effect mainly of providing the gloss and of sealing the grain. It is true that all polishes tend to darken the wood, and that a certain amount of toning can be given by using dark or light polishes or by introducing colouring matter into it. But it is in the preliminary staining that the basic tone is given.

The reason is fairly clear. Stains tone the grain but do not hide it, whereas coloured polishes are necessarily partially opaque, and this is bound to hide the grain. Remember that the finish should bring out the beauty of the wood, not hide it. As in all things, there are exceptions, and perhaps the most obvious is that of ebonising, when the intense blackness can only be produced by using a black polish. Even here, however, a preliminary black stain is essential.

CHAPTER II: PREPARING THE WOOD

TO produce a good finish the wood *must* be properly cleaned-up first. No matter what skill is used in polishing, the result will be a failure if the wood is not accurately and thoroughly prepared. Remember that, far from hiding blemishes, polish serves to magnify them. It is rather like a faulty mirror or sheet of glass. You know how the imperfections are at once obvious, causing reflections to be distorted. It is due to the glass not being flat; and exactly the same thing applies to polished wood. If the latter is not flat it will be at once noticeable. Plane marks, rounded edges, bruises, and so on advertise with alarming clarity the worker's lack of skill or patience.

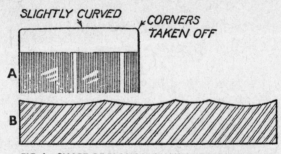

FIG. I. SHAPE OF PLANE IRON WHEN CLEANING UP.

The cutting edge should be *slightly* curved and have the corners rubbed off. If the edge is too rounded the resulting surface will have a series of hollows as at B.

It is assumed that the surfaces and edges are true; that is, straight and square. This, of course, is a matter belonging rather to the constructional side of woodwork. In other words, it is taken that the trying-plane has been used so that a surface meant to be flat really is at least approximately so. It may, and probably does, show plane marks, tears in the grain (pronounced " tares "), and other small imperfections, but these are minor blemishes which the cleaning-up will correct. In fact it is to remove these that the cleaning-up process is undertaken.

Planing. The smoothing-plane is used for cleaning, and its cutter should be given a super-keen edge. Finish off on a fine stone, and remove the burr by stropping on a piece of leather dressed with the finest emery powder and oil. The edge should be almost straight as at A, Fig. 1—a very slight curve does no harm—and the corners should be taken off to prevent any possibility of digging in. If the edge is too round the wood will show a series of hollows as shown in exaggeration at B, Fig. 1.

Set the back iron as close as you can to the cutting edge, especially when dealing with tricky grain which is liable to tear out. This reduces tearing to a minimum. Give the cutter a minimum projection, and, if the mouth is adjustable, set this fine. You are now ready to go over the surface. The purpose of the operation is to remove marks made by the trying-plane, and, in doing so, to avoid tearing out the grain as far as possible. It will be realised that the

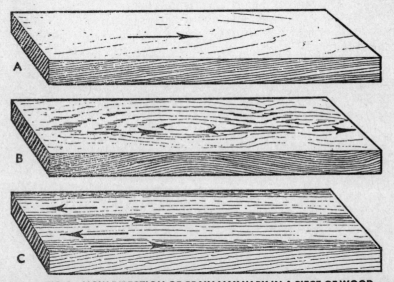

FIG. 2.   HOW DIRECTION OF GRAIN MAY VARY IN A PIECE OF WOOD.

At A the direction in which to plane is obvious. At B the grain undulates so that tearing out is inevitable whichever way the plane is worked. The same thing applies to C, in which the grain runs in alternate directions in streaks side by side. Tears are pronounced "tares".

trying-plane cannot have its back iron set too fine, because it would offer too much resistance.

Difficult grain. Some woods plane better in one direction than in the other, and you can generally tell this by examining the edge. At A, Fig. 2, for instance, it is clear that the planing should be in the direction of the arrow. Working the other way would inevitably cause the grain to tear out. In other woods the grain undulates as at B, so that the planing will be *with* the grain in parts and *against* it in others. Here the best plan is to go over the whole surface in one direction, then reverse the wood and plane locally the torn-out parts. Even so a certain amount of tearing is inevitable.

Another kind of wood has the grain running in streaks so that tearing out is inevitable whichever way it is planed. C, Fig. 2, is an example. The streaks may be anything from about $\frac{1}{8}$ in. up to some 1 in. wide, and it follows that any shaving may have half a dozen or more streaks in it, so that when planed in one direction every other streak will tear. When planed the other way these will become smooth whilst the others tear out. The only plan is to set the plane as fine as possible and just plane in the direction which seems to give least tearing.

What tears are. In this chapter we hear a lot about tearing out and we may just consider what tears are. Look at Fig. 3, which shows a section of wood being planed against the grain. The latter runs at a slope, and as the shaving is raised by the cutter, it endeavours to split along the grain in advance of the cutting edge. The split

FIG. 3.   HOW TEARS IN GRAIN ARE FORMED.
The grain runs down so that the shaving is torn up in steps.
The drawing shows the appearance of the tears on the
surface.

develops a short way, when it is caught up again by the cutter, broken, and a fresh cycle of events started. The surface thus presents a series of sloping steps as shown. The closer the back iron is set the smaller the " steps," because the shaving is broken almost as soon as it is raised. This robs it of its strength and prevents the split from developing. A fine mouth also helps because it stops the shaving from lifting far in advance of the cutting edge.

Scraping. Even with the most finely set plane, marks due to the shape of the cutter are inevitable. The purpose of the next operation, scraping, is to remove these and to take out tears created by the planing. Go over the whole surface regardless of whether there are any tears or not, taking special care at the edges. It is a little awkward to start the scraper at the near end of the wood, and the only way is to hold it askew so that part of it rests upon the wood.

In the case of difficult woods of the kind shown at C, Fig. 2, the best plan is to work over the whole surface in one direction, reverse the wood, and work the other way. Even so some woods are very difficult, especially those of a woolly texture. It is frequently a matter of coaxing out by individual attention to each tear.

It should be remembered that tears show as imperfections whatever the finish. On an unfilled surface they are easily visible, and when the grain *is* filled it means that all the tears are filled, so that the surface shows almost as much filling as real wood. This robs the wood of its beauty, and is a source of danger in that the filling may absorb too much oil, and this may cause sweating at a later date.

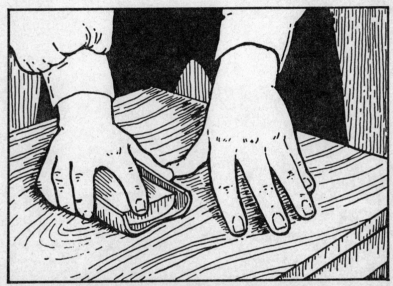

FIG. 4. USING THE CORK GLASSPAPER RUBBER WHEN CLEANING UP.
The cork gives to small inequalities in the surface. If glasspaper is held in the hand the edges are liable to be dubbed over.

Glasspaper. You should now have reached the stage when the surface is free from both plane marks and tears, and there are only the minor imperfections left by the scraper. These are removed with glasspaper. The latter is wrapped around a flat cork rubber, this preventing the edges and corners from being dubbed over, and ensuring a still further levelling effect by rubbing harder on the high portions than the low parts.

For the usual run of woods start with middle 2 grade, giving a thorough scouring *with* the grain. Do not be satisfied with a single rub over every part. Go over several times using plenty of pressure as in Fig. 4. Follow with No. 1½ grade, repeating the process, and finally use No. 1 grade.   This will give a satisfactory result for most woods.   Soft woods such as deal need nothing finer than No. 1½ grade.   Incidentally these soft woods cannot be scraped successfully as there is too much give in them.   Glasspapering follows directly after planing.

When oak is to be french polished it receives the treatment just outlined, but when it is to be left " natural " or to be waxed, many workers prefer to use no glasspaper at all, leaving the work straight from the scraper.

In the case of very light woods, such as satinwood, avoid using

FIG. 5.   CLEANING UP MOULDING WITH SHAPED WOOD RUBBER.

The use of a rubber prevents the corners from being dulled over.   It is advisable to damp the moulding first and allow it to dry before cleaning up.   It prevents the grain from rising when stain is applied.

glasspaper which has previously been used for a dark wood.   It will cause dust from the latter to be forced into the grain, producing a dirty appearance.

Veneered work.   Veneered surfaces cannot be planed; they must be scraped and then glasspapered.   The important point is to make sure that all glue is removed from the surface, as this would prevent stain from taking properly.   Take care not to scrape too vigorously locally or you may go right through to the groundwork beneath.

Some veneers have no definite directions to the grain.   Burr walnut is an example.   When finishing this use nothing coarser than No. 1 glasspaper, and rub with a circular movement. Follow with *flour* grade, again rubbing in circles. Quartered panels and other built-up designs also have the grain running in various directions, and the only plan here is to rub the long way of the panel, finishing with flour grade paper so that the scratches made by the glasspaper are very fine.

Machined surfaces. Wood which has been machine planed should always be damped with hot water before being finally cleaned, even though it has been machine glasspapered. The reason is that the machine cutter is under a certain pressure, and this is transmitted to the wood as it cuts. If the work is stained the moisture releases the stress and the wood swells, leaving a number of fine ridges across the surface. This is very noticeable if the plane cutter should have a gash in it. The ridge thus created may be planed and glasspapered away, but when stained it will immediately become visible again. By damping the wood with hot water these marks are raised and they can then be cleaned away. Any subsequent damping with stain will cause no further harm.

Mouldings. If machine-made these must be damped with hot water as just described for machine surfaces. Otherwise when stained they will become horribly rough and show bad machine marks. Incidentally, remember to use specially shaped rubbers for glasspapering mouldings, as in Fig. 5.

When mouldings have to be mitred it is always an advantage where practicable to stain and partly polish them first. Corners are always the most difficult part of polishing, and by polishing mouldings in long strips and mitreing round afterwards a lot of awkward work is avoided. A typical example of where this is an advantage is in the latticed or barred door of a bookcase or china cabinet. It is much easier to polish the mouldings in long lengths and mitre and fix afterwards.

STOPPING

Plastic wood. Nails are best avoided on the show parts of cabinet work, but they cannot always be helped. They should be punched in and the holes stopped. A popular stopping to-day is plastic wood, normally obtainable in tubes. It is pressed into the hole, left to harden, and levelled. As it shrinks whilst drying out it is essential that it is made to heap up slightly and allowed to dry thoroughly before being levelled, otherwise it will pull below the surface. In the case of a deep, wide hole, the stopping should be built up gradually, otherwise the centre will remain soft. Either natural or coloured stoppings can be obtained. One great advantage this stopping carries is that stains of all kinds will take over it. This means that the stopping should match as near as possible the colour of the bare wood.

Beaumontage. Another good home-made stopping is beaumontage, a mixture of equal parts of beeswax and crushed resin and one or two flakes of shellac. It is heated in a tin, thoroughly mixed, and poured into the corner of a tin box lid, where it will set hard like a stick of sealing wax. Before completely hardening, it can be rolled in the palms of the hands. To use it heat the end of a pointed rod of metal, and hold it over the nail hole. Place the stick of stopping against the metal. It will melt and run down into the hole. Allow it to stand up slightly and level when cold with a wet chisel. Finally rub down with glasspaper. Do not rub too vigorously or the heat generated may melt the stopping. Fig. 6 shows the stopping being applied.

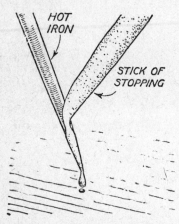

FIG. 6. USE OF STOPPING.
A hot rod is held against the stick of stopping so that the latter melts and runs.

Stopping can be made in either natural colour or it can be coloured with powdered colours to match the wood. Remember that it is the colour of the wood *after* staining that has to be matched, because this stopping will not absorb stain. For reddish woods like mahogany use red ochre or venetian red; for oak to be stained dark, vandyke brown or burnt umber are suitable. You will soon collect a series of stoppings of various colours. Sealing wax makes a good stopping if a suitable colour can be obtained.

Ready-made stoppings in coloured sticks to be melted in can be obtained; also soft stoppings which have only to be pressed in and left to harden.

Larger holes if filled with stopping should be scored with an awl to give a grip. If shallow it will be necessary to deepen the depression somewhat, as otherwise the stopping may drop out. Putty should not be used as a stopping except for unimportant work. It takes a very long time to become really hard, and, even if this is not regarded as an objection in itself, it means that it will probably shrink below the surface a long time after polishing. Another point is that it will not take stain. Putty is really suitable for painted work only.

Polisher's putty. For light woods a good stopping can be made from dried whiting mixed with white polish to the consistency of putty. It is worked into the defect with a knife or pointed stick. It dries in about half an hour, when it can be levelled with chisel and glasspaper. Allow as long as possible to harden to avoid sinking. One advantage of this stopping is that spirit stain will take over it.

Cheap stopping. For unimportant work—shelves, fitments, and so on, a quite good stopping can be made from plaster of paris and glue size. It sets fairly quickly, and will absorb a water stain.

Heel ball. At a pinch you can use this. Either run it into the defect with a hot iron, or melt it in a tin and apply with a pointed match-stick.

Bruises. If a bruise is not too deep you can frequently take it out with a hot iron and damp rag. Place the latter over the place and rub the iron locally over it. This will cause the fibres to swell and may take out the bruise.

Grease and glue. It is most important that all traces of these are removed before any finish is begun. They may prevent stain from taking properly, and in the case of chemical staining or fuming may result in light patches being left. The normal cleaning-up process normally removes glue, but examine the surface closely, especially round tenoned joints which are set in and cannot therefore be planed afterwards. Look over veneer closely also. Grease does not often occur, but is sometimes found when a job has been set aside for a long while. If in doubt glasspaper afresh. In mechanical parts such as drawers, slides, rule joints, and so on do not apply any lubricant until after staining and polishing.

Final preparations. The most difficult parts of work to polish are internal corners and angles. It is always policy therefore to reduce them as far as possible, partly by arranging to apply mouldings and other parts after polishing (whenever this is feasible), and by making the job in separate parts so that they can be polished individually and assembled afterwards. With the same idea in mind, take the job to pieces as far as is practicable. Pull out drawers, unscrew doors, take off tops and edgings, and remove all fittings so that the rubber has a clear, unrestricted path.

In some cases stain must be used before assembling. Take, for instance, a panelled door or back with solid panels. The edge of the panel *with* the grain should be stained before gluing up, so that in the event of shrinkage the panel will not show white where it pulls out of the grooves. Actually it would be an advantage to stain and polish the whole panel before gluing up, but this is not always practicable. It is unnecessary in the case of work to be waxed because the polish can be scrubbed into the corners without difficulty.

CHAPTER III : STAINING

KINDS OF STAINS

ALTHOUGH furniture is sometimes polished without any preliminary staining, it is usually advisable for work which is to be french polished. It ensures the whole thing being of even tone, especially when different varieties of the same wood have been used; it helps to bring out the full beauty of the grain; and it darkens the work to a shade which will wear better in use than the light natural colour.

Staining differs from painting in that it does not conceal the grain. Its purpose is to darken the tone, whereas paint forms an opaque and entirely new surface.

Kinds of stain. There are several ways of staining wood, and we give here the chief methods. We can then consider the merits of each.

Water Stains.	*Wax Stains.*
Oil Stains.	*Varnish Stains.*
Spirit Stains.	*Water Coating.*
Chemical Stains.	
Fuming.	

Of these only those in the left-hand column need be considered seriously for normal furniture polishing. Those in the right-hand column come in occasionally for special work and are dealt with later, but they are generally unsuitable for work which is later to be polished.

Apart from the special materials such as bichromate of potash, which depends on chemical reaction, any stain can be used on any job. So-called oak stains are usually of a rather greenish colour suitable for a Jacobean finish, and if this happens to be the colour you want for a job not made in oak it is quite in order to use it, but other stains may be better. Similarly a walnut stain so labelled by the maker might be very useful for some jobs in mahogany or oak.

Water stains. These stains are the best for some reasons, the chief being cheapness, their capacity to cover more surface gallon for gallon than any other type of stain, good penetration, and clarity of colour. Water-stain powders can be obtained in a great variety of colours from any of the polish manufacturers, and by varying the quantity of water used with each powder, an infinite number of shades can be produced. They can also be obtained ready-mixed, and by adding water or mixing stains together the tone can be varied

12

at will. When powder stain is mixed allow plenty of time—an hour or so—before using because some ingredients are dissolved more readily than others, and if used too soon the resulting colour may be different from that anticipated.

Walnut crystals. A stain used almost universally is that made with walnut crystals. When made into a strong solution with water, it produces a deep and rather cold brown. Incidentally, it can be made more penetrating and slightly darker by the addition of a little ·880 ammonia (ask for " point eight-eighty ammonia "). Used alone in water, however, its lighter shades are often useful on oak to produce pale golden tones in conjunction with garnet or button polish. Further notes on making the stain appear on page 201.

With the exception of walnut crystals few men nowadays make up their own stains. So wide a range of reliable proprietary stains is available that it is not worth while.

One disadvantage of water stains is their liability to raise the grain. To prevent this, it is policy to damp the surface with clean water after cleaning-up, allow to dry, and then glasspaper down afresh. When the stain is applied after this any roughness will be reduced to a minimum.

Oil stains. These are oil-soluble dyes dissolved in turps, naphtha, or similar oils, and may be obtained in a great number of colours which again may be blended to produce any particular tone. Though not so penetrating as water stains, they are useful in arriving at a colour quickly, and they do not raise the grain. Mahogany oil stain is a rather deep red in its strong state and is made lighter with turps. Browns, both warm and cold, black, greys, and lighter green stains are useful for taking the red out of mahogany and can all be obtained from the manufacturers of polishing materials, and are moderately inexpensive.

A point to note is that when it is proposed to wax polish wood after oil staining it is essential that the latter is first fixed with a couple of rubbers of french polish. Its purpose is not to produce a shine but merely to fix. If this is omitted it is quite possible that the waxing will remove the stain in patches, since the wax may be mixed with the same medium as the stain. This is an important point and should be carefully noted. It is unnecessary in the case of water stains.

Spirit stains. These are not widely used in the trade because they need confident handling, and have a tendency to fade. It will be realised that the spirit with which they are mixed dries out rapidly, and it is difficult to keep an edge alive, especially when a large surface has to be covered. One advantage is that they are not liable to raise the grain. They can be obtained in powder form ready for mixing with spirits. They dry out more rapidly than either water or oil stains. When it is suspected that a surface is greasy or when a previous finish has been cleaned off, spirit stains are handy in that they take better than water stains.

Chemical stains. Strictly speaking these are not stains in the ordinary sense of the word. They produce their effect by chemical action, and the colour of the chemical frequently has no connection with the colour produced in the wood. They are included here because they virtually act in the same capacity as a stain.

Bichromate of potash. This is the chief of the chemical stains. It depends upon chemical reaction with the tannic acid in the timber. It is obtained in crystals of a reddish orange colour, and a concentrated solution is made by steeping the crystals in water. The resulting solution is of the same beautiful tint. Water can be added to the concentrated solution when lighter tones are required. Only certain woods are affected by it, the chief being mahogany. Oak too is darkened, though the resulting shade is rather greenish and cold. Deal is not affected by it.

In a strong solution it produces on mahogany a cold, deep brown, though different in hue from that of walnut crystals. The colour in part depends on the original type and colour of the timber. Thus Cuba and Spanish mahoganies would be much redder and deeper than Honduras when stained with the same strength of stain. On white oak it produces (with tannic acid) a rich brown similar to fumed oak. This is covered more fully when dealing with the latter process. Black water stain when diluted is also very useful for various greys, as well as to tone down other stains, as for example bichromate.

Generally speaking, there is no stain that can be guaranteed to give a certain colour unless all the facts are known regarding the timber used. As seen above, mahogany takes bichromate of potash differently according to its particular variety, and it will therefore be realised that pattern pieces of different timbers stained with various strengths of different stains will be of the utmost value when it is required to know the stain to be used for a job in hand. These patterns should be labelled with details of the process. Some mahoganies are scarcely affected by it, and if mixed woods are used in the same job the result may be patchy. See also notes on page 18.

Ammonia. This if used in liquid form will have the effect of darkening the wood, especially oak and mahogany. The effect is slight, however, and the more usual plan is to obtain the effect by fuming. This is dealt with separately. It is useful for mixing with water stains in that it has the effect of driving the stain more deeply into the grain. Do not use it with the bare fingers as it can be very painful.

Sulphate of iron (green copperas). Used to kill the redness of mahogany when latter has to resemble walnut. The crystals are dissolved in water which becomes a muddy greenish tone. When first applied the effect is scarcely noticeable, but on drying the wood assumes a bluish grey tone. See further notes on page 111.

It can also be used to give oak a blue-grey tone. Try the strength on a spare piece of the same kind of wood and wait until it dries to see the effect. If too strong the colour will resemble Air Force blue. It turns sycamore to a grey tone, thus producing " greywood " or " harewood." If filling with plaster and water has to follow, always fix first with two coats of white french polish. See also notes on page 18.

Aniline dyes. These are obtainable in powder form in a wide variety of colours, including black, blue, bismarck brown, vandyke brown, green, red, maroon, and purple. They are powerful stains and require great care in their use. Some of the colours are unorthodox so far as woodwork is concerned, and should be used cautiously or startling results may be produced. Generally it is advisable to keep to the proprietary stains already listed. The black, however, is useful for ebonising. They can be obtained soluble in water, spirit, or oil, and the correct medium must be used. Vinegar must be added to the water aniline to fix the colour. Spirit aniline dye should have a binder of french polish. Turpentine is used for the oil aniline. For further details of mixing stains, see Chapter XLIV.

Permanganate of potash. This makes a cheap stain. It is obtained in small crystal form, and is dissolved in warm water. It imparts a rich warm tone to oak, but the colour is fugitive. In a short time it fades and is not recommended for important work.

FUMING

This is a darkening process in which ammonia gas reacts with the tannin in the timber. It gives a beautiful tone to oak, and has the great advantage that, since no liquid is applied to the wood, the grain will not be raised. White oak when so treated turns to a grey weathered colour, which, when rubbed with linseed oil, becomes a rich brown. Chestnut also, being rich in tannin, reacts beautifully to the process; while mahogany and walnut become somewhat browned. White oak and red oak should not be used together in any article that is to be fumed, for the latter wood contains less tannin than the former, and the work becomes of uneven colour in consequence.

The chamber. The process is quite simple. Any cupboard

that can be made airtight can be used, or a special box can be made. For large work, a big cupboard or small room may have to be made airtight by covering cracks and holes with gummed tape. The chamber should be the smallest that will accommodate the work, because the fumes are rapidly dissipated. The work and one or two saucers containing the ammonia are placed in the fuming box, which is then closed up and allowed to remain so until the colour is dark enough. Use ·880 ammonia (ask for " point eight-eighty ammonia "). In the case of large work put down three saucers well spaced from each other. Details of a simple home-made fuming box are given in Fig. 38 on page 104

A dowel of similar wood to that being fumed is made a tight fit in a hole in a side of the box. It projects inside an inch or two and makes a useful test piece, saving opening up and allowing the gas to escape. To test, put a small amount of linseed oil on to the dowel or an inconspicuous corner of the job, when it will turn to a brown tone. Alternatively, wet your finger and touch a small portion of the work. This will reveal approximately the finished shade. If not dark enough the process must be continued, more ammonia being added as the first becomes useless, for as the gas is liberated the liquid turns to water.

No overlapping of parts should be allowed or there will be light unstained parts. Therefore see that all surfaces are placed so that the gas can reach them. The time taken is anything from one to forty-eight hours, depending on the colour desired and the size of the fuming box. Another point to note is that the surface must be clean and free from grease or glue, as these will prevent the gas from becoming effective, and the result will be a light patch.

Use of acid. The process may be quickened by coating the wood with tannic or pyrogallic acid in solution of 1 oz. tannin powder to 1 quart of water, and $\frac{3}{4}$ oz. pyrogallic to 1 quart of water. Pyrogallic acid treatment gives a redder tone than the tannic acid, while a mixture of the two gives a slightly different shade from either. Acid-treated timber is generally of a more even colour when fumed than that not so treated.

Bichromate with or without a little black stain added is quite good for matching up any uneven portions, the strength of same depending on the shade required. The whole job is then papered well down. As this process penetrates well into the wood there is no need to fear light patches, but care should be taken with edges.

As mentioned in connection with water staining, the grain should always be raised with water and well sanded when dry before commencing operations at all. This, of course, is unnecessary when the work is to be fumed only, without the use of tannic or pyrogallic acid.

Rubbing with a mixture of one part linseed to three parts turps is the next operation, all excess being wiped off well. The job is allowed to dry for twenty-four hours before any finish is attempted. Wax polish generally follows fuming, though there is no reason why french polish should not be used if this finish is preferred.

Wax stains. When a piece of furniture is to have a waxed finish it can be darkened or toned to a different shade by the use of a wax stain. This stains and polishes in one operation. Wax stains are seldom used in the trade for direct staining from the bare wood, but are handy for toning a job which has already been stained and which is not of quite the desired tone. They are obtained ready made and are applied freely and allowed to dry out thoroughly. It is advisable to allow at least a day for this, because no effective shine is possible until after all liquid has evaporated. Use a cloth rubber free from fluff when polishing. A dull, eggshell sheen should be produced.

Varnish stains. These are virtually varnish to which colouring matter has been added. They are largely opaque, so that the grain beneath is almost entirely concealed. They are therefore entirely unsuitable for figured woods, since the beauty of the grain is lost. They can be used for cheap-grade woods, though even here the result is inferior to that of clear varnish applied after staining.

The chief value of varnish stains is in covering over a poor and dilapidated finish. Take, for instance, a kitchen chair which originally had a varnished or polished finish, but which is now badly knocked about. To strip off the old finish would be a long and difficult process. By using a dark varnish stain the old finish and all defects are entirely covered up and a gloss produced at the same time. If used on bare wood it is advisable to give a preliminary coat of glue size first. Otherwise it will sink in unevenly and produce a patchy result, especially on softwood.

Water coating. Strictly speaking this is not stain at all, but is dealt with here because the coating is intended to answer the purpose of a cheap stain. It consists of one of the powder colours (ground in water) mixed with water, with size added as a binder. If the powder—umber, red ochre, or black, etc.—is merely mixed with water it will be left as a deposit on the surface as the water dries out and can be brushed off. The size binds it, and it adheres to the wood as a sort of distemper, entirely opaque. All grain is thus covered up. This gives it a value for some work because defects are covered up as well. It is thus handy for backs and unimportant jobs where inferior wood may have been used. It is entirely unsuitable for work to be french or wax polished.

EFFECT ON VARIOUS WOODS OF
GREEN COPPERAS AND BICHROMATE OF POTASH

	Green Copperas	*Bichromate of Potash*
Oak	Strong grey-blue tone.	Brown shade, greenish in some varieties.
Mahogany (Honduras)	Used weak gives walnut shade. Do not overdo strength.	Varying shades of brown. Some species affected more than others —one fiddleback variety not affected at all.
Mahogany (Cuban)	Darkens, but turns only slightly grey.	
Chestnut	Strongly affected like oak.	Strongly affected like oak.
Teak	*Slight* darkening and greying.	Almost unnoticeable effect.
Ash	Turns light grey-blue.	Darkens to yellow-brown shade. Not very attractive.
Beech	Turns light grey-blue.	Darkens to yellow-brown shade. Not very attractive.
Hornbeam	Gives strong grey-blue shade.	Slight darkening to yellow-brown. Not very attractive.
Birch	Turns light grey-blue.	Turns to yellow-brown. Not attractive.
Peroba rosa	Slightly darkens. Used strong would probably give greyish tinge.	Gives yellowish tinge and spoils colour.
Sycamore	Gives grey tone.	Turns yellow-brown and spoils colour.
Obeche	Gives grey-blue shade.	Turns yellow-brown.
Akomu	Turns grey-blue.	Gives dirty yellow-brown colour.
Danta	Gives grey tone rather like walnut.	Deepens to brown tone.
Niangon	Similar effect to Honduras mahogany.	Similar to mahogany, but not so marked.
Box	Very slight darkening.	Slight darkening only.
Satinwood	Little or no effect.	Slight darkening. Rather more pronounced than box.

WATER stains have a drawback in that they raise the grain, but this can be largely eliminated by first sponging the timber with water and papering down when dry. The grain having thus been raised and sanded, the stain can be applied without much subsequent papering and therefore less fear of light patches.

Applying the stain. With a brush or rag fairly wet but not dripping, work quickly *with* the grain, as in Fig. 7, and only over such an area as can be conveniently handled. Wipe off with a soft

FIG. 7. HOW BRUSH IS USED WHEN STAINING A WIDE PANEL.

The panel shown here is in plywood and can be stained after assembling. In the case of a solid wood panel fitting in grooves, the edges parallel with the grain should be stained before the framework is glued up. If practicable the whole panel can be stained first.

rag in the same direction to even the colour, taking out any lines or marks previously made.

Speed in working is essential because dried edges inevitably leave marks, especially when a heavy stain is used. Keep the edge alive —that is, do not allow it to dry out before the adjoining surface is covered. It will be realised that if it should dry out it will not be so noticeable *with* the grain as across it. That is why you should always work in the same direction as the grain.

Using bichromate. Bichromate and also ammonia-bound walnut stain need careful handling as they bite quickly, leaving very often the mark of a careless sweep of the rag across the work. Work as wet as is convenient and wipe off immediately the surface is covered. Incidentally, bichromate should never be used if there are any open cuts on the hands, as this often leads to skin trouble : otherwise it is harmless.

Oil stains. Oil stains are best applied with wadding, but they are simpler to handle. Speed, however, is an important factor in applying all stains. When the oil stain is dry it should be given a thin " wash in " with the polish to be used, to prevent the filler when applied from taking out any of the stain. It is applied with a piece of new wadding. If the work is stained too dark the polish wash can be omitted. The filler will lighten it up a shade. A still better plan is to soak a clean piece of wadding with turps and wash off as much as possible of the offending stain. Should this be over a patch (as, for example, a sapwood streak) care should be taken not to lighten the surrounding stain. After this lightening process the wash of polish can be used.

Spirit stains. These are the most difficult to work because they dry so rapidly. An edge will often dry out before it is possible to cover the adjoining surface. Small areas present no special difficulty, but it is advisable to avoid spirit stains on a large surface until you feel confident enough to work rapidly. The temperature naturally affects the handling : a hot, dry atmosphere causing rapid drying with consequent increased difficulty of handling.

Brushes. For large areas a flat brush is the most suitable (see A, Fig. 8). If you do a lot of work it is as well to have two of different sizes. You will, of course, have to keep separate brushes for oil and water stains. A fitch (B) is handy for picking out small mouldings and similar parts, whilst the pencil brush (C) comes in for small details. Always clean them out after use.

Do not use good quality brushes for strong chemicals such as potash, lime, soda, etc. The bristles will soon be destroyed. Instead use a grass-hair brush.

System of working. Plain surfaces are fairly straight-forward in their treatment. Begin at one side and work gradually across to the other. Don't begin at the middle because this means that you have two edges to keep alive. Neither finish the whole width at one end and work down, as joins across the grain are very noticeable. The exception is in the case of narrow strips or panels which can be easily handled.

In panelled work there is a correct order in which the staining should be done.   Begin with the panels, starting against the moulding at one side and working across as in Fig. 9.   Deal with all four panels in this way first.   Finish off each stroke straightaway by drawing the now nearly empty brush towards the top moulding then towards the bottom.   If this is not done there may be a tendency for such parts to turn out light owing to the brush sweeping the stain away from the ends.   Immediately afterwards rub over with the rag.   Note that the latter must not be dry, but must be damp with stain.   The object is neither to add to nor take from the stain on the wood, but is rather to level it.

Now follow the short uprights marked 2 in Fig. 9, care being taken not to let the brush run past the joints at top and bottom.   A piece of card held level with the joints will help to prevent this.   Wipe the card dry before using it for the next joint or you will mark the wood. Rails (3) follow, the same precautions being taken at the end joints. Finally, the mouldings are picked in, the fitch tool being handy for this.

End grain.   Being very open this is liable to soak up more than its share of stain, and it therefore tends to be darker than the rest of the work.   To prevent this a small quantity of stain weaker than the rest should be made up, and this used for the end grain.   In this way an even tone is assured.

FIG. 8. BRUSHES FOR STAINING.
A. Wide brush for wide surfaces. B. Fitch for picking in mouldings. C. Pencil brush for small work.

For the same reason carvings generally need a weaker stain than the rest of the work, there being a lot of end grain exposed.

Matching.   Having covered the work with stain it must be matched up as far as possible, so that when the job stands in its natural position all parts when in the light are approximately the same tone.   It will be found that rails of tables and other parts where the grain runs horizontally will be lighter than those parts in which the grain is vertical and must be re-stained after the first coat is dry.   This second coat will, in all probability, have to be weaker than the original stain, but this must be adjusted to the particular job in hand.   The idea is shown in Fig. 10.

One word regarding quartered panels. These, no matter how stained, will always appears dark and light, according to how they are viewed, one way or the other. They must therefore on no account be re-stained.

When matching up or judging the depth of a stain, the work should

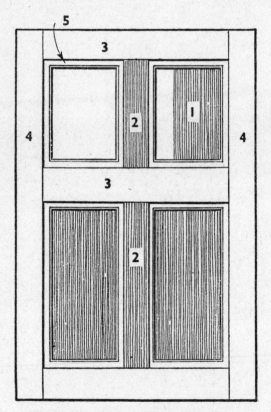

FIG. 9. ORDER OF STAINING PANELLING.
The numbers show the order in which work is done; panels, short stiles, rails, long stiles, and moulding lastly.

always be viewed in a position similar to that it will occupy when finished. Thus a door must be held in a vertical position for the colour to be seen properly, while table tops and similar parts should be placed horizontally at about the correct height from the floor. Never judge work that is standing on the work bench, for it always appears several shades lighter in this position.

Darkening. Sometimes a part of the work will appear light, possibly owing to a different grade of wood having been used or to the presence of sapwood (actually the latter never should be used : it is immature wood). A second coat of stain applied locally may darken it, or it may be necessary to use another stain. Make sure, however, that the colour is the same; otherwise even though you reduce it to the same depth of tone, the colour may be different.

HORIZONTAL GRAIN APPEARS LIGHTER THAN VERTICAL GRAIN

**FIG. 10. HOW POSITION AF-
FECTS TONE OF STAIN.**

After staining, the horizontal parts generally appear lighter than the rest, and need darkening. It is there-fore essential that the work is stood upright in its normal position when being viewed, otherwise a false appearance will be obtained. For instance, if placed on its side, the normally vertical parts will seem light.

As a last note on staining, always make up rather more stain than you actually need. Nothing is more disastrous than to run out half-way through a job. It may and probably will be quite impossible to obtain an exact match. Another point is to avoid splashing when applying the stain. Keep unstained parts well out of the way or cover them over. It may be impossible to get rid of these marks entirely. Finally, allow all stains to dry out *thoroughly* before starting any later process such as filling in the grain or polishing. Dampness in the wood may cause trouble later on.

It may happen that a part is too dark, and then bleaching is necessary. Oxalic acid is used. This is obtainable in crystal form, and a fairly strong solution of about 1 oz. to half a pint of hot water should be made up. Wash this over the dark parts, taking care not to let it run beyond. Several applications may be needed; in bad cases a rag soaked in the bleach can be left on the wood.

When finished, wipe well with clear cold water to remove all traces of the acid, otherwise the latter will attack any finish subsequently applied. As a further precaution it can be neutralised with borax, 1 oz. to a quart of warm water. Note that oxalic acid is a poison, so that contact with the fingers should be avoided. See notes on page 206.

Bleaching. A popular effect is the bleached finish in which such woods as oak, walnut, and some varieties of mahogany are bleached to a light shade and finished with either white or transparent french polish. It looks most effective and is reliable, but it should be realised that not all woods bleach well. Some cannot be bleached at all. The following table gives notes on some of the better-known woods. Generally the darker and denser woods are difficult; also those of a greasy nature:

These bleach easily	These may require two applications	These bleach with difficulty or cannot be bleached	
Ash	Mahoganies	Cherry	Padouk
Beech	Oaks	Rosewood	Iroko
Elm	Walnuts	Zebrawood	Satinwood
Avodire		Ebony	

Oxalic acid mentioned above will lighten the colour only slightly, and for any serious degree of bleaching it is necessary to use one of the more powerful proprietary bleaches, such as *Blanchit*, *Bleach white*, *Ultra-bleach*, *Vita-bleach*. These are of the two-solution type.

Two-solution bleaches. The No. 1 solution is alkaline, usually dilute caustic potash or dilute ammonia. No. 2 is usually high per cent hydrogen peroxide. All alkalis tend to darken wood and so, often, there is a preliminary darkening effect with No. 1. Its purpose, however, is to cause the chemical reaction with No. 2 which does the actual bleaching. This commercial two-solution bleach is reliable and is the one we recommend. However, for the benefit of those who like to make up their own, No. 1 could be made from ·880 ammonia and 5 parts water, and No. 2 from one part hydrogen peroxide 100 vol. and 2 parts water.

Other bleaches are oxalic acid (3 oz. to the quart of hot water), hydrogen peroxide 100 vol. alone, chloride of lime, sodium perborate, and several of the better-type household bleaches.

Depth of penetration. With special vacuum apparatus it is possible to bleach throughout veneer thickness at the most. This is done before the veneers are laid. For ordinary application such as we would employ the surface fibres only are whitened. It is essential therefore to complete the tool finish and sand to requirements before bleaching or there will be a serious risk of cutting through.

The procedure. For all bleaches it is first necessary to check for finger and glue marks, etc., as these would resist the bleach. No. 1 is given five minutes to soak in, then No. 2 is applied evenly along the grain. It is necessary to wait until complete drying before the effect can be observed. The process may then be repeated as required. Usually with fresh bleach one application is sufficient. It is necessary then to remove any chemical residue by wiping with warm water or methylated spirit. With some bleaches a white deposit may remain after this neutralising stage. This is removed by papering and dusting. Hydrogen peroxide need not be neutralised.

Any painting out or faking should be done before polishing. The polish itself must be trade quality white. Coloured polish will merely undo all the work of bleaching. For light finishes such as the ivory bleached mix well into each pint of polish a level teaspoonful of powdered Chinese white. Use this until the job is about half bodied, then continue with the white polish by itself. For finishes like light contemporary oak, tint the first coats of polish to give the brilliance and shade required. Apart from this follow the usual procedure. Do not use rubbers containing any colour.

A bleached job will stand up well provided the correct procedure is employed. Insufficient drying time will cause subsequent blistering due to trapped volatile elements. Always allow at least two days for drying. The risk is greater on solid timber where there is no glue barrier to prevent deep penetrations into the pores. Failure to neutralise properly may cause black areas to develop in time on some woods, especially oaks, and may induce bubbles or wrinkles in the film. Bleached timber should not be left unfinished longer than is necessary or it will tend to darken again. It is often impossible to bleach out local markings. These should be painted out.

Surplus bleach. Excess bleach should be discarded as return to the main container will accelerate deterioration. Metal reacts with bleach so containers must be non-metallic. Bleach will spoil good brushes, therefore use white fibre or grass brushes or cloth swabs or sponges. It is possible to use No. 1 and No. 2 mixed equally for a one-solution bleach but this mixing must be done just before application and the mixture must not be stoppered.

Bleaches must be kept from the skin. Any spots that do get on should be washed off immediately. Rubber gloves should be used. A mask should be worn when sanding bleached surfaces. Bleaches are unstable and will deteriorate rapidly if left unstoppered. They should be stored in a dark, cool place; even under the best conditions they remain fully effective for only about three months.

Stopping. To make good defects such as cracks, nail holes, etc., use ivory-coloured hard stopping made with molten beeswax and rosin and coloured with flake-white powder. A little polish pigmented with Chinese white and if necessary a touch of another colour is suitable for painting out surface faults in the timber.

Cheap imitation of bleached woodwork. A fair imitation which would not deceive anyone who knew better is possible on wood which is itself fairly light in colour. This should be wiped with a 50/50 mixture of flat white paint and turps or white spirit so that the grain still shows. When hard the surface is polished in the usual way.

CHAPTER V : FILLING IN THE GRAIN

THE main purpose of a filler is that of filling the pores of the timber in order to save polishing costs, both material and time. A filler is not absolutely necessary, for the timber could be made quite " full " by the use of polish only. In fact, this was the method used when french polishing was first introduced. The probability is that this still is the most reliable form of polishing. However, apart from the quantity of polish used, on some timbers the time taken would be too long for all normal purposes, and so use is made of the various materials, such as plaster of paris, etc.

PLASTER

Plaster of paris is one of the oldest fillers in use, and is effective. It is cheap, and the *Superfine*, which is the grade of plaster used as a filler, can be purchased at any oilshop. Before filling in with plaster give the wood two coats of french polish (after staining). This serves the double purpose of fixing the stain and of lessening any liability for the filler to turn white in the grain at a later stage owing to absorption of the oil. Allow to dry out for several hours before applying the filler.

Application. The best way of using it is as follows : Put the plaster in a fair-sized shallow box, so that it can be taken out on a damp rag conveniently. A bowl of water is placed alongside the box. A piece of rag or canvas for applying and several other pieces for wiping off are all that are required.

Wet the rag, dip it in the plaster, and apply to the job with a circular movement, bearing moderately heavily as in Fig. 11. If there is too much water in the rag dip again in the plaster until the mixture on the wood is a fairly thick paste. Allow the plaster a few seconds until it begins to set, when, with a conveniently sized piece of clean canvas, rub off briskly across the grain. Remember that plaster takes only a very short time to set hard, and the rubbing off should be done before this occurs.

Care should also be taken to see that only that surface which can be rubbed clean in time is covered with filler. Go over the whole job, section by section, making sure to clean out well all corners and mouldings. A scrubbing brush is a great help in dealing with mouldings and similar parts, and a sharp-ended stick for the corners. Pay special attention to awkward places, because nothing looks worse

than choked-up angles and corners.   Fig. 12 shows the stick in use.
Carving is not filled at all.

Use of oil.   Allow the whole to dry thoroughly.   The entire
surface will appear white.   Soak a piece of wadding in raw linseed oil
and cover the job all over with a thin film of oil.   Paper the work
thoroughly, when the plaster and oil on the surface will combine into
a thick paste.   When the entire surface has been papered wipe the
whole off with a soft rag.

Colouring.   There are one or two special considerations with

FIG. II.   APPLYING FILLER TO SURFACE WITH DAMP RAG.
Work the rag with a circular movement, covering every part of the surface, and rubbing
the filler well into the grain.   Avoid an unnecessary deposit on the surface.

regard to the above, which deals with filling with the white plaster.
Actually the natural plaster is only used on very light colours, as
natural walnut, etc., when the oil, the only purpose of which is to
" kill " the plaster, should be white mineral oil—which is water
clear.   Linseed oil would impart an unwanted colour to such light
work.

On darker colours, brown walnut or red mahogany for instance,
the plaster can be mixed with vandyke brown powder colour or rose
pink respectively.   Just sufficient colour should be added to tone
down the whiteness against the dark ground.   Linseed oil, not
white oil, is used in these cases for killing the plaster.   If these oils
are not used, the plaster on the surface is very difficult to get off,

and has a disconcerting trick of appearing through the polish at a later period.

Canvas. A little advice as to choice of canvas will be of assistance. Choose the loosely woven stuff that can often be obtained from the greengrocer. Hard-surfaced hessian is of no great value as it will not take up any of the plaster, but tends to shift it from one place to another. The open-grained stuff can be pulled and shaken out and made to serve again.

PROPRIETARY FILLERS

Next in order of merit come the various proprietary fillers. These consist of a basic substance such as silex, china clay, whiting, etc.,

FIG. 12. CLEANING FILLER OUT OF AWKWARD CORNERS.
A small stick of wood is used to remove unwanted surface filler
from mouldings and other angles and corners.

mixed with turpentine, a drying oil, and certain other ingredients, varying, of course, with individual makers. These fillers originally came from America, and a reliable brand is " Wheeler's," which is stocked by most polish suppliers. They are supplied as a very thick paste in tins with air-tight press-in lids, which, incidentally, should always be pressed well home when the tin is not in use.

Application. The paste is thinned with turps to a workable consistency. Too much turps, however, is useless, as insufficient filler is carried into the grain. It is applied with canvas, in the same manner as plaster, and rubbed off similarly across the grain as soon as the filler has gone dull, which effect will be quite obvious as soon as it is used.   When the work is clear of filler the surface is rubbed, with a piece of rag as a final operation, set aside, and allowed to dry for at least twelve hours if the best results are to be obtained.

As to colour, these fillers are stocked in oak, mahogany, and walnut, though some makers prefer the colour names such as brown, red, natural.   The last named is something the colour of putty.   Should these colours need modifying they can be thinned with a suitable oil stain instead of turps.   Alternatively, after thinning with turps, add a powder colour, as, for example, gas black added to red filler, so making various browns according to the proportion.

Filling and staining.   This type of filler can often be used to combine the two operations of staining and filling, when all the considerations in connection with oil staining will apply, for example, staining any sapwood.   Indications as to which filler should be used for the various colours cannot be more than general owing to the large number of different shades that have been developed. Roughly, however, where the general tone is red, use a red filler.   When brownish, a dark or light brown filler.   The various greys and naturals should be filled as light as possible with either natural patent filler or white plaster.

Filling oak.   Oak can be filled in or not according to the result desired.   Some prefer the oak to be quite open in the grain.   The most general method for furniture is to semi-fill the grain with chalk, as follows.   To a pint of the polish to be used add a handful or so of french chalk.   Then coat in the work all over with a brush, keeping the mixture stirred each time the brush is dipped into it and avoiding running.   When dry, paper well down, dust off, and the job is ready for the subsequent operations.   This chalk mixture when dry sets quite hard, and it will be found that papering afterwards leaves the surface satin smooth.   Incidentally this chalk-polish coat is ideal for washing in the interiors of wardrobes, etc., that are to be finished light, button polish being used.   Any running or tears allowed to set when doing the work will show quite plainly and be unsightly.   The button polish used in this case is a special cheap variety made especially for the job.

Fillers for softwoods, etc.   For the close-grained timbers such as pine, spruce, birch, the filler used can be one of the proprietary fillers used thinner than normal, but on account of the smallness of the pores, a coat of size is more effective.   This, however, cannot be applied after an oil stain.   The size can be either glue or patent size thinned down until it no longer feels sticky when rubbed between the fingers.   The general idea is to allow the liquid to sink into the timber and not to form a film over the stain.   If the size is not kept thin, this object is defeated. When the job is dry it should be papered smooth and dusted well down.

Stopping. So far, only filling the grain has been dealt with, but often a bruise or two will creep in even with the best cared for work, and to fill these up " stopping " or stick shellac is used. The latter substance may be obtained in white, button, or garnet varieties, while " stopping " is made in red, brown, white, and several other shades. They are used by melting with a hot iron, and held over the offending place, allowing the molten substance completely to fill the dent. The surplus which invariably piles up must be cleaned off with a sharp chisel, and finally with glasspaper grade " 0. " A little oil with the papering is a great assistance, and in both cases a cork block should be used to ensure all being level.

When the bruise is a shallow one, it should be well pricked with a needle or something similar to form a key for the stopping, or there will be a tendency for it to be pulled out when worked over. When unable to obtain either substance quickly, a piece of suitable coloured sealing wax may be used, but this is a very brittle substitute. The colouring of these filled bruises will be dealt with later, so no notice should be taken of them if they show up greatly against the ground colour.

General notes. Paper the work lightly with No. 1 or 1½ paper before filling, and be certain that the job is free from dust when filling, as otherwise there is often a tendency towards muddiness of colour.

When the patent filler has been used, rubbed off, and is perfectly dry, it is also good to paper down any raised grain or particles of filler still adhering; and after all fillers, before proceeding with any further polishing, all dust and grit from the surface must be removed.

For those who would like to mix a paste filler of their own, the following is quite good :

    1 quart boiled linseed oil
    1 pint gold size or brown japan
    1 gill turpentine.

Mix these ingredients together and add china clay or silex little by little until a stiff paste is obtained. Allow to stand twenty-four hours, when it may be thinned with turpentine as required. Do not mix too much at once, as after a week or two the mixture hardens and is not so good for completely filling the pores. The silex may be obtained from all polish supply houses. Other notes on fillers are given in Chapter XLIV.

POLISH FILLING

After staining, charge a rubber freely with polish and work on to the wood, passing from one part of the work to another, until the surface shows signs of becoming too tacky for further working. Lay aside for a few hours to harden and ease off any dust or specks with fine worn glasspaper. Dust the surface and go over the work with a mop brush charged with a thick, heavy-bodied polish, taking care not to work too long in any place and avoiding streaks or tears.

Allow to dry for at least two hours and paper down to a smooth dull surface. Dust again and smooth this coat with several rubbers of thinned-out polish. This will ease out any irregularities and at the same time force the polish into the pores. Once again allow to harden for several hours, and repeat the brushing, following with the rubbing. Yet a third application may be needed. A little fine pumice powder placed between the wadding pad and the covering rag will help in grinding the surface down flat. The work then passes to the bodying stage of polishing as described in a later chapter.

CHAPTER VI: FRENCH POLISHING—FADDING

THERE are three chief ways of finishing when french polishing ; stiffing, spiriting, and the acid method. In all three the preliminary processes are the same. It is only the final finishing-off stage that varies. Actually there is a fourth way of finishing—glazing, but this is generally confined to cheap work, and to such parts as cannot be dealt with by the rubber. Details of the process are given on pages 56-7.

We outline here the stages involved in french polishing.

THE STAGES IN FRENCH POLISHING
STAINING
FILLING-IN
FADDING
COLOURING
COATING
BODYING

STIFFING   SPIRITING   ACID FINISH

It has already been mentioned that in some cases, oak in particular, the filling-in process may be omitted or a semi filling-in given. The colouring, too, can be left out providing the whole job has been made not only from the same kind of wood but from the same variety of that wood. This, however, is seldom possible and the purpose of colouring is to bring the whole to an even tone. Some workers omit the coating process when the work has not been coloured. Regarding the choice of the finishing-off stage, most beginners seem to prefer the spiriting method, as being the simplest, but in reality there is not much in it.

MATERIALS

First, a little as to materials.

Polishes. The type of polish used will be either button, garnet, white, or transparent, depending on the colour desired. Button is yellowish in colour and finishes rather golden. Garnet is a dark greenish brown, and finishes much warmer and darker in tone. White is of a creamy hue and over light grounds tends *slightly* to grey the work. Transparent white is water clear and finishes much the same as would water with regard to tone.

Making french polish. All polishes can be obtained from supply houses, and there is little economy in making them yourself. For those who prefer to do so the following recipes are reliable. In all cases shellac is dissolved in methylated spirits or methylated finish (see page 199), the resulting shade of polish depending upon the kind of shellac used. Some manufacturers add certain gums and other ingredients, but the object is generally to build up a body and cheapen the cost. Shellac makes the best polish.

The following shellacs are used in accordance with the tone required. They are arranged here in order of colour. White, orange, button, garnet. Button polish is inclined to be rather muddy, but has the reputation of being harder than the others.

White polish, 6–8 oz. bleached shellac to 1 pint methylated spirits.
Orange polish, 6 oz. orange shellac to 1 pint methylated spirits.
Button polish, 6 oz. button shellac to 1 pint methylated spirits.
Garnet polish, 6 oz. garnet shellac to 1 pint methylated spirits.

The shellac and spirits are placed in a corked bottle and left until the shellac is dissolved. This will take several days. Agitate the bottle from time to time to help on the process. The quantity of shellac can be increased to make a heavy-bodied polish or varnish.

General rules for their particular use may be put roughly thus. Never use button over dark warm stains, as it tends to cloud over and obscure the grain. Garnet is the best general polish for this work. Button is useful, however, in golden walnut and similar tones, while for the lighter colours use white or transparent white, toning if necessary with a little of either of the warmer polishes. Red polish, either bismarck or red sanders, is used to give greater warmth. This is dealt with under *Colouring*.

A wine bottle fitted with a cork that has a fair-sized groove or cut in one side is first class for holding the polish (see Fig. 13). The latter should run quite *freely* through the cork.

Wadding and rag. As to wadding, that bought at a polish supplier's is certain to be good, but if purchased elsewhere, say a draper's, that known as unbleached wadding should be asked for. Bleached wadding, medicated cotton wool, and similar materials are useless owing to their compressing into a tight and unresponsive mass when charged with polish and used as a rubber.

Rag is important, though guidance in its selection is difficult as polishers themselves differ in methods of handling, and where one can use a coarse-grained open rag, another using the same material is hopelessly at sea.   Select for a beginning a fairly fine-grained linen with a substantial body or thickness.   An old dress shirt is ideal. All coloured rag and that with a fancy grain is useless.

Oil.   Oil can be of two kinds : raw linseed or white mineral oil. The latter is the better, as it does not thicken appreciably on exposure to air and is less greasy.   Linseed can be used if white oil is not available.

FADDING

This is the preliminary polishing process and is very important, though not so highly critical in its application as the later finishing process.   There are several methods of " fadding," but perhaps the best is a modification of that most generally used in furniture polishing.

Experimental work.   Regarding the actual work to be polished it will perhaps be best if pieces of timber (say six of about 12 in. by 8 in.) are pinned to the bench or a board and worked in rotation.   This will be much easier in the beginning, for corners will be entirely eliminated until proficiency in rubber handling is attained, and if unsuccessful the work can be cleaned off without spoiling anything of value.   Birch ply or mahogany would make a good beginning.

FIG. 13. BOTTLES USED TO KEEP POLISH.

Note that a V-groove is cut in the side of the cork to enable polish to be shaken out.

Making the fad.   For applying the polish initially a piece of wadding some 9 in. square is soaked in polish and allowed to dry.   This is subsequently softened in spirits, and the surplus wrung out well.   By using this instead of a new piece of wadding, the adhering to the surface of the inevitable hairy threads will be eliminated.   Fig. 14 shows stages in making the fad.

Shape conveniently to fit the hand, dip up fairly wet with polish, and flatten on the back of a piece of glasspaper.   This serves the purpose of evenly distributing the polish over the surface of the fad. Apply to the work along the grain at the top edge, working gradually down and covering completely once only as shown at A, Fig. 15. If the fad works dry before covering, dip up again.   Allow a moment or two to dry, then with a piece of fine paper work all over the surface, when anything underneath such as a filler, etc., will be exposed. Clean off well and proceed as before, working *with* the grain and bearing fairly heavily. The quantity of polish in the fad should be such that its path on the work is obvious but leaves no runnings or any wet patches.

This process is carried on several times when the shellac film will show up quite clearly. If care is taken and not too much polish at a time is used, the fad will show no tendency to stick or leave pieces of wadding on the work. If this happens, wet the finger and rub round and round over the offending place, when the wadding will

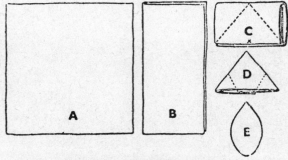

FIG. 14. HOW WADDING IS FOLDED.

Take a piece of wadding 9 in. square, A, and fold along centre, B. Fold side over about 3 in. and the remaining 3 in. on top, C. It will be found that of the two long sides, one has a ragged edge and this should be kept to the bottom, X (C). For final shaping, folds are made along the dotted lines away from the worker (C). To form the heel the point of the triangle should be held between finger and thumb of the left hand, while with the right, grip like a pistol, turning in the two corners while so doing (see D and E).

It will be more convenient for practising if the wadding is soaked in water instead of polish, as it will be just as effective, without dirtying the hands.

generally roll up and come away. If unsuccessful, a piece of glass-paper will remove it, but this should be done when a little drier.

Use of oil. Up to the present no oil has been used. This is to ensure that the timber has been completely sealed and that there is no oil layer between it and the shellac. If oil had been used it would have probably been held by the pores of the timber and have broken through the shellac at some later period in an attempt to dry, thus cracking and spoiling the work.

However, for a good groundwork more polish is required than is put on by three or four fads used until dry, and here for quickness a little oil is used. If the worker feels confident of putting on sufficient polish without oil, so much the better, and with the aid of occasional papering down the work can be kept flat. The majority of workers, however, will use oil.

With the fad, collect the oil and spread all over the surface, when a smear will result which will vary according to the wetness of the fad and the quantity of oil. Working with a moderately wet fad, the smear should be quite obvious when viewed by looking slightly along or across the surface towards the light. It might be stated here that polishing at any stage while learning should always take place as near a window as possible during daylight. If in artificial

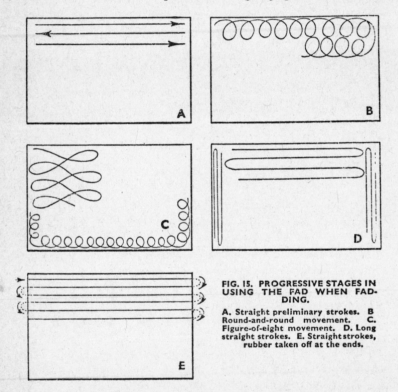

FIG. 15. PROGRESSIVE STAGES IN USING THE FAD WHEN FAD-DING.

A. Straight preliminary strokes. B Round-and-round movement. C. Figure-of-eight movement. D. Long straight strokes. E. Straight strokes, rubber taken off at the ends.

light, the worker should view the smear in the direction of the light source. Looking down at a surface from immediately above only the colour is seen and any blemish or smear is invisible.

Movement of fad. Having worked the oil all over, increasing the initial quantity if necessary, the fad should be worked round and round in fairly open circles, such as at B, Fig. 15, using a small figure-of-eight motion for the edges. Work all places evenly, keeping the head on a low level so that the surface is seen. Pimples, formed by polish fixing particles of dust to the surface, should be eased gently off with a piece of oily paper. When, using pressure, the polish is difficult to get on to the work, dip up again. The smear will probably be streaked with bright patches now, which shows that the

FIG. 16.   STAGES IN MAKING THE RUBBER.

Take piece of rag 9 in. square, and place over wadding, with the heel a couple of inches from back edge. Hold as at A, firmly. Place fingers as at B underneath rag, where second finger presses against point, while finger and thumb draw rag taut.   Left hand can now be disengaged to take up the position shown at C, where finger and thumb hold the point and rag closely together.

With point held firmly folds shown at D can be made, first from the dotted lines to position shown, and secondly that marked edge I to the heavy dotted line at the face of the rubber. In first fold the right thumb plays a big part in obtaining crease at the point which is so desirable, it pressing back while forefinger rolls rag over.

Hold all tight in the left hand, and place the heel and ends of rag as in E, where thumb does not grip tightly and fingers only act as a support. If rubber is kept at a right angle to the palm, the binding turns at the end may be made by turning the rubber away from the worker, much as using a screwdriver.

fresh shellac is taking off the oil.   If the pores are still open, a little more oil should be used.   When it is obvious that there is plenty of polish on the surface and the pores are well filled, change the " round and round " for long ovals or figures of eight as at C, Fig. 15, gradually changing to D.

At this stage the smear should be all over with no bright shellac streaks, much the same as breath on a glass, with the difference that the curved path of the fad will show quite plainly.

Using the rubber.   Now take a rubber, hold in the left hand by the heel, turn back the rag on the face, dip up well and re-make. Fig. 16 shows the stages in making the rubber.   The inner cotton wool is folded as in Fig. 14.   Flatten on glasspaper to distribute the polish and pick up any that has squeezed out.   It should be so charged that when the point is squeezed between finger and thumb

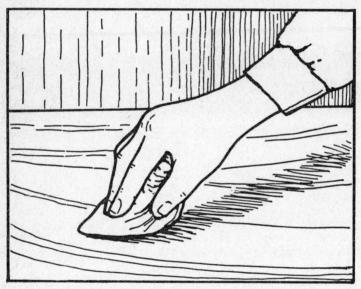

FIG. 17.   HOW TO HOLD THE RUBBER WHEN FRENCH POLISHING.

of left hand the polish just comes through the rag.   The rubber is held with the forefinger at the point quite straight, the thumb at the heel on the left-hand side, and the other fingers curled towards the heel on the opposite side as in Fig. 17.

The rubber, with a gliding motion to prevent sticking, should be placed in the top left-hand corner and moved across to the other side much the same as at D, Fig. 15, not pressing too heavily at first but using a gentle touch, when bright streaks, such as were seen when using a wet fad, will appear.   The oil is now being taken off and this is just what is required.   Continue as at D until none but a few thin streaks are left.   To attain this, the rubber may have to be dipped up again, but not before the first charge of polish is nearly used.

Taking off the oil. To remove these last few streaks the rubber is dipped up about half strength and used as at E, Fig. 15, where the lines show the path of the rubber, which is taken off at each stroke. The curves at each end show the easy approach of the rubber at the beginning of the stroke and the arrows the direction. Each stroke is the width of a rubber, and each should overlap the other by a small margin to ensure all surface being covered. Do not hurry this taking-off process by using very wet rubbers or oil will be buried.

The resulting surface should now be bright and perfectly free from oil. If not free the last process should be continued until it is so. The brightness will in all probability be marred by small lines corresponding with the grain of the rag and perhaps an obvious mark where the rag has dragged, for in this process the last taking off of oil is accompanied by a slight resistance to the rag as the oil get less.

If, after fadding, the rubber used fails to take off oil appreciably, it is in all probability due to the rag. This is judged largely by the feel, which should be an easy but definite pull. As the oil becomes less the surface feels drier, and the pull becomes greater. If at any point in working the rubber does not feel as if it is gripping the work, examine the face of same. If it is beginning to get shiny, too much oil is being used and such surplus may be wiped off the timber with a clean rag. This will probably take off too much, but this must be judged by experiment. If, on the other hand, there is no sign of shiny oil on the face, change the rag, for that which has no " pull " allows the oil to remain on the work.

General remarks. Remember to keep a constant eye on the surface and to dip up only when the rubber or fad requires it. In the first stages of putting on the polish, pressure plays a big part in forcing the shellac well into the pores. Several very wet fads will not achieve what one fad well used will do. After each dip-up, go first gently and lightly, and as the fad gets drier use more pressure until finally, if required, assist with the left hand over the right.

Fads and rubbers. To make perfectly clear, the difference between a fad and a rubber is that the latter has a rag over the face, while a fad is the plain wadding.

A good rubber tin is a snuff tin (2-lb. size) which has a close-fitting *easily removed* lid, and which will keep rubbers soft for months.

One vital point regarding rubber handling. Never put the rubber down deliberately, always glide on and take off in the same way.

CHAPTER VII : FRENCH POLISHING—COLOURING

WHEN work is stained, even though the utmost skill is used and the greatest care taken, almost invariably a patch or two will occur; or a rail or leg become noticeably light after a coat of polish. In any case few stainings give the exact shade required. The object of colouring, then, is to even the colour generally and tone to the particular shade required.

Colours. The main materials needed for the job are a supply of powder colours, spirit dyes, a good colour brush, and a pencil brush. Of the powder colours, gas black or vegetable black is a necessity ; also sanders or bismarck red polish. When the black and red are combined with polish, a great variety of browns and greys is obtained. The spirit dyes are obtainable in brown, scarlet, mauve, green, yellow, and other shades.

Brushes. The colour brush should be a No. 6 or 7 camel hair mop, quill bound with a wooden handle. It can be obtained bound in a long quill, the latter forming the handle, but this is not so good, lacking balance and rigidity. A good brush is not expensive and will last a lifetime. A pencil brush can be bought for a copper or two, but the cheapest are of little use. They will never give a good point, and the hair is so soft that it will not put colour where it is wanted.

Before using a new colour brush, soak it in polish for a couple of days in a jar with a cardboard lid to set the hair. Force the handle into the board so that the hair is a little way from the bottom of the jar. This prevents the hair being set in a bent position, so ruining it. When soaked, squeeze out the surplus, bring hair to a point, and set aside for a day. When used, no hair will come out, and the brush will be in ideal condition. For the first week or so of use it should be softened in polish and not spirits, so as not to wash out the setting polish so carefully worked into the roots.

Example—mahogany. For an example we will take a piece of plain mahogany which has been stained to a deep brown with bichromate stain. This has been fadded with garnet polish to the point where there is a good film of shellac on the surface, but not a high shine. This latter shine is to be avoided because it catches the light and makes the viewing of the plain colour more troublesome.

It should be placed in the position that it will ultimately occupy, either vertically or horizontally and on, or some distance above, the floor. It should be pointed out that, if timber is coloured at floor level, for example, when it is to occupy a position some few feet above it, it will be found several shades lighter than desired. This should be borne in mind in all colouring operations. Place the work as near a window as is comfortable to ensure a good light. Artificial light is useless for good colouring, as accurate matching is impossible.

Making the colour polish. To half spirits and polish add a little gas black to make a medium strength grey. Warm this up with a touch of bismarck or red sanders, making a brown on the greenish side. (A colour is more easily judged by touching the brush on the back of the hand or the back of brown-coloured glass-paper. White paper or " o " paper gives a wrong sense of colour.)

Take a piece of old fad, make it into a small compact shape, and flatten out well. Now lightly charge with a brush full of colour and again flatten well out, touching the surface with a little oil. Here enter judgment and skill. Look at the timber; notice just where the lightest place is, and apply very lightly the dark colour-fad to the spot. It must be done in such a manner that the colouring is not an ugly patch. If the grain is more or less parallel, it is a simple matter to follow the light streaks, using only a portion of the fad on the narrow parts and the whole surface on the wider parts.

Irregular shapes. Where the stain is very irregular, such as concentric ovals and wavy, indented curves, the fad must follow the lines exactly, and if a darker patch intrudes skip it and start again just above. Do not go over the dark place just because it is in the path of the fad. Any wide places can be worked round and round. Cover each place once and then pass on to the next, working in this manner until the work assumes a more even appearance.

Use of brush. It will probably be found that there are one or two places that are too small for the fad to work without darkening some spot that is already on colour. Here the brush comes in. Dip into the colour, squeeze out with the finger against the side of the jar, and bring to a point. Apply to the spot delicately, spreading the hair just the right amount as the streak widens out.

This brush control needs some practice, but it is soon acquired, provided the brush is held at the tip of the handle or as near as convenient. This brings the hand away from the surface, allowing a good view of what is taking place. If also the arm is extended it is easier to judge how things are looking. Looking at a colour near the work gives a false impression, but if colouring is done at arm's length the necessity for getting back continually to view is eliminated. This brush work is known as " picking out."

Warmth of tone. Having toned down and picked out the light spots and patches, the work is now viewed for warmth. There are probably a few places that have not the same amount of red as the rest. These are toned in the same way as when using the dark fad, only this time a new piece of fad dipped up with red is used. This is never used full strength, but is thinned with polish to a pink. Just dip up with strong red, add to the fad the same amount of polish, and squeeze out flat.

Having warmed up the whole job until even, judge whether it might require a general warming, and if so, work the whole with a slightly round-and-round grain-following motion. This warming, however, must be carried out carefully, for a too red patch means an ugly glare, and red is a very strong colour effecting a considerable difference quickly. In tinting up, allowance must be made for the garnet polish, for this polish imparts considerable warmth to the work.

General darkening. It has been assumed so far that the darkest part of the work as stained is, apart from a tint, the shade desired. This is not necessarily so. Indeed it might be many tones lighter than expected, for stain under shellac looks different from the original stain colour. Should this be so, darken all over with the dark fad before evening up and picking out. This may on moderately straight grain be carried out " up and down," but on a variegated birch-type grain, a more grain-following round-and-round is better. If following the grain seems unnecessary, try a dark fad up and down parallel with the edges.

The main thing is to work gradually with weak colour so that the wood assumes its final tone slowly but clearly. Too strong a colour obscures the grain, and if too warm makes the work coarse. Working in the same place continuously will result in taking off the colour first put on, and, until dry, the lightened patch will refuse to colour at all.

Fiddle-back mahogany. So much for plain timbers. Fiddle-back mahogany, especially when quartered, needs careful colouring. Never use a brush, but rather a fad of colour used *with* the grain or figure and viewed from square in front. A view at an angle will result in a change of colour. This timber cannot be coloured so that it will appear the same shade from all angles. It can only assume one colour from directly in front.

Quartered work. Take a table top in quartered veneer. Viewed from one side two diagonal quarters are dark. Colour it to make even and then turn it round. It will be seen that the two opposite diagonals are now dark. Colour these and you will be turning it round in a year's time because of this shadowing of timber. In these cases treat the quarters on their merits : even the two light ones to match each other, but not darkening down. Even up the dark ones similarly and the job is done.

Making a pattern. In colouring jobs, always make a pattern if possible of similar wood. This will save carrying the colour in the mind's eye—always a doubtful business. Sides, ends, and all parts can then be matched accurately. Suppose a nest of tables is to be coloured. Fetch the large top to pattern and bring down the others to match. Then colour the stand all round. Put the smaller tables " in nest " and see what wants doing to the front leg faces and inside back legs. Colour down. Separate and colour, say, the left-hand side legs and include faces of opposite legs. Colour them side by side and match one with the other. Continue round the other sides to complete. If each stand is coloured individually, there is generally a different colour for each table in the nest. It will be appreciated that matching one part with another is just as important as toning down and picking out to make even, but is a part of colouring most easily forgotten.

Walnut. Straight-figured walnut is coloured just as mahogany, but there is little or no red put into the black, which must be very weak. This refers to the lighter, more delicate tones to which walnut lends itself so perfectly. If, however, it is being coloured a dark, warm brown this lack of red in the colour is unnecessary. Vegetable black is better for walnut as it is not so intense a black and is therefore better for the grey tones.

In figured walnut " grain-following " colouring is most essential, as any muddled figure due to colour-fading could not possibly be allowed. In a burr timber a round-and-round motion is best, as there are no definite shapes to tone down, but merely lighter places gradually shading into the dark colour. Here, again, the colour should be clear, for the burrs can easily be obscured by muddy, careless colouring.

Fixing. When the colouring is completed it should be fixed, after a short period, with a new clean rubber of the polish to be used. It should be applied lightly and quickly so as not to disturb the colour.

Spirit colour. There are one or two considerations in colouring which do not come under darkening or picking out. When matching a colour it is often found that there is a particular cast which cannot be obtained using black and red. Here the spirit colours come into use. First, those colours which kill red. Spirit yellow used weak and in the usual manner will turn any too red tone to a less fiery, more orange shade. Spirit green does the same, turning the red to a brownish hue. Spirit blue acts similarly and is mostly used for walnut if too fiery.

These colours are made by adding a pinch of spirit-soluble dye to polish. About a saltspoonful to a pint of polish is amply strong. These powders may be purchased by the ounce from any polish supply house. In using, err on the weak side and use sparingly, particularly green and yellow. Spirit mauve is useful for taking the greenish cast from certain types of walnut, etc., and is applied before any other colouring. Spirit brown will give a brown cast to a coloured job which does not quite reach the desired tone of the pattern. Because these colours look pale when mixed thinly, do not think that there will be no effect. Unless used thin there will be too much effect.

Painting—solid opaque colours. So far the colouring has been transparent. There is another necessary method for treating such places as polished bruises or discoloured streaks. This is done with solid colour, using the pencil brush. The main colours used are red lead, raw umber, brown or burnt umber, yellow ochre, yellow chrome, and orange chrome. All these are cheap colours and may be purchased in small quantities from polish supplier or oil shops.

The usual method of mixing for small bruises and so on is as follows. Put a brushful or two of polish on to the back of a piece of glasspaper; then with the damp brush pick up a little of the necessary powders and work them into the polish to make a thinnish mixture approximately the colour of the job. No exact combinations can be given, but the following general hints might be useful. Red lead, red polish (strong) and black with polish will serve for dark mahogany colours. Brown umber, yellow ochre, and a little chrome yellow will serve for some walnut colours. Yellow ochre alone in polish is also good for walnut. Red lead mixed with spirit green gives a kind of greenish yellow useful for golden walnut. This last is a good example of green " killing " the red.

A great deal of judgment is required in mixing the correct shade, but always use too thin than too thick, giving a second touch if necessary when dry. These solid colour mixtures are useful in painting out edges of plywood, etc. In this case the paint is put on thickly after the grain has been well waxed up and papered off smoothly. Mix up a colour approximately the general tone and paint the edge thoroughly, allowing to dry well. Mix up a darkish brown mixture, not too thin.

Dry the brush after dipping in this colour, so that when the point is stubbed against a piece of glasspaper or the hand the hair divides into several separate points. Work across the ground colour of the edge in a kind of diagonal manner, when each point of the brush will form a type of grain, though not too formal.

General. Always work slowly and gradually. Corners should not be worked right up with a fad but as near as is convenient, finishing the actual angle with a brush. Toning down (if not too large patches are entailed) may be done with a brush, but never should the latter be dipped up very wet, or the colouring will be uncontrolled.

Always wash out thoroughly with spirits after solid colour, for if left to harden the brush will be ruined. After using in ordinary polish colour, point the hair with the fingers and allow to dry. This method keeps the brush in shape, and it can always be softened with spirits when necessary.

COATING

This is the general term for varnishing, which follows fadding or colouring and assists in providing a thick groundwork quickly. It is best applied over a fadding in which no oil has been used. If, however, oil has been used, but has been *thoroughly taken off* with the rubber, varnish can be used without fear of sweating. This coating may be omitted if desired, but it gives quite a saving of time. It normally follows the colouring stage, but if the latter is omitted it follows the fadding.

Kinds of varnishes. Spirit varnishes are used and the best of these are naphtha, crystal, white hard, and stick. The first two are fairly quick drying. Hard varnishes can be applied either with a brush or a rubber.

In use they should be thinned down roughly to the following proportions : 1 part varnish, 1 part polish, 1 part spirits; which mixture will be about right for charging the rubber. If still too thick add more polish and spirits. A rubber which has been previously used for polish is best, as it is already soaked and the varnish can be put on the face only without making a rather sticky mess of the rest of the wadding. The rag used should be the thinnest and most open possible, but without lint. When charged (with a brush dipped up wet and wiped on the face) the rubber is made up, when the varnish should, on the slightest pressure, come through very easily.

Using varnish rubber. The method of using is similar to the last process in fadding, working absolutely straight, taking the rubber off at the end of each stroke, and with as light a touch as possible. If a place is missed do not attempt to touch it up, but wait until the whole has been covered, then begin again at the top and give a second coat, when the dry patch can be covered.   It will be found probably that several times over will be necessary to get a really good coat, and in this event the rubber will have to be dipped up several times, for no pressure is used to make the varnish flow.

Brushing the varnish.   When using a brush, a No. 7 or 8 bear's-hair mop is ideal, and the varnish made a little thicker by lessening the spirits.   Coat in quickly (with not too wet a brush) and as flat as possible.   While still wet, dip up a polish rubber with a little spirits and lightly stroke the surface in exactly the same manner as varnishing with the rubber.   This spirit rubber should be fairly wet, and the " rubbing down " not continued after the varnish shows signs of pulling up.

Always remove cover of rubber
when recharging with polish.

CHAPTER VIII: FRENCH POLISHING—BODYING

UP to the present the work has been given a moderately flat groundwork, coated or not with varnish, and it now remains to flatten further and increase the body of shellac, and bring its surface up bright and clean. The latter term means entire freedom from rubber marks, pimples, and dust.

Glasspapering. If the work has been coated with varnish, a supply of Oakey's 7/o garnet paper is essential. This paper has a fine grain which leaves few deep scratches and at the same time has twice the amount of " cut " on polish of any other grade of sufficient fineness. A good substitute is a fine garnet sander belt which has been used and discarded. The thick backing is peeled off, leaving a thin fine-cutting paper. If not coated, ordinary grade " o " paper may be used if the above is not available. This grade has very little " cut " on varnished work.

Cut down the work well, using a cork block or the flat of the hand. Using the tips of the fingers on flat surfaces is to be avoided as far as possible owing to uneven pressure and consequent waviness in the final surface of the shellac. Having flattened the surface, dust off well and cover once with a new rubber dipped up fairly wet. This brings the job back to colour and shows up any small holes and bruises.

Stopping small holes. These are now stopped up with either Japan wax or beeswax. The former is easier to put in, but the latter holds better. The best way of applying is with a penknife, picking a little up on the point and pressing well down in the hole. Alternatively a piece of wax may be rubbed over the hole until it is effectively stopped, but this method does not always ensure a complete filling to the bottom of the hole and the wax often sinks at a later period. Whichever method is used all surface wax must be cleaned off thoroughly, or polish applied will eventually " break up " during bodying and leave a very ugly depression which will entail a great amount of building up later.

To clean off, remove all lumps carefully with a knife, afterwards papering with a piece of " o " paper. When all is free from wax, the stopped hole may be smoothed with the back of the paper. Care should be taken that no oil is present when waxing, for it will be found that the shellac will not cover and the wax will either pull out or remain dull and dirty.

After stopping all holes and bruises, the wax must be fixed with a wet rubber applied straight and without oil several times, or the various places may be picked out with a small pencil brush charged lightly with polish.   Care should be taken that no unsightly ridge of polish is formed around the hole when using this brush method. Having made sure that all the wax is sealed with polish the bodying proper may be commenced.

System for rubber movement.   Apply oil with the finger just as in fadding, collecting it with a fairly wet rubber and distributing over the work.   Work up now with a round-and-round motion, covering every part evenly.   The centres should be worked in fairly

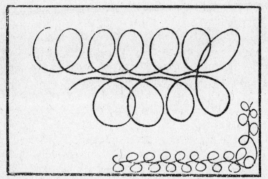

FIG. 18.   ROUND-AND-ROUND MOVEMENT OF RUBBER.
Use large circles for the centre of the panel and use either
small circles or small figures of eight around the edges.

large circles while the edges are best done in either quite small circles or figures of eight.

The parts usually missed are the edges that cross the grain and the corners.   Evenness may, however, be attained by a simple system.   Work the centre in rows of circles backwards and forwards until the whole is covered *once* except for a margin of, say, a rubber width all round.   Without taking the rubber off, move it to the nearest edge and work figures of eight along it once until a corner is reached.   Work two or three circles here, moving on in the same way up the next edge and so on until the first edge is reached, when the centre is begun again as before and the whole operation repeated. In this way every inch will be covered once, and as the rubber moves away, each place is given a few moments to settle before being touched again.   Fig. 18 shows the idea.   When using the six practice pieces, of course, after each piece is covered once the rubber is moved to the next, and so on.

The rubber.   So much for the systematic covering, but there is an equally important point to be watched at the same time. This is the smear and the state of the surface. As was mentioned in " fadding," the smear is dependent upon the amount of oil and the quality of rag. If a good piece of linen dress shirt is being used this may be taken as the best obtainable. If not, however, be sure that it is fairly thick, of a moderately fine grain and definitely not woolly. If good textured, though thin, it may be doubled and will work well.

Pull of the rubber. To give an approximate idea of the pull of a piece of good rag, take a mirror, polish well with a rag, and rub the heel of the hand (in circles as in polishing) on its surface. It will be found that there is a distinct resistance to the flesh of the hand, yet not so strong as to make the circular motion awkward. The hand, if very moist, should be dried so that the correct feel is obtained.

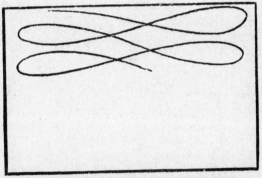

FIG. 19. LONG FIGURES-OF-EIGHT MOVEMENT.
This follows the round-and-round movement. If preferred a long oval movement can be substituted.

To see the opposite effect of no pull, thoroughly wet the glass and rub as before; it will be seen that no pull or grip is possible. This latter is very similar to the feel of a rubber when using too much oil. There is no grip; the polish is just squeezed out of the rubber, and as the rag has no power to pull it where required, the resulting surface is far from presentable.

Exactly the same thing happens when the oil quantity is correct and the rag is bad. However, if oil is *gradually* added until a good smear stays on the work there is no fear of excess, and if the " pull " is not requisite change the rag. It should be pointed out that polishing is not a science but an art, and good polishing depends *entirely* upon the worker's sense of touch. If the above experiments are carried out they will provide the worker with a good knowledge of what the professional has learned slowly by experience.

As to the state of the surface, this should always be viewed by keeping the head well down and looking along the work towards the light. The nearer the worker is to a window the clearer will any blemishes show up. As each fresh rubber is applied to the work the pressure is light, gradually increasing as the polish becomes less. The rubber should not be dipped up again until considerable pressure is needed. After each dip up, the smear will show a tendency to be taken off, and while more shellac is required on the timber, a little more oil should be added to keep the smear as before.

Avoid a wet rubber. If a wet rubber is used carelessly or with too much pressure, the polish squeezes out at the point and sides, and unless noticed at once and flattened out will settle hard enough to form a ridge which will be difficult to eliminate, and therefore care

FIG. 20.   LONG STRAIGHT PATH OF RUBBER.
As the work proceeds the figure-of-eight movement (Fig. 19) is changed for long straight strokes as here.

should be taken that these rubber marks or " whips " do not occur.

Again, using a wet rubber in a dusty situation will probably result in a very inferior " pimply " surface, for as the dust settles the rubber passes over it, acting as a fixative. With the dry rubber method the surface is never wet. Therefore, as the dust settles, the edges of the rubber pick it up easily and pimples are avoided. Obviously these edges should be wiped occasionally to ensure that no dust will work its way on to the rubber face.

Rubbing continued. So far we have cut down the surface, waxed it, sealed it, and begun a body in wide, slow-moving circles. Now this process should be continued until each rubber becomes fairly dry, dipping up again and again according to the depth of body required.

We will suppose that three rubbers have sufficed to fill up any open grain and give a substantial thickness of polish to the work. Now a fourth rubber will be required finally to improve the surface. The round-and-round is changed to the long ovals and figures of eight, as in Fig. 19, until all traces of circular movement have gone, changing then to a straight up and down motion, though, of course, turning on the work and not taking the rubber off (see Fig. 20).

The ends. To ensure the ends being properly bodied, the rubber may be taken up and down these occasionally, though if this is practised too often there will be obvious signs of a cross-movement which will spoil the effect. However, when all signs of circles and curves are gone the straight work is continued until the rubber is quite dry. Dryness of same is easily gauged by touching the lips with the rubber face. If dry there will be no cold spirits apparent but a slight warmth due to friction.

Taking off the oil. The oil is now right on the top and to complete the body, so that it may dry, this oil has to be taken off. This may be done with a piece of clean soft rag, *very slightly* moistened with spirits, which is rubbed lightly all over. This causes a slight dullness, but as it is only a body this does not matter. Alternatively, use the final polish method of taking off as in " fadding."

When dry, ease down with a piece of old oily paper, dust off, and begin again, taking off the oil at the end of each body and allowing about twenty-four hours for drying. About three bodies should be enough and in the last one, instead of wiping the oil off for drying, it is allowed to remain.

Pulling over. The object of the preliminary circular motion is to pull the polish flat. When polish is put on *with* the grain it tends to pile up between the pores, making ridges or what is called ropiness. Thus very small hollows are formed, which, however, are very apparent on a shiny surface. With pressure and a cross-grain circular motion, the tops of these ridges are flattened and forced into the hollows and any open grain. This is known as " pulling over " and is obviously very necessary.

Grinders. To quicken the " pulling over," if a pinch of super-fine pumice or silex is added evenly under the rag to a *medium* wet rubber, greater pull is obtained and therefore greater flatness and brilliance. When first applying one of these pumice rubbers or " grinders," go gently at first, for the initial wetness forces the pumice through quickly and with excessive pressure there is a liability of tearing-up. As the polish decreases, the grittiness lessens and pressure can be increased safely. Incidentally, a grinder is a fine method of working down a stubborn rubber mark.

At this stage you now pass to one of the three finishing processes: Stiffing, Spiriting, or the Acid Finish.

STIFFING

THIS is one of the three alternative methods of finishing french polishing. The work has passed through the stages of *Staining*, *Filling*, *Fadding*, *Colouring*, and *Bodying*, and has now to be given the final shine.

Dip up the rubber half strength, flatten well out, and examine the face to ensure freedom from wrinkles and dust. Press the face with

FIG. 21. STRAIGHT MOVEMENT WHEN STIFFING

Note that the rubber is taken off at the ends and is glided
on again so that it overlaps slightly the previous stroke.

the thumb to see that there is a sufficiency of polish to flow freely, yet not enough to run. Glide it on to the top left-hand corner and *lightly* make one straight motion to the other side, when the rubber is again glided off, as in Fig. 21. Come back in the same way, over-lapping, say, half an inch.

Cover all the surface in this way once, and start again at the top and work down. On about the third time the smear will have reduced to a few streaks. The rubber is dipped up again similarly, and these last few oil marks are removed in exactly the same way, leaving the surface clear and bright. There may, however, be a few marks caused by a drag of the rubber, but in an hour or so these will dry out.

It will be noticed that as the oil is gradually taken off the pull becomes stronger until, in the very last finishing strokes, there is a distinct stiffness and the absence of oil is very obvious. The name for this process is now clear.

Straight strokes. The great thing in stiffing is a light touch, and the more delicate this is the better the result. The other factor is absolute straightness of stroke. It will be apparent that in work with straight edges, any curves will be ugly, but it will be obvious that if the worker stands at the middle of one edge and moves his hand to his left and right, the strokes will be arcs. A better plan and easy way of avoiding this is to stand at one end and " stiff " away from and to himself, when he will be able to sight a straight rubber path. On long work the arm is kept rigid and the worker moves bodily along, or alternatively, works at the centre of one side and keeps the face of the rubber at right angles to the top edge by moving the wrist.

Do not, however, try to " stiff " with a grinder or trouble will ensue. In any case a grinder is always too hard for stiffing, which latter needs a soft, pliable rubber. Make up a good " stiffer " and keep it in a small airtight tin away from all bodying and grinding rubbers. Always use the new " stiffer " for bodying for a few minutes after making, to put it in compact shape and to force the polish everywhere in the wadding.

SPIRITING OFF

Spiriting is the second of the three methods of finishing off french polish. The preliminary building-up stages in this finish do not vary much from those of other finishes, but since spiriting gives a high gloss a little extra flatness is as well. The final body needs a little more care. Cutting down with a piece of worn flour paper is all that should be necessary to avoid scratches showing through the final shine. The work at this stage should be free from pimples, etc. Oil on the paper will assist in the papering. When smooth and clean, the whole should be wiped with a soft cloth to remove grease and dirt.

First spiriting operation. Now for the actual work. Take the hard rubber and dip it up with half spirits and half polish, taking care not to be too free with the spirits. Flick a *little* oil on the job, collect with the rubber and begin to work the whole surface. The great thing in this work is even pressure which gradually increases as the rubber dries. The beginner usually manages the gradual increase correctly, but where he goes wrong is that his circular swings outward are heavier than the return swings.

Path of rubber. However, to continue with our final body, carry on in circles, straightening out every now and again to see how things are progressing, and, as the rubber dries, change to figures of eight and long straight turns until completely dry.

Oil. During this body there should be sufficient oil to produce a thin steamy smear which follows the rubber and dries back a little when left. The smear should be the full width of the rubber. When the latter is quite dry this smear will be very faint and delicate.

Spiriting. This follows the above immediately. Take out the spirit rubber and hold it to the lips. If it is just sharp and cold to the lips it is dipped up enough. If it is quite dry, sprinkle a few drops of spirits on to the palm of the hand and apply to the rubber and cover with the rag. (The way to make this rubber is described later.) Use a full-length sweeping motion as lightly as possible, until it is obvious that the rubber is not so wet as to burn the polish and take off the oil too quickly.

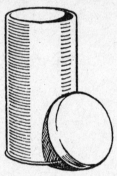

Pressure can be increased, using figures of eight, and, when confidence is obtained, circles; but it is better for the beginner to stick to figures of eight and long turns, which will ensure no rubber marks. Continue until quite dry when the oil smear should have disappeared and the surface appears mirror-like. For a final burnish, dip the face of the rubber into vienna chalk and work in long strokes. This will effectively

FIG. 22. RUBBER TIN.
The tin should have a tight-fitting lid so that it is air-tight.

clear the work and allow a good clear surface to show.

We can now deal with a few of the important points, many of which apply to any finish.

Rubbers and rubber tins. For the " spirit rubber," wash out an old rubber thoroughly free from polish, and allow to dry. Remake and dip up with spirits, covering the whole with a piece of fine old damask table-cloth. This is the finest and softest rag for spiriting, but, failing this, use fine-textured good linen. There is usually, however, an old damask cloth about that is beyond service and is invaluable for this work.

A substitute for washed-out wadding is medical cotton wool which automatically hardens when dipped up. Regarding tins, keep one for fad and general bodying rubbers, and separate ones for spirit rubber and " half-and-half " rubber, as the harder bodying rubber is called.   In this way the important rubbers will always be in good clean condition.   Fig. 22 shows a rubber tin.

Purpose of spiriting.   The idea of this process is gradually to burnish the surface of semi-soft shellac without disturbing the layer, and at the same time to lift off the thin film of oil, a job that has been partly done by the half-and-half rubber.   It will be clear then that any surplus wetness of spirits will straightway render the surface soft, preventing all further attempts at burnishing.   The correct " dip up " will come with practice, but to err on the dry side is good, for more spirits can always be added.   If the rubber is too dry, it will be apparent from the half-and-half smear going as if a piece of cloth were being rubbed over it, leaving just a dullness.   Too wet a rubber takes off all the oil at each stroke, leaving bright streaks.   The chalk may also be used just before all the oil has disappeared.

THE ACID FINISH

Here we have the third method of finishing a french polished surface.   The building-up processes are as previously described. They are :   *Staining*, *Filling*, *Fadding*, *Colouring*, and *Bodying*. When the acid finish is to be used it is essential that no colouring is attempted *after* bodying, as otherwise the acid may attack the colouring matter and have the effect of bleaching it.

To seven parts of clean cold water add one part of sulphuric acid, distilled water being the best for the purpose.   Shake the acid and water to mix thoroughly, and spread the mixture on the surface of the work with either the palm of the hand or with a piece of butter muslin.   Have ready a pounce bag filled with vienna chalk and dust the chalk all over the damp surface.   Next burnish up the work with the palm of the hand, working to and fro in the direction of the grain. As it dries out, dust the chalk off the surface with clean dry rag, which will bring the work to a fine finish.   The weak acid kills the superfluous linseed or other oil which has been used to lubricate the polishing rubber, and in due course the acid is killed, absorbed, and dried off by the chalk.   Some workers use a piece of new chamois leather instead of the palm of the hand for the final burnishing up.   Use precipitated chalk if vienna chalk is not available.

Sulphuric acid varies in strength and should any pitting or pock marks of chalk appear on the work, it is safe to assume that the acid mixture is too strong, when it should be diluted with water. Furthermore, if large quantities of colouring matter have been used during the bodying-up process, the acid method of finishing will bleach the bismarck or other colouring anilines which have been used. It is therefore advisable to stain and match up all the job correctly to the required shade before bodying-up the work.

When making the acid mixture it is the best practice to add the sulphuric acid to the water drop by drop. The pounce bag is made by tying up two thicknesses of muslin like a miniature plum pudding, the vienna chalk being of course tied up inside. When the pounce bag is dabbed on to the work a certain amount of the chalk escapes through the mesh of the muslin. Fig. 23 shows the pounce bag.

The acid process is used in two different ways. Where work has been somewhat hurried and a slightly excessive amount of oil has had to be used, it is the usual practice to body up the surface and reduce the polish with methylated spirits until the worker almost reaches the stage where all is ready for spiriting-out. He then allows the work to stand overnight (about twelve hours), and proceeds to use the acid finish to remove his surplus oil. The work is finished off by the legitimate spiriting-out process. The second method of using the acid finish is first to spirit out the job and, after laying the work aside to harden up, finish as previously described.

FIG. 23. POUNCE BAG.
This is filled with fine vienna chalk, and is dabbed on to the surface.

Amateurs who have had no experience with the acid finish are advised to use the process after the final bodying-up and prior to spiriting-out. This will give them the opportunity of clearing any specks or other defects with a little polish applied to the spirit rubber before the final burnishing of the surface with neat spirits. When the final burnishing is done by the acid process, the best workers complete their job with a few drops of clarified ox-gall sprinkled on a piece of soft rag, and used similarly to a furniture reviver. This to a great extent prevents any fingermarks appearing on the completed product. Ox-gall can be obtained from any butcher's slaughterman, and this will last the polisher until it turns bad. The ox-gall should be put into a wide-mouthed bottle and filtered through crushed bone charcoal before using. A piece of white blotting paper may be folded up like a triangular toffee bag, the crushed bone charcoal being placed in the interior.

GLAZING

This is really yet another method of finishing of french polish, but it is rather in the nature of a cheap and easy finish, and is not so permanent. However, it has its uses where a shine is required quickly, and is suitable for small work. The operations of *Staining*, *Filling*, *Fadding*, *Colouring*, and *Bodying* are carried out first, though, since glazing is generally used for cheap work, it is usual not to give so full a body. However, a reasonable foundation must be built up over which the glaze can be applied.

What glaze is. Glaze is made by dissolving gum benzoin in methylated spirits; it is used for imparting a final gloss to a french polished surface instead of spiriting-out the work. Gum benzoin is the product of the *Laurus benzoin* of America and the *Styrax benzoin* tree of Sumatra, and is one of the gums used for burning as incense in churches.

Preparation. In appearance gum benzoin resembles pieces of white nut. The white pieces vary in size from the size of a pea to the size of your thumbnail. The flakes are all stuck together with the twigs of the tree and other foreign substances, somewhat like lumps of white nut toffee. The more white the gum contains the better its quality.

When procured it should be crushed and placed in a wide-mouthed bottle, with sufficient methylated spirit to cover just nicely the mass of benzoin. Cork the bottle, place it in living-room temperature, and shake it from time to time over three days. Then strain the mixture and bottle it for future use. If it can stand for a month, so much the better, because a solution of benzoin improves with keeping.

By preparing the mixture in this way all the white benzoin will be dissolved and the twigs and other refuse may be thrown away after it is strained. Glaze can also be obtained ready-made.

How glaze is used. To use the glaze it should be diluted with methylated spirits until the colour is similar to champagne. It may be applied to the bodied-up surface by means of a french polishing rubber, or by means of a low velvet pile textile such as white velveteen. Do not use a coloured velveteen, because the dye may run. The rubber or pad should be used in straight sweeps in the direction of the grain, from one end of the work to the other, and the pad should make paths so that the lines are parallel to each other. Care must be exercised to avoid too much overlapping of the paths, otherwise the glaze will be picked off the surface as quickly as it is deposited.

Allow the glaze to dry for five minutes or more, and then repeat the action of the rubber in such a manner that it will cover any small spaces which have been left between the paths of the first application, and proceed until the surface has been glazed to a bright finish. The rubber should contain more liquid than is usually used in a charged french polish rubber, as glazing really consists of applying a thin coating of benzoin spirit varnish to give a gloss.

The blind corners of framed polished panels should be picked-out with glaze by applying it with a No. 3 artist's pencil brush, or by using the glaze on a small piece of cotton wadding which has been spun or folded on a spent match stalk.

Other methods. Another method of using glaze is to mix it half and half with french polish in the last stages of bodying-up, and apply it by using the rubber in long, straight paths. This gives a stiffed-up appearance to the job and eliminates spiriting-out for cheap work.

Glaze is usually used for the edges of shaped brackets, spandrels, etc., where it would be next to impossible to spirit out these small and narrow surfaces.

Piano makers use both benzoin glaze and a speciality varnish known as " China varnish " for the edges of their work, and some very proficient workers are successful in spiriting-out a surface so glazed. Glaze improves with keeping up to three years.

Burnishing. The usual workshop method of producing a piano-type finish is by the process known as burnishing. There are many burnishing agents such as *Supersol* or *Belco* liquid polish. In all cases the liquid is shaken well and applied in close loops and finally straight strokes with wadding or a soft rag. These are really super-fine abrasive and polishing agents and are effective only when the film is properly bodied and completed with the rubber.

Dull finish. This effect comes somewhere between the full gloss finish and the dull eggshell effect, and can be varied. Carry the work through to the full gloss and allow to harden right out from twenty-four to forty-eight hours. Wrap up a small piece of the finest grade steel wool (it must be fine) and apply some ordinary washing soap or wax polish to it to lubricate and to lessen the bite. Apply to the surface evenly. Alternatively, any really fine abrasive such as whiting, *fine* pumice, or crocus powder can be used with a rag. In some cases a definite direction to the marks of the abrasive is desirable, and the method given on page 78 can be used.

CHAPTER X : FRENCH POLISHING—THE AWKWARD PLACES

THE previous chapters have covered the general processes of french polishing, and they can be applied to all straightforward jobs. Most work is not so simple as this, however, there being awkward corners, mouldings, carvings, etc., in which the path of the rubber is restricted. The despairing cry of the conscientious amateur is that he cannot obtain really sharp, clean corners. If the reason is simple, the remedy is equally so. Here we deal with some of these difficult jobs.

Dirty corners. When first putting rubber to timber, the polish is naturally squeezed into the corners to take off the dryness, and then for some time all interest in these ceases, the rubber taking a quadrant path instead of entering the awkward angle. The excuse for this is that by piling up polish in these places, they become sticky and therefore look dirty. After bodying the main surface for some time, the rubber is once more worked into the angle, and then left for another period.

Obviously what must happen is this : the first corner-working puts polish there which does not dry immediately. Meanwhile the dust that settles on the main surface is worked by the side and point of the rubber into the only place it can remain undisturbed—the corner. When it is considered time to give these angles their second working, there is quite an accumulation there, and the polish that is now squeezed into these places effectively fixes all the dust, leaving an ugly, dirty mixture that only glasspaper will remove.

In the rubber making explained on page 37, it is seen that there is a fairly sharp point, and in holding the rubber it is recommended that the forefinger be placed right at this point. This is the main factor in keeping the corners clean. The point will enter conveniently and the forefinger will guide and hold it firm. The second point is : work each corner as many times as the main surface is covered. That is to say, cover all over once, then all sides and corners and repeat throughout the job. If a small patch were left in the centre of a panel, to be worked over once to every six times of the rest, it would be expected that there would be a bad, dull patch, yet curiously enough, this reasoning is never applied to the corners.

Path of the rubber. One or two points regarding rubber handling might be of value here in connection with these awkward places. Always approach a corner from along one of the sides, never work diagonally into it. The best way is to follow a system and work all the corners in the same way.

Take for example, a tea tray with square, unmoulded sides. Begin in the left-hand top corner, this being the easiest for a right-handed man and therefore begun most confidently. Start about 6 in. from the angle along the top edge and work a steady stroke right into the corner, and without stopping come back along the same edge for 2 in. Still without stopping, work right into the corner again, though this time the rubber point is taken down the left-hand side for 2 in., back into the corner again, and then right along this side ready for the next corner. When they can be worked without sticking, etc., a very small circular movement can be made in the angle before coming down the second side. This movement

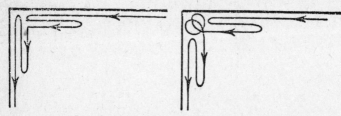

FIG. 24. FIRST CORNER MOVEMENT.   FIG. 25. SECOND MOVEMENT.
These two movements at the corner are carried out one after the other without stopping. Proper forming of the rubber with its pointed end is essential.

will clearly *have* to be *very* small, with the rubber point and forefinger jammed right into the angle.

These motions are pictured in Figs. 24 and 25, but it must be borne in mind that the lines of the rubber path are to be all on top of each other and *right into* the corner, not separated as shown.

Bodying the tray should now be straightforward, but when it comes to stifling, a method is needed both for the centre and corners which will work cleanly, for as the oil gets less the tendency towards dirty work becomes greater. At this stage, let us assume that the job is just on the point of completion, just the final strokes for taking off the oil being necessary.

Stiffing the work. Begin with the rubber a little from the right-hand top corner. Draw it towards the centre, gliding off as this position is reached. Put the rubber at the opposite end and make the stroke also to the centre, gliding off as this stroke meets the first, as in Fig. 26. Continue right across the job. If a stroke were begun from the end and continued right across, there would be difficulty in taking the rubber off at the exact instant, for the rubber cannot now glide off the edge as on the plain flat surfaces. By this method, however, each complete stroke has two beginnings, and the places where the rubber is taken off merge in cleanly.

For the corners, put the point of the rubber into the angle, work to the corner, and straight down the other side to half-way, working the next corner similarly, and making the strokes meet in the centres of the sides, as Fig. 27. In Figs. 26 and 27, the ends of the strokes are shown as curves, but this is only to show that the rubber is glided off, not picked straight up. The latter would result in a print the same shape as the rubber.

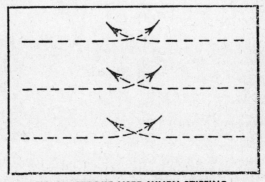

FIG. 26. STROKE USED WHEN STIFFING.
Start the rubber at one end and glide it off just past the middle. The path is straight throughout.

Mouldings. Mouldings take a long time to work up unless done in the proper way; those with several members seldom finish cleanly when worked up solely with the rubber. Work up a little with a fad, and when convenient give a coat of varnish with a brush. Not thickly, but just enough to hold up. When picking up the work next for bodying, take a small piece of fad and wring it out dry in a rag. It should be quite soft, not sticky. Dip up lightly with polish, add a little oil and a little fine pumice powder. Work out on the back of the glasspaper, and work into the members of the moulding with the thumb. (There is usually a projection or an edge handy that the fingers can run along to form a gauge and obtain some pressure.) Work this fad backwards and forwards until the whole becomes burnished up thoroughly.

It will be found that this method will get up a moulding more quickly and flatter than any other way. Beware of too much oil, for this quickly puts on a beautiful shine, but will soon get very dull.

Too much polish is too sticky.   Add pumice until there is a nice
" bite " ;   more than this will just tear up.   When all is flat and
bright, run a nice, clean, soft rubber down the members once or
twice to remove the oil and the job is done.

As mentioned earlier, when mouldings can be polished in a length
and mitred and fixed afterwards a much cleaner result is possible.

Treatment of carving.   This method of burnishing applies to
some kinds of carving such as the shells often used on Queen Anne
legs and apron pieces.   With deep carving, such as leaves and flowers
well recessed, burnishing is not possible for the varnish would be
difficult to apply nicely and the more inaccessible spots would be

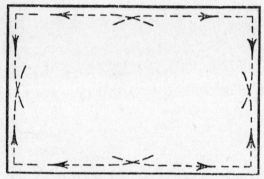

FIG. 27.   DEALING WITH CORNERS AND EDGES.
The curves in both Figs. 26 and 27 are only to show how the
rubber is glided off.   The actual path is straight, the rubber
being lifted straight off.

hard to get at with a fad.   This type of decoration is best either
stained and oiled or rubbed in cleanly with a pigment in oil and the
surplus rubbed off with a cloth leaving the upper portions lighter.
This, of course, is done after polishing the surrounding timber,
and care must be taken not to touch the carving with polish or the
stain will not take.

Drawers, backs, etc.   A word or two regarding the finishing
touches to furniture when polished.   First, the insides of drawers,
wardrobes, etc., should be cut down and fadded up.   When a job
is begun by fadding, it is usual to coat inside the drawers, etc., with
button polish plus a handful of chalk.   When finishing is begun
these coated portions are nicely dry and the chalk helps in a smooth
surface.   Clean fads should be used and all dust got out carefully,
for these natural-coloured interiors mark very easily.

Next give a coat of polish and a smooth down to stained undersides of plinths. Cut down with glasspaper the bottom edges of doors, wax up, and paper smooth. The backs of all pieces should have been stained and can now be eased down and fadded well up.

The unseen places. Such parts as mirror-bars on dressing tables are usually either stained with walnut stain, varnished, and stiffed, or else painted out to the approximate colour of the job and finished as above. The great thing in all these unseen details is *finish*. A job roughly stained below, generally with runnings from the glued blocks, unvarnished and rough, is nothing to be proud of. A table, whether dining or occasional, that has its undersides rough to the touch is apparent to everyone who has occasion to move or touch it, and casts no credit on the craftsman.

Polished angles. Now a word about the polished portions. There should be nothing wrong with these except the angles. These when polished by the best man always look the least bit dry. This is overcome by dipping a piece of oily wadding in the gas black and mixing into a thickish black grease. Then rub it down all corners and angles and rub off with a soft clean cloth. This wadding makes a very ugly black streak when put on, but it comes away easily enough, leaving the merest suspicion just where the rubber couldn't get.

While the wadding is still to hand, pull out each drawer, if any, and with the thumb and finger to guide the wadding, make a strip of black down the drawer side, a quarter of an inch wide where it meets the front. This prevents the side from showing white and makes a neater finish when the drawer is an easy fit.

This black oil is also used at the hollows of beads and mouldings that are impossible to reach with fad or rubber. Just rub in the black and polish off with a clean rag. This eliminates the dusty effect that small worked beads are so prone to have.

Note on stiffing. The only point that needs stressing is a delicate touch when stiffing panels. Always go lightly and try to feel what you are doing. When placing the rubber at the ends to make the stiffing strokes, place it accurately first time and move off immediately. An instant too long and you had better let the job dry and body-up again.

Although a tea tray was taken as an example, it might be pointed out that polished tea trays are not to be recommended unless covered substantially with glass to prevent marking. In this connection it might be a help to know that all work to be under glass should be finished much redder to allow for the greenness of the latter.

CHAPTER XI: FRENCH POLISHING—HOLDING THE WORK

A FEW hints on holding various pieces of work whilst polishing will be of assistance to those who have never actually seen the inside of a polishing shop. As all the appliances or gadgets discussed are of the simplest form, they can be easily made by any handyman.

Bench. For general purposes the bench should be much higher than that of the joiner or cabinet-maker, otherwise both the back and the arms of the polisher will soon become cramped and fatigued.

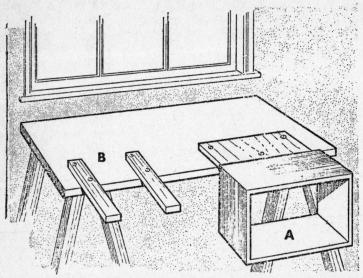

FIG. 28. BENCH USED FOR POLISHING IN POSITION NEAR WINDOW.
The worker should face the window as this shows up the path of the rubber. The battens are screwed on to enable drawers and boxes, etc., to be dealt with.

For a man of average height, the bench should be about 3 ft., and if possible it should be under a window as suggested in Fig. 28. The top of the bench should rest on trestles, so that all may be conveniently moved for washing and dusting out the workshop. Cover the top with two or three thicknesses of good brown paper. The paper may have its edges glued. In time, the several thicknesses of paper will form a somewhat soft but firm surface and there will be little or no tendency for work to become scratched on its underside, provided that the bench be frequently dusted. Several pairs of pad sticks should be kept at hand, these varying in length from 15 in. up to 22 in.

Drawers. For supporting drawers of dressing chests and sideboards, two pairs of trestles should be made to a height of about 20 in. so that when drawers are placed upon their backs the fronts will be about 3 ft. high. If the trestles are made about 16 in. long on their back bone they will hold two drawers, one in front of the other; thus, two pairs of trestles will accommodate four drawers.

Small drawers, wireless cases, and similar pieces of furniture may be suspended on temporary battens which project from the

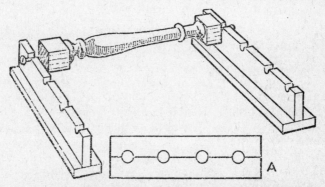

FIG. 29. BRACKET BOARDS USED AS A CRADLE FOR TURNINGS.
The uprights are made as shown at A, a saw-cut being made through the
holes. They are screwed to the horizontal pieces.

bench top, these being screwed to the bench as suggested in Fig. 28. (B). The box (A) can thus be partly bodied up on its top and right-hand side. When the polish is too soft for further rubbing, the box may be lifted off the battens; or, if it is small, it can be turned round so that the other two surfaces are brought into position. By adopting this plan the box can be continually revolved, as it were, thus bringing the dry surfaces into a comfortable position for the plying of the rubber.

A narrow (say 6 in.) drawer could be laid upon the two battens B, Fig. 28, whilst the front face is bodied up; and the moment it appears too soft to continue the rubbing it can be quickly removed and another drawer could occupy its position on the battens. Several pairs of these battens may be fixed on the bench or benches so that several drawers or boxes can be polished by working first on one and then on another.

Turned work. For polishing the pillars of sideboards, columns, and turned spindles, which may be square, round or octagonal, loose bracket boards (Fig 29) are used. These, being self-contained, may be laid on the bench at any convenient distance apart to accommodate any length of pillar. The bracket supports are roughly

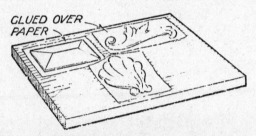

GLUED OVER PAPER

FIG. 30. CARVINGS GLUED TO BOARD.
The paper beneath the carvings enables them to be levered up after polishing.

made by nailing $\frac{3}{4}$-in. or 1-in. boards together, and the vertical pieces may have holes bored through them before they are sawn into two pieces, as suggested by the inset drawing (Fig. 29, A). The turned pillars may have a fairly large round wire nail driven into each end so as to form an axle, upon which they can be freely revolved with the left hand whilst using the polishing rubber in the right hand.

In many cases the worker will find that pillars, columns, and spindles already have turned wooden pins upon their ends when they come into the polishing shop, and when this is the case the wooden dowel pins can be used as an axle on which to rotate the turning. This eliminates fouling the end of the turning with a nail hole.

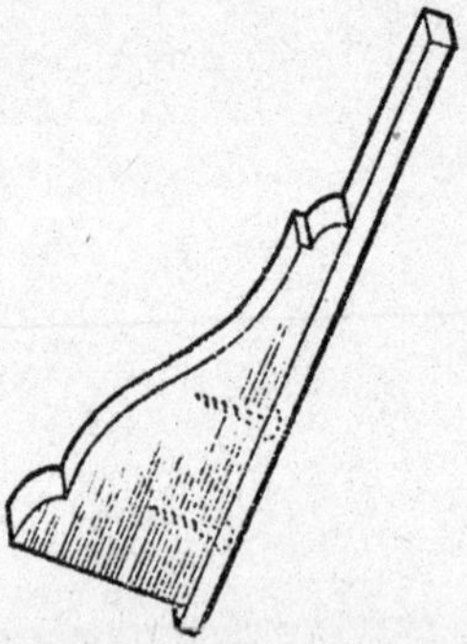

Carvings. For polishing small pieces of carving similar to those shown in Fig. 30, it is usual to fix them on to a piece of clean board by gluing them down with a piece of newspaper inserted between the back of the

FIG. 31. POLISHING A BRACKET SCREWED TO A BATTEN.

carving and the polishing board. This holds them firmly in position whilst they are stained, glasspapered, and polished. When completed, a well-worn table knife blade pushed between the carving and the board will cut away the thickness of newspaper and thus release them.

Brackets. Small decorative brackets and similar pieces which have to be polished on two sides and one edge are generally mounted as shown at Fig. 31. Small pieces of hardwood laths are kept for the purpose, and two screws secure the handled laths to the bracket. The handle is held in the left hand and the bracket moved first to one side and then to the other, so that both sides and the front edge can be polished without having to hold it in the fingers.

Tenter hooks. A metal tenter hook is illustrated at Fig. 32, and a few of these are useful for holding panels on to a temporary polishing board. Tenter hooks are also used for fastening long lengths of moulding on to the boards as at Fig. 33, one being used at each end of the moulding. Several lengths of moulding are of course fastened one behind the other on a 10-in. or 12-in. board, and the polisher plies his rubber on them, one after the other, and then picks up another board of mouldings and works on it whilst the previous lot are drying off.

FIG. 32. TENTER HOOK USED TO HOLD DOWN WOOD WHEN POLISHING.

Laths. Where a number of cot, table, or chair laths have to be polished on both faces and both edges, a quite good idea is to fix a narrow and thin strip of wood on the bench with a couple of panel pins. Pick up a lath and hold it with the left hand and use the rubber as suggested. Revolve the lath with the left hand

FIG. 33. MOULDINGS FIXED TO A BOARD WITH TENTER HOOKS.
The mouldings should be extra long so that marks made by the tenter hooks are cut off. In some cases the mouldings can be glued down over strips of paper.

so as to bring each face of the wood into contact with the rubber. When too soft for further working (which will mean about two rubs on each face of the lath) rear it at an angle against the wall and pick up the next lath. By the time you have got to the end of a row of say twelve laths, they will be hard enough for you to begin the process all over again. Thin-shaped cabriole-pattern table legs may also be manipulated in a similar manner.

Heavy work. All heavy carcase work having sharp square edges should be protected in the polishing shop by fixing strips of wood on to them as at Fig. 34. The strips should be about $\frac{3}{4}$ in. by $\frac{1}{4}$ in., and may be fixed with panel pins. The laths should stand back about $\frac{1}{16}$ in. from the polished face so that they are clear of the rubber. If these laths be not fixed on to square carcase work there is great danger of the edges becoming bruised. Good cabinet work

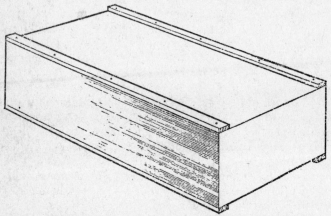

FIG. 34. STRIPS FIXED AT EDGES OF HEAVY WORK FOR PROTECTION.
These are desirable in large carcases which would easily be bruised at the edges. They are nailed on to the plain sides.

has often been spoilt at its joint lines by the polisher failing to take these or similar precautions.

Sweep out your polishing shop every week with damp sawdust and have the floor washed with soap and water. If you can afford to have your shop covered with linoleum, do so. See that the place is properly heated in cold weather, otherwise your polish will chill and bloom. Remember, too, that dust, cold, and damp are the polisher's enemies, so try to avoid them.

CHAPTER XII: CONTEMPORARY FINISH

THIS consists of a semi-gloss finish with a slightly waxy appearance. The commercial finish is cellulose lacquer containing a wax element which gives a satin appearance and waxy feel. Usually this is preceded by a sealer and colour coat, the grain being left unfilled. The finish is therefore of a simple nature but cannot be reproduced exactly without the special lacquer and equipment to spray it. It can, however, be matched exactly by hand methods, the finish obtained being superior to the factory variety.

On this furniture the colour varies from nearly natural to golden oak and even light daffodil. The main problem is to match this colour precisely. So little colour is involved that it is not advisable to use stain. Earth colours or pigments are also unsuitable because the finish required is almost perfectly transparent. We must, therefore, resort to aniline spirit-soluble crystals, using these as a dye to tint the initial coat of polish to the shade required, not as a spirit stain. Spirit soluble crystals are available readily in various shades of yellow such as canary, old gold, and cadmium, these particular yellows being roughly as the name suggests. It is essential to have one or preferably two of these dyes at hand, canary (light yellow) and cadmium (rich yellow) being the most suitable.

Aniline dyes are bright in colour. We must therefore use them with care and discretion. One-half ounce would probably last the average home craftsman for the rest of his life. They are best kept in strong solution in a bottle, two gills of methylated spirit to the half ounce being a suitable proportion. If the bottle is shaken well and allowed to stand undissolved crystals will collect at the bottom. It is the saturated solution above—and this may not look yellow—which must be used for tinting.

Preparing the colour coat. This is done by observation then trial and error on scrap oak. We should expect to do this in minutes but it may take the inexperienced an hour. The important thing is to get it dead right. The work can then be tackled with complete confidence. Begin by brushing one coat of button polish on to scrap. Now compare with the job to be matched in clear daylight. Most likely it will not be yellow enough. We use button polish for this first coat because its particular cast is nearest to requirements. Finishing is done with white polish.

Now decide which yellow dye is nearest. The amount of polish

69

required to colour say a bedside cabinet is, to use a familiar measure, about one-third of a cupful. To this add a quarter-teaspoonful of the dye. If it is proposed to use the crystals dry then dissolve a tiny pinch in a little methylated spirit and add this in the required amount to the polish. Apply one coat to another piece of scrap, force dry it near a fire for a minute or so, brush on a few coats of white polish, and test again. Most likely minor adjustments will be required.

Slight darkening may be achieved by adding a little garnet polish; or making the first one or two finish coats garnet or button; it may be required to add a little more dye to strengthen the colour; perhaps a little more of a different yellow is required. It is essential not to use too much dye. The quantity suggested will tint strongly and still leave the film perfectly transparent. If you are slow about matching it may be necessary to make up the polish quantity with spirit. When completely satisfied and not before apply the colour coat. Use a rag which can be discarded. If you use the mop you are sure to get the colour on the next job where it may not be wanted. Allow an hour or so to harden up.

Faking. The next thing is to make good any defects. There may be a joint that is not perfect, perhaps a few panel pin holes, or

MODERN STYLE TABLE WITH PLYWOOD TOP

Plywood edges are sometimes blanked out with a neutral colour.
Poster paint is suitable and takes the finish well. Smooth the edges
with glasspaper before application. Earth pigments in french polish
are also suitable and can be mixed to match

a minor defect in the timber. Plastic wood of the water soluble type seems to be a favourite with readers but the colour range is not adequate. We can overcome the difficulty by adding a little ochre to a knob of the stopping. Mash together with the blade of a screwdriver and a spot of water, and fill the holes. Hard stopping tinted with ochre would be suitable. In either case the colour is unlikely to be exactly right, but we can remedy this by touching in when hard with a little of the dyed polish mixed with a spot of ochre.

Surface defects, such perhaps as a dark mineral streak in the timber, can be touched out in the same way. Here again judgment and observation are required. Add just enough ochre to a little of the dyed polish to conceal the mark, still leaving the grain visible through it. Complete blanking out should be necessary only on such as a spot of stopping which does not match up. When satisfied with the touching up leave everything to harden, and apply a sealer coat. This will usually be white polish but may even be garnet, depending on the colour plan decided upon. The purpose of the sealer coat is to reduce the risk of lifting any colour when bodying is started.

Finishing. The bodied film will harden much brighter than required. The aim now is to produce the satin appearance and waxy feel. For this use steel wool. This is a simple abrasive but even with it fatal mistakes can be made. It is possible for particles of the steel to become embedded in a soft film where they can oxidise and ruin the work. It must therefore be used only on a hard film—never on one which is uncured or which is permanently soft such as ordinary varnish. The wax used can be furniture wax.

Dip a pad of No. 1 steel wool in the wax and rub firmly in straight strokes along the grain. Rubbing is easy because the design of this furniture is simple but the usual care must be taken at corners and edges. The steel wool and wax will cut the surface to the required satin sheen. Complete the job by rubbing with a soft rag in the same way. Note particularly that slight differences between the finish on the hand and factory films will not be noticeable but differences in shade will be immediately apparent. The key to success is therefore exact matching of the shade.

Notes :

1. Aniline dyes will stain the fingers deeply. The stain is harmless but unsightly and may take a few days to disappear.

2. A misplaced crystal of these dyes—which are usually equally soluble in water—can cause serious staining to clothing or carpets.

3. Steel wool is made in grades 000, 00, 0, 1, 2, 3, 4. No. 0 is more suitable than No. 1 for beginners.

4. If a full grain finish is required filling should be done before the colour coat. A suitable routine would be:

(*a*) Apply a wash coat.

(*b*) Ten minutes later fill the grain with *Alabastine* tinted with 10 per cent as much ochre. Next day sand to the white with No. 1F paper, remove dust, and apply the colour coat.

CHAPTER XIII: FRENCH POLISHING—TURNED WORK

WHEN turnings are built into furniture they have to be polished in the same way as the rest of the job, being bodied up and spirited out or stiffed. In the case of very small spindles glaze is useful, especially when they are so close together as to render the use of the rubber difficult. In some cases, however, it is practicable to polish them before assembling, and this can be done on the lathe.

The lathe. For polishing, the lathe should generally be run slowly, and in the case of Jacobean twisted turnings the strap or belt should be thrown off the pulley and the work revolved with the left hand whilst the rubber is applied with the right hand. Two wooden brackets, with iron centre pins on which the work can revolve, will turn out polished work much more quickly and smoothly than by the hand method. More freedom is obtained by revolving the turning than by excessive wrist manipulation, and for glass-papering the grain of the timber or for the first or subsequent coatings of polish, it is much easier to hold the glasspaper against the profile of the turned members than to rub them down when in a stationary position.

The pieces to be polished should be turned up according to ordinary routine, and the centre marks of the head and tailstock should be left untouched so that, after the staining process is completed, the work can be re-chucked or centred for sanding down the raised grain.

The stains used may be oil, water, or spirit. They should be slightly weaker than is usually the case, because much of the turned work will show end grain and consequently it will take the stain more readily. Some workers rub the large end grain members with a piece of ozokerite composition candle partly to fill up the pores and thus prevent the stain striking too deeply into the wood. This method makes for more even staining. Water stain should not be used in this case.

Filling. The filling-in is applied with a brush or rag. It is rubbed in the accustomed manner whilst the pulley of the lathe is revolved by hand. During this process the belt is discarded. Afterwards the belt may be put on the lathe and the work slowly treadled whilst the surplus filling is wiped away with an old rag.

Several turnings, one by one, are treated in this manner and they are then set aside to allow the filler to harden off. They are after-

72

wards given a coat of thick brush polish which can be applied with a fine sponge or a camel hair mop brush. When hard, the work is re-centred in the lathe and it is carefully glasspapered down with No. 1 paper.

Polishing. Ordinary glasspaper may be used dry, but if the worker prefers to use the "wet or dry" variety he may sparingly apply a little white mineral oil on to the woodwork. Wipe the work clean with a dry rag whilst it is still revolving, and take a cotton wadding polishing rubber without a rag covering and charge it freely with polish. Do not use a new rubber for the purpose; an old rubber is preferable. Revolve the work slowly and apply the rubber to the inequalities of the turning, re-charging it with polish as may be thought necessary.

When the pores of the wood appear well filled up and a fair body of polish has been applied, give the work another coat of brush polish. When dry, carefully ease off any dust specks or roughness with spent glasspaper and again use the polishing rubber. The polish on the rubber which is used at this stage of the work should be fairly thin so that it will level up and amalgamate with the under-coat.

When the pores of the wood are choked up and a good body of polish has been obtained, use a piece of new soft folded wash-leather as a spiriting-off rubber, and moisten this with a mixture of one part of polish to four parts of methylated spirits. Run the lathe at a moderate speed, and the moistened chamois leather will soon burnish up the body of polish to an excellent finish.

It is possible to french polish with the wood revolving in the lathe, but it calls for experience. Special polishes for the purpose can be obtained, but although the initial application is simple there is danger of pulling off more than is put on until the knack is acquired. Run the lathe at the slowest speed and lubricate the charged rubber with linseed oil. Fair pressure is needed, but you have to learn when to leave the work to harden. When a fair body has been built up it is left to harden and is finished by burnishing with *Supersol* or a fine abrasive motor car polish. Many tool manufacturers finish by holding a rag moistened with saliva over the revolving wood.

Wax polish. A suitable polish for turned work can be made by shredding 2 oz. of beeswax and working it into a thin paste by the addition of turpentine. Then mix 2 oz. of gum sandarac in 1 pint of methylated spirits and thoroughly dissolve it. Add the spirits-sandarac solution very gradually, stirring it into the wax compound. Whilst the lathe is revolving apply this mixture with a piece of old woollen blanket.

The finish is then obtained by friction, using a soft piece of old linen rag for burnishing up the surface. Beeswax and turpentine are better dissolved cold; heat appears to denature this type of polish whilst in the making. Cornice poles, cornice pole rings, cornice pole ends, and turned handles for all kinds of tools may be expeditiously and economically polished or polish-cum-spirit varnished in the lathe.

Carnauba wax is often used. It gives a brilliant and attractive gloss, but does not wear particularly well and once damaged or marked is not easy to correct unless it can be re-chucked and re-polished.

A lump of carnauba wax is pressed on to the revolving wood, the heat so generated by friction causing the wax to melt and spread on to the surface. This will leave a film of wax on the wood which will be patchy and uneven. A knot is tied in a piece of fluffless rag and this pressed on to the revolving surface and passed slowly across it. This will spread the wax evenly and build up a bright shine. A certain amount of pressure is needed, especially at the start to generate enough heat to spread the wax, but afterwards it should be only enough to burnish the film of wax.

A cheap mahogany stain and filler for common spruce or deal table legs can be made as follows : 1 oz. of burnt sienna, ground in water, ¼ pint of stale beer, and ½ pint of warm water. Add hot liquid glue to thicken and act as a binder and filler, about 1 oz. or a good tablespoonful of glue to the pint of stain. If too dark a mahogany colour add more water; if too light add more burnt sienna. Burnt sienna can be obtained in 1-lb. tins, ground to paste form in water, at any drysalters or paint stores.

Tool handles. These nowadays are generally cellulose dipped, but for those who wish to follow the older method the following is satisfactory.

Immediately after the handle has been turned and glasspapered it is wiped over with raw linseed oil whilst still revolving at a slow speed on the lathe. The oil is applied liberally with a piece of old woollen blanketing or a pad made from knitted underwear.

Filling. The work is next filled in (whilst still in the lathe) by applying a dry or almost dry filling which is made by mixing dried whiting and powdered pumice stone with a suitable pigment, such as yellow ochre for oak, venetian red for mahogany, and a mixture of rose-pink and venetian red for black walnut.

For ash wood handles all that is required is a slight pinch of lemon chrome or yellow ochre to prevent the whiting and pumice showing too white in the grain of the wood. Boxwood does not require any filling in, and rosewood may be filled with a dark mahogany paste deepened by the addition of a little brown umber.

When the turned work has been well oiled, the worker takes a piece of coarse rag and dips it into the dry powder and rubs this into the wood, which is slowly revolving. The oil sucks up the whiting, etc., and the filler in this way effectively seals up the pores of the wood. If the worker does not care to apply the filler in a dry and dusty state, he should mix it to a very stiff paste with a little turpentine and a spot of gold size. After filling the work it should be set aside to harden off. Allow it to stand as long as possible whilst proceeding with the remaining handles.

The next operation is to coat in the handles with a coat of half-and-half spirit varnish and french polish, and allow this to harden, he coating being applied with a gilder's mop brush across the grain of the wood. Re-chuck the handle in the lathe, wipe it over with linseed oil, and glasspaper it smooth with No. 1 glasspaper according to the roughness of the grain. With a piece of engine waste wipe away the scum formed by the glasspapering process whilst still slowly revolving the lathe mandrel, and then hold a fairly moist rubber of polish to the surface of the wood. If a better finish is required give another coat of brush polish, repeat the glasspapering, and bring up the final finish with a piece of woollen rag which is charged up with thin polish.

Finish for wood salad bowls. Here the risk of food becoming tainted has to be considered. Some take the view that the timber, in addition to the usual turning requirements, should have no unpleasant taste or smell and that the bowl should be used in the white. The bread-board is quoted as a similar case. Others think that a finish is necessary and that the bogey of food being tainted by it is largely imaginary. Probably this is so when sycamore is used.

For those who wish to leave the bowl in the white we suggest buffing with swarf or shavings after sanding. This will put a smooth gloss on the surface. Darker woods could be buffed with a piece of teak cut at an angle to the grain. Teak has, and would impart, a smell which some people find unpleasant. It is specially noticeable during buffing but soon disappears. Either finish will last only until the bowl comes into regular use.

The following are briefly the finishes we suggest:

1. An oil finish, sealed, filled, and then skinned over with boiled linseed oil. Sealing stops the oil from soaking in which would make the oil smell persist for some time. Filling gives a dense surface to start on. The oil is applied sparingly with the lathe turning at

high speed. A really tough thin skin can be built up in a few stages.
When cured there is no smell.

2. For the white woods use three or four coats of cellulose lacquer.
The grain is filled and the lacquer wet flatted, the final coat being
burnished. All of this is done on the lathe.

For a simple finish use two coats of *Valspar*, flatting in between.
The varnish is applied by rag with the bowl rotated by hand or at
low speed. These finishes will stand rinsing under a tap and regular
wiping. They will prevent staining with items such as beetroot
and possible cracking due to dampness. The same finish should be
used both inside and out, and the same work should be put into
each. (But the inside could be dulled.)

We have to remember that wood is not the perfect medium for
these bowls and that common sense is needed in caring for the finish.
Olive oil for cleaning the inside is useful and will keep the varnish
film in good shape. It will also impart a suitable aroma to the bowl.
When thorough cleaning is necessary use a wash leather with a
minimum of soap or detergent, rinsing under the cold tap, and
finally drying with a cloth.

CHAPTER XIV: FRENCH POLISHING—EBONISING

THIS consists of staining and polishing black various woods to
imitate real ebony. Although the grain is entirely concealed in
the operation, not all woods are suitable for the purpose. Real ebony
is exceptionally close-grained, and it would not do therefore to use
a coarse, open-grained wood, because the filler would inevitably
sink in time and reveal grain completely unlike ebony. The process
is one of the most disagreeable in french polishing, because of the
unsightly state into which the fingers get.

Suitable woods. Apple, pear, cherry, holly, and sycamore are
excellent for ebonising, but may be difficult to come by. American
whitewood and birch take the finish very well, the former especially,
though it suffers from the disadvantage of being rather soft and liable
to bruise easily. Mahogany is widely used in the trade and is quite
successful, except that the grain is rather liable to show in time.

Staining. After thoroughly cleaning up, the wood is stained.
Incidentally, this cleaning is important because any blemishes will
show through. Be specially careful to get rid of any tears as the
filling will probably sink later. Take off sharp edges and corners
because these are liable to be rubbed and show light. You can use

any proprietary black oil, spirit, or water stain, or you can make up one with aniline dye (see page 201). There is an advantage in using water soluble dye, as will appear later. Make a good heavy stain, go over the whole surface, allow to dry, and give a second coat. A little ammonia in the stain will help to drive it into the grain. For a small object use artists' Indian ink.

Filling the grain. This now follows. You can use a black paste filler such as that supplied ready made by polish houses, or you can use plaster. It is when the latter is used that the advantage of water

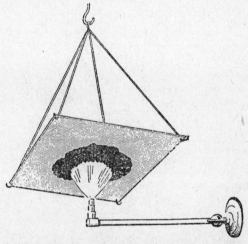

FIG. 35. MAKING GAS BLACK FOR BLACK POLISH.
The tinned plate is suspended above the gas bracket so that
a black deposit is formed.

aniline dye is felt, because the same stain can be used for mixing with the plaster (instead of clear water), this turning it black and avoiding white specks showing through. Use it as already described in Chapter V, except that the rag with which the plaster is applied is damped with the black stain instead of water.

Black polishing. This proceeds on the same lines as described in the general french-polishing chapters, except that black polish is used throughout. There is the fadding, bodying, and either stiffing or spiriting. No colouring is needed, of course, because the whole thing is built up to an intense black by the black polish. Work up to a good body and attain a brilliant gloss because, although the work is dulled later, it must have the foundation of a good polish.

Black polish. You can obtain a ready-made black ebony polish, and most men prefer to use this to save the bother of making their own. However, for those who care to make it the following is reliable. Dissolve about ½ oz. of black spirit aniline dye in 1 pint of white french polish. Wrap a piece of Reckitt's washing blue in muslin and dip it into the polish, squeezing it so that a little of the blue is dissolved. This gives the polish a more intense colour. The whole should now preferably be strained through muslin to get rid of grit and any undissolved powder.

If preferred, gas black can be used. You will have to make this

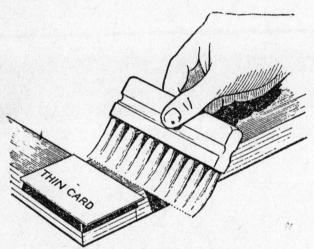

FIG. 36. DEALING WITH CORNERS WHEN DULLING.
The thin card placed in line with the joint of the framework so that the
line scratches run in line with the grain.

yourself. Suspend a piece of bright tinned plate over a gas burner fitted with the old type of fish-tail burner as in Fig. 35. An incandescent burner is useless. After an hour or so a black sooty compound will appear, and this should be carefully removed and stored for use. This is added to the polish in place of the aniline. It gives an excellent dead black and is free from grit. It was widely used by polishers in the Victorian period when ebonising was popular. The preliminary staining can also be done with the gas black, and in this case size should be used to act as a binder.

Finishing. When the polishing is completed it will have a brilliant gloss. This, however, is not characteristic of ebony, which looks at its best with a fine, eggshell gloss. This effect is produced by covering the surface with superfine scratches by means of the finest pumice powder.   Put the powder into a box and lightly dip in a broad brush with soft bristles.   Draw this lightly along the surface of the polish in *straight* lines, thus making a series of fine scratches.   It takes practice to keep the direction straight, and it is important because the path of the scratches is strongly defined.

The direction of the scratches should be along the length of the wood.   This is generally simple for such parts as legs, but is rather more complicated for, say, a door frame.   The best procedure is shown in Fig. 36.   Place a piece of thin card with a straight edge level with the joint and take the brush straight across this.   The wood beneath is thus protected.   To finish the other member place the card over the other side, again level with the joint, so protecting it. Incidentally, some people prefer to take off the brightness of ordinary french polished work by finishing with this scratching method.

One of the troubles against which the beginner runs is that, in rubbing down, he removes the black stain and polish at the edges. Matters can be helped by taking off the extreme sharpness before staining, but in any case care must be taken not to rub such places with glasspaper.   Re-stain and body-up afresh with black polish.

CHAPTER XV: FRENCH POLISHING—INLAID WORK

TO get the best results, inlaid work should be polished natural colour as far as possible, no stain being used and no colour in the polish.   However, there are occasions when the main wood must be darker than natural colour, and the problem is to apply the stain without also darkening the inlay.   Take for instance, say, a mahogany sideboard with satinwood inlaid bandings and strings.   The old school of cabinet-makers picked their rich Spanish mahogany veneers as they were cut from the log and thus to a great extent they did away with staining the surface.   A weak red oil was applied to the work, quickly wiped off the surface, and the wood then polished from start to finish with white polish.   No filling-in preparation other than polish was used.

Coating-in.   In the present case if the worker prefers to use bichromate of potash water stain (probably because the mahogany is of a moderately soft texture and somewhat pale in colour) it will be necessary to coat-in the boxwood lines with (*a*) a moderately thick white polish, (*b*) a clear cellulose lacquer, or (*c*) thin glue which is mixed similarly to size. The mixture (*a*, *b*, or *c*) would be applied with a No. 2 or No. 3 soft-bristle pencil brush such as is used by the water-colour artist.

This picking-up or lining-in process will have to be done quickly and very carefully, and the polish, cellulose, or glue-size must not be allowed to run on to the mahogany ground. Cellulose is the best and most modern method, because water stains, oil stains, and spirit stains if carefully and quickly applied will not affect it and re-dissolve it. Size is liable to be lifted by water stain, but resists oil stain.

Staining. After coating in the white lines with at least two coats of cellulose lacquer or white polish, the work can be given a bichromate of potash stain, the surplus being wiped away with a soft cloth. The bichromate stain will not strike through those portions of the work which have been coated. If thought desirable (after the stain has dried), the worker may rub into the wood a little red oil on those portions which appear to require a little more darkening or colouring-up. If a cellulose solution is used to coat in the inlays fill in the work with any good make of mahogany wood filler and body-up in the orthodox manner.

Polishing. Most of the polishing should be done with a white or transparent polish. Should the cellulose or polish-coated parts of the work stand proud of the groundwork after the first bodying-up has been done, wipe over the affected parts with white vaseline oil and proceed to level down the ridges with No. 0 glasspaper. The glasspaper is applied by folding it around the finger-tips.

When thick polish has been used as a protective coating, it will be found that the further application of the thin polish which is used in the embodying rubber will re-dissolve and work up the protective coating quite level with the body. When a thin coating of glue has been used to protect the inlay it will be found necessary to wash it away with warm water after the first bodying-in has been applied by the polishing rubber. The work calls for care and discrimination.

Toning. If it is felt that the work needs toning this can be done by using garnet polish for one or two rubbers. Inevitably this will also darken the inlay and for this reason any such toning should be kept to a minimum, the required tone being obtained as closely as possible with the stain.

Another method of obtaining a rich shade on mahogany is to fume the wood with strong liquid ammonia whilst the furniture is kept in an airtight ante-room or large box. If the mahogany is of a suitable character to take the fume, one obtains a rich effect on the groundwork, the boxwood or satinwood lines and banding being unaffected by the process.

CHAPTER XVI: FRENCH POLISHING—MISTAKES IN STAINING AND POLISHING

YOU can frequently learn a great deal about polishing by the mistakes that other people make. We therefore give here some of the blunders that are often made.

Stains. For a stain to be of any value when used alone it must be even in colour, and therefore will not stand much papering after application. Yet time after time timber is water stained without any previous attempt at grain raising and cleaning off. The result is that the surface is either streaky in colour or very rough. Damping down, then, is an essential point.

Next comes the application of certain varnish stains, the composition of which is unknown. In real polishing, varnish stains must not be considered. They are probably intended for rough work which needs toning down, but, used as a basis for further working, the result is generally hopeless. Again, these mixtures are difficult to apply evenly, either in thickness of coat or in colour, both faults giving trouble.

Home-made stains. Many readers like to make up their own stains, and a recipe that many try to follow is one using japan gold size plus turps and required colour. It is obvious, however, that this is really going to produce a type of thin paint. The colour, being mostly opaque and insoluble in the oils, must remain largely on the surface, held there by the small amount of gold size. Apart from the grain being partly hidden, the oil size is not good as a basis for further work. Black japan and turps for oak, though considered a good colour by some, is useless, for the black japan purchased is mostly brunswick black which never really hardens—a disastrous state under polish. If this is ever used, however, owing to awkward conditions, give a very long drying period and apply as thinly as practicable.

General materials. There is one great point in buying all polishing materials, and that is to buy from a manufacturer or retail polish house. Oil shops can often supply good polish, but they usually fail in stains of a good workable type. Materials bought from a good supplier are those of the professional, and the stains will not fade or leave objectionable deposits on the timber, as might often happen with some stains put up cheaply.

Lastly, the beginner is advised to leave spirit stains alone. In the hands of the expert they are capable of good results, but with the amateur much work is utterly spoiled.

Filling-in. Fillers seems to give trouble, though there is little that is difficult in their use. A word as to plaster. This should not be used over oil stain. Obviously oil and water together will cause complications. This caution includes stains that have been fixed with polish. Plaster also should be applied with water and not methylated spirit, the latter drying far too quickly for convenience.

Oil should be rubbed on *before any papering off*, and remember that oil stain cannot be substituted for linseed oil. Any colouring before papering may be done by using alkanet stained linseed, but nothing else.

Oil stains (fixed) need paste filler, and an appropriate shade of filler should be chosen for different timbers and colours. A filler may be toned by mixing into it a powder colour made into a paste with oil.

French polish. In the polishing proper there are many reasons for the job failing. First, a good coat of polish should seal the grain before oil is used. As to oil, either white mineral or linseed is good, but care should be taken not to use boiled linseed oil—the common boiled oil of painters. Use raw linseed oil.

Polish is important, and quite a number of people like to make their own, but unless something is known about the type of shellac, its quality, etc., the experiment is not always a success, and it is therefore advisable to purchase good trade-quality polish. So far as the type of polish is concerned, there is a tendency to use orange shellac polish for *every* purpose, as this shellac is the commonest in oil shops. Orange polish has a limited application owing to its strong yellow colour on the timber. It is useful in golden colours and for toning, but it is impossible for a very dark walnut, mahogany or general brown oak, owing to this yellow cast acting as a cloudiness to the dark stain. Garnet or brown shellac polish is easier to use and gives a far better " stiff " than button ; so when the colour is right use garnet.

This polish, when used much on the one job gives a very golden brown cast, though clear and transparent. If this is not desired mix white polish with the garnet or finish with white, preferably transparent white.

Avoid " easy-to-use " polish put up at a low price. Much of it has oil already mixed with it, and for a serious worker this is a real inconvenience, for the inside of the rubber becomes charged with a percentage of oil, and when " stiffing," oil can never be really taken right off.

THE faults outlined below are in some cases caused by incorrect working during the polishing process and in others are the result of bad treatment. Some of them can be treated successfully, but others may require stripping or scraping and polishing afresh.

Sweating. This shows itself in the form of fine cracks developing in the film of polish, and is caused by imprisoned oil breaking through to the surface. It may be caused by the use of too much oil during the polishing; failure to work out the oil; use of adulterated shellac in the polish; or a greasy filler. The latter fault is aggravated when the grain is of a large and open character.

Once the fault shows itself, the probability is that it will continue for some time, even after treatment, because oil will still exude through the cracks in the shellac. It may persist for several months.

For a start, wipe over the surface with a soft, damp cloth, and rub on a reviver (see page 200). In slight cases this will clear the trouble, though several applications will probably be needed as the oil continues to exude. If this fails, wash the surface with luke-warm water and fine pumice stone powder with a little soap. Then re-polish the surface. It is advisable, however, to leave it until the sweating has continued for some time.

" Chinese writing." A series of cracks running in all directions on the polish is known as Chinese writing, and is generally the result of the layers of polish drying out unevenly. It may be the result of polishes of different makes being used on the same surface, one having a different drying contraction from the other. Nothing can be done about it short of stripping and re-polishing. If the surface is plain the simplest plan is to scrape off the polish and clean up afresh. For a difficult surface with carving or other awkward detail the better plan is to use a proprietary stripper, brushing or scraping off the polish as it softens. Follow the directions given with the particular stripper used. Clean up with glasspaper and polish afresh, staining and filling in the grain in the usual way. Fig. 40, page 122, is an example of Chinese writing.

Scratches. If these are slight, that is, they do not reach right through the film of polish they can be eased down with fine glasspaper and re-polished. This generally means that any colouring in the polish is removed and fresh colouring is necessary. When the scratch is deeper, coloured wax can be rubbed into it. A single rubber of polish (without oil) is applied, and the wax coloured to the exact tone with polish suitably tinted with powder colour and strained. Professional polishers usually keep bottles of tinted polish which they can mix to obtain an exact match. This colour is fixed with another coat of clear polish after it has dried. It is allowed to harden for several hours, after which it is polished afresh. In any case it is difficult to conceal scratches entirely, and if the surface is badly scratched scraping with the steel scraper, cleaning up, and repolishing is the best plan. To help hide small scratches without repolishing a pecan nut kernel or a brazil nut can be rubbed over them. The nut is broken, the oil will exude and take off the whiteness.

White heat marks. Placing a hot plate on a polished surface will cause this, or it may be caused by the spilling of hot water. Mix equal quantities of linseed oil and turps and apply to the surface with a cloth, allowing the liquid to remain a while on the affected place. Alternatively, try camphorated oil. Wipe off the oil and rub on a little vinegar to remove all traces of oil. The process may have to be repeated several times. If this fails try the flashing method on page 85.

Glass ring marks. These are caused by glasses damp with spirits being placed on the surface. In slight cases rub down lightly with fine worn glasspaper and re-polish. Bad cases are the result, as a rule, of the part having been rubbed vigorously with a rag whilst still damp, this removing the polish and with it the colouring. This needs patching and it must be retouched with the pencil brush as described on page 130. Never work the brush in a circle. It will only show the more. Work always with the grain in short strokes as described. Professional polishers often remove the centre with spirits, colour it, and build up level with the general surface. A brush is used to remove the centre, this being frequently drawn between the fingers to keep it clean and so prevent muddiness. A couple of coats of polish applied over the coloured patch with a brush will soon bring it flush.

Ink stains. Rub over the stain with weak nitric acid. This will probably cause the stain to turn white, when it should be rubbed dry at once with a soft cloth. If the white does not come away try rubbing with camphorated oil.

Iodine stains. Dissolve 3 oz. of hypo-sulphite of soda in a pint of warm water and apply with a piece of cotton wadding. Leave on the work and allow to dry naturally. It may be necessary to strip off the polish locally. Two or three applications may be needed.

Water marks. Sometimes drops of water falling on to a polished surface and being allowed to remain will cause lightish marks. Wipe over with camphorated oil, rubbing well into the surface. Repeat the process if necessary and wipe off the oil with a dry rag. The application of a little vinegar will remove all traces of the oil. It may be necessary to body-up afresh afterwards.

If the above fails try flashing the area.

(a) Set the table top vertical, or nearly so.

(b) Warm a small soft rag and rub lightly over the marked area a few times.

(c) Soak the rag in methylated spirit—have it wet but not dripping —and sweep it up over the area and clear.

(d) Quickly set the meth. film alight at the bottom. Cover the marks and adjacent area this way in strips.

It is important to light the meth. film at the bottom or it may burn down and damage the film. The treated area may dull slightly but can be restored soon afterwards with furniture polish.

Simpler alternative:

(a) Polish the area with Brasso much as you would for metal, but do not let the liquid dry white.

(b) Damp a soft rag slightly in meth., leave it for a minute or so, then rub the area quickly and firmly along the grain.

White streaks or clouds. Dampness is usually the cause of this, and it may be the result of water stain not having dried out thoroughly, polishing in a damp atmosphere or even in a draught. The colour can sometimes be restored by rubbing over with half-and-half linseed oil and turpentine. Work if possible in a warm room. Alternatively, try equal quantities of linseed oil and methylated spirits. It will probably be necessary to body afresh. In bad cases nothing short of rubbing down and re-polishing will be effective.

Fading. This is generally the result of exposure to the sun, though dampness may cause it. Rub down the upper surface of the polish and colour afresh. Body afresh and spirit or stiff off.

Finger marks. A french polished surface should be quite hard after a few days. If it shows finger marks it is a sign that it is greasy. Probably too much oil has been used, or perhaps it has not been worked out. Possibly, too, the polish itself contains some adulterant which prevents it from hardening. If it is the polish that is at fault little short of rubbing right down and starting afresh is likely to be of much use. If the trouble is due to excessive oil wipe over with vinegar to remove the surplus oil, or use the acid finishing process (see page 55). Then body-up afresh.

Dullness. When dullness clouds over polish after a day or two of its application it is generally due to the use of too much oil or to its not having been worked out properly in the finishing-off process. Try spiriting-off afresh (page 53), or finish by the acid method (page 55).   Sometimes it may be caused by too much spirit having been used in spiriting-off.   This will leave the path of the rubber showing in a dull track.   Allow the work to harden for a few hours, and try spiriting afresh, using only a suspicion of spirit (see Chapter IX).   If this fails, rub down lightly with worn glasspaper, body-up afresh, and spirit-off again.

Bruises.   Since the wood itself is crushed it is clear that treatment of the polish is not likely to be effective.   If the polish has come away it is sometimes possible to help matters by placing a damp cloth over the part and putting a hot iron over it.   The steam generated will cause the fibres to swell.   If the polish is unbroken the method is of little value because the moisture will be unable to penetrate the polish.   In any case do not attempt it if the wood is veneered.

The only really satisfactory plan is to scrape off the polish, level out the bruise, and polish afresh.   Alternatively, you can cut out the wood locally and let in a fresh piece.   If these methods are too drastic you will either have to fill it with wax or just ignore it (and this is probably the better plan).   Wax is always liable to drop out, especially if the depression is shallow, though you can help matters by scratching the bottom to give a key for the stopping.   Give a single coat of polish without oil, tone with coloured polish applied with a brush, and body-up.   It is tricky work and you may find that the filling shows up worse than the bruise.

Spirit marks.   Caused by spirits being dropped on to the polish. If allowed to dry out naturally no great harm is done.   A rub with glasspaper and re-polishing is all that is needed.   If rubbed off whilst wet after it has been on long enough to soften the polish the latter is rubbed off, generally including the colouring.   Rub lightly with fine, worn glasspaper and colour if necessary with tinted polish.   Then body up locally.   In slight cases no colouring may be necessary.

Dirt.   Wash the work with warm water and soap and dry off thoroughly.   Now go over the whole with one of the revivers given on page 200.   An excellent cleansing reviver is the No. 5.   Afterwards keep it in condition with a furniture cream (page 201).

Soft polish.   This is often only discovered when an ornament is placed on the surface and allowed to remain several hours.   It leaves an indentation of its shape.   The fault is known as " printing " and the usual cause is that the film is too plastic.   Many polishes are adulterated with gums, resulting in a film that fails to harden.

There is no method of hardening the film.   If it fails to harden in a week at the outside it will have to be cleaned off and the surface repolished with best trade-quality polish.

CHAPTER XVIII : FRENCH POLISHING—TERMS USED

BODYING. The middle and a most important process in french polishing, in which the film of shellac is built up to a good depth with a surface bright and clean (page 47).

Colouring. The second stage in french polishing, during which the work is brought to an even colour by the use of coloured polish applied with either the rubber or the brush. Any light patches are darkened and bad colours corrected (page 40).

Cut down. When a polished surface is rough or uneven it is levelled or "cut down" with fine glasspaper. Sometimes an abrasive such as pumice powder is used instead, this being applied with a piece of felt.

Dip-up. Polishing rubbers are usually charged by removing the cover and shaking polish on to it. In the initial stages of fadding, however, the fad sometimes needs more generously charging and it is dipped into the polish, hence the term.

Dulling. When a good body of polish is required without a brilliant shine, the work is finished normally and the surface then dulled with tripoli powder lightly dusted along it with a dulling brush. The latter is a wide, soft, and long-haired brush (see page 78).

Fadding. Sometimes known as " skinning-in." It is the first stage in polishing, when polish is applied fairly generously with a " fad." The latter is plain wadding with no cover. It is dipped into polish and allowed to dry. This prevents hairs from adhering to the work when it is subsequently dipped-up and used (page 32).

Filling-in. Preliminary process before actual polishing is begun. The open grain is filled with plaster of paris or paste filler (page 26).

Glazing. An inexpensive and quick method of finishing french polish; also useful where the rubber cannot be used properly (page 57).

Grinder. A polishing rubber with a little fine pumice powder beneath the rag to increase the pull (page 51). See also "pounce bag " and "pull-over."

Kill. This term is generally used to denote the toning down of an unwanted colour. For instance linseed oil is used to " kill " the whiteness of plaster-of-paris filling (page 27). In the same way green copperas " kills " the redness of mahogany (page 111).

Pounce bag. This is a piece of rag filled with the finest pumice powder and tied around the top as shown on page 56. It is sometimes used in bodying french polish to level a surface and take out any roughness. It is dropped lightly on to the surface causing a little pumice to be deposited. Only the slightest amount of powder is needed. It serves much the same purpose as a grinder (*q.v.*).

Pull-over. When polish is put on *with* the grain it tends to pile up between the pores, making ridges or ropiness. To remove these a cross-grain, circular movement is adopted, this flattening the tops of the ridges and filling in the hollows. The operation is known as "pulling over." To quicken the process a little superfine pumice powder is put beneath the rag of the rubber. The rubber thus becomes a grinder (*q.v.*). Alternatively, the pounce bag can be used (*q.v.*).

Ropiness. A series of ridges formed on the surface when the rubber is used *with* the grain. It is corrected by a pull-over (*q.v.*).

Rubber. The distinction between a rubber and a fad is that the former has a covering of rag whilst the latter is merely a piece of wadding (see fadding). For details of making a polishing rubber, see page 37.

Sizing. The application of glue-size, usually on softwood, to prevent polish from sinking (see page 113).

Skinning-in. Another term for fadding (*q.v.*).

Solid colour. This is polish which has been made opaque with colouring matter as distinct from a tinted transparent polish. It is used when the grain has to be covered or painted out (see page 44).

Spiriting-off. A method of finishing off french polish. Methylated spirits is used to take off the oil (see page 53).

Stiffing. One of the finishing-off processes in french polishing in which all traces of oil used in bodying are removed (see page 52).

Stopping. A substance used to fill in defects such as nail holes, small cracks, etc. It may be plastic wood or beaumontage (see page 9). It should not be confused with filler (see "filling-in").

Whips. When the rubber is too fully charged polish may exude at the edges, causing ridges or "whips" to be formed. They should be flattened out at once before they have time to harden.

CHAPTER XIX: WAX POLISHING

WAX polish can be used for any wood, though it is more usually associated with oak. It gives a fine eggshell shine which is most attractive, and there is a tendency nowadays to revive its use. One of its advantages is its ease of application combined with the fact that it can be renewed at any time. A drawback is that it does not keep out dirt as well as french polish, so that items that come in for a lot of handling are liable to become soiled. This applies especially to light unstained woods. The wax is rather liable to absorb dirt, and subsequent rubbing forces it into the grain of the wood. Matters can be helped by giving a couple of rubbers of white french polish before applying the wax. This seals the grain and if it becomes necessary to clean the surface dirt is easily removed.

Fixing the stain. If the work is to be stained, this is done first (see Chapter IV). If an oil stain is used, this must be fixed with two rubbers of french polish, otherwise the wax polish may pull off the stain in patches owing to the turpentine acting as a solvent to the colouring materials of the stain. First rub the surface well with coarse rag to remove any oil or grease left by the stain. Of course, the stain must have dried out thoroughly. The polish is unnecessary in the case of water stain, though, as already mentioned, it helps to keep out dirt. Some workers prefer to build up a slight shine with french polish before waxing, as it means that a shine is built up more rapidly than when wax only is used. If this is done it is important that white polish is used for light woods, otherwise the work will be tinted.

No filler is required for wax polish because the wax itself acts as a filler, gradually being forced into the grain with continued rubbing. If, however, there is a reason why the grain should be filled in quickly add some cornflour to the polish. This is suitable for light woods. At first it will give a dull appearance, but this will pass when the filler has had time to harden and ordinary wax polish is used.

Ingredients for wax polish. The best polish is made from beeswax and pure American turpentine (failing this turps substitute). Sometimes a little carnauba wax is added to harden the polish; or a small quantity of rosin can be used for the same purpose. Paraffin wax is sometimes added to lower the cost, but it is doubtful whether any polish is so good as that made from pure beeswax. Petrol is sometimes added to speed up the evaporation. Use the kind made for lighters. In its raw state beeswax varies from a deep yellow to a brown shade, and this is suitable for polishing dark woods. For light, unstained woods bleached wax should be used. To give an antique effect lamp-black powder should be mixed in with the wax polish until the whole polish is black. Then when this is applied the black is deposited in the grain and corners. Never use it for new work.

Carnauba wax is very hard and may be difficult to dissolve. It is best mixed with an equal quantity by volume of ordinary beeswax. Shred both waxes. Put the carnauba in a container and cover with No. 1 white spirit. Set the container in water which should be heated and kept hot until the wax dissolves. (Guard carefully against the fire risk.) Now double the volume in the container by adding white spirit then put in the beeswax. This will dissolve much more quickly, after which stir well and allow to set. It should set to paste consistency. If too hard for easy application it must be dissolved again and more spirit added.

Wax polish recipes.

Light wax polish. Bleached beeswax and turps.

Extra light wax polish. Paraffin wax and turps.

Dark wax polish. Raw beeswax and turps.

Antique wax polish. Raw beeswax, lamp-black, and turps.

A little carnauba wax can be added to the light, dark, and antique polishes if desired. Rosin should be used with the darker polishes only. The consistency should be about that of butter in summertime. If stiffer than this it will be difficult to spread evenly. To any of these polishes a little petrol can be added.

Making wax polish. The wax is dissolved in the turpentine, being shredded first to help the process. It can be speeded up by using heat. Stand the vessel in a bowl of hot water so that the wax is melted. Never place it over a naked flame because of the danger of a flare-up. If rosin is being used, this should be melted first, and the wax added little at a time, the mixture being stirred thoroughly. Whilst still hot the turps is added. Also the petrol, if required.

Applying the wax. A brush of the shoe-brush type with fairly stiff bristles is the best means of applying the wax. Scrub it well into the grain, using a fairly generous quantity, and making sure that it is spread evenly and every part is covered. The stiffer the paste the harder the scrubbing will have to be. The point previously mentioned about oil stains drying out thoroughly is important because oil will effectually prevent a shine. Hence the rubbing with the coarse rag to remove any surface grease before fixing with shellac polish. The same necessity for water stain drying also applies, but there is no need to rub with a rag since water stain leaves no deposit of grease.

When the wax has been applied, set aside the work for as long as possible—twenty-four hours or more. The reason for this is that no shine is possible until the turps has completely evaporated. If the polish contains petrol the waiting time can be cut down. Now with another shoe brush burnish the surface, brushing well into angles and corners. Finish with a cloth rubber free from fluff.

It may be that the first application will reveal a somewhat uneven spread of polish, but this can be corrected by a second waxing carried out similarly to the first. The oftener polish is applied the better the result. Later applications can be with rag only.

Apart from home-made polishes there are many excellent proprietary polishes available. Some of these dry out more rapidly so that it is not necessary to wait so long before polishing.

Carvings. In the case of carvings care has to be taken not to choke up the smaller interstices with wax, and a quite good plan is

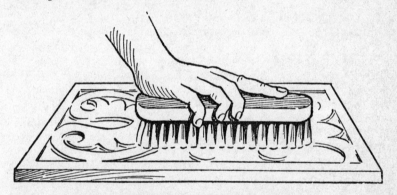

FIG. 37. USE OF BRUSH FOR POLISHING WAX.

A brush of the boot-brush type can be used for both applying and polishing the work. For carvings the brush need only be drawn across a lump of wax.

to use a lump of beeswax only. Draw the brush across this a few times so that the bristles collect a certain amount of polish and rub well on to the work. Follow with the polishing brush and rubber.

Incidentally, never apply french polish directly over a waxed surface, because it grips only the wax and may come away in flakes if rubbed later. The reverse can always be done. In fact, most furniture polishes have a basis of wax.

In the case of the antique wax polish, the process is much the same, but do not scrub it too vigorously out of angles and corners, because the object is to deposit the black in these places.

CHAPTER XX : OIL POLISHING

OIL POLISHING is simplicity itself, and it has its advantages over french polishing, wax polishing, or varnishing. There is no danger of an oil-polished surface cracking or blistering, like either french polish or varnish; nor will it show marks, especially marks made with water, as does wax polish. To do the work requires a great deal of time and a considerable amount of friction in its application. It is mostly used on plain surfaces, owing to the amount of rubbing which is needed to do the work in a proper manner.

Oil polishing is almost obsolete to-day because of the labour and time it involves.

The treatment consists of rubbing oil into the wood with a soft rag. It is vigorously rubbed; and the application must be continued at intervals, preferably daily, for some five or six weeks if a good job is required. Either boiled or raw linseed oil may be used, and the rubbing at each application must continue until the surface is dry. When this has taken place daily for a few weeks the result will be a most durable surface, comparatively dull as regards gloss.

Oil polishing is most useful for table tops, bar tables, counters, and spirit cabinets. A dining-room table with an oil-polished top, and the side and legs french polished, will make a most satisfactory job. If the top is french polished it is liable to become marked if hot dishes are placed upon it, but the same hot dishes may be placed upon the table with impunity if it has been oil polished.

To prepare the oil. Put the required quantity into a vessel over a fire or stove, and gently simmer (not boil) for a quarter of an hour. Then take it off and add one-eighth of turpentine. It helps drying if about 1 teaspoonful of terebine is added to $\frac{1}{2}$ pint of the mixture. For a table top or other surface which is large and level, rub some of the oil well into it, and then polish with a rubber made by wrapping a quantity of felt or flannel round a brick or other suitable block, the purpose of which is, by its weight, to relieve to some extent the polisher from using his muscles in applying pressure. In applying the oil to the wood do not saturate or flood it, but scrub it in and afterwards rub long and hard. Of course the wood will absorb the oil, even after several applications. It will need much patience to bring it up to a good glow; in fact, it might be said that the work is never finished. An oiled surface will always bear more rubbing than it has had, and will not deteriorate by friction. It can always be rubbed over again at any time with the oil, and will be improved by so doing.

The reason that turpentine is added is that it helps it to dry more quickly than it would otherwise do. Some polishers recommend boiled linseed oil, others raw, while yet others will advise various proportions of the two. Boiled oil dries more quickly but it never seems to completely harden. Some workers add a small quantity of terebine to boiled oil, but, although it does harden out, it may soften at the slightest heat—even from the fingers. All told it is safer to use raw linseed oil and allow longer intervals for drying. If, after a good polish has been obtained, the work begins to sweat, rub some methylated spirits in.

Open-grained woods. In polishing open-grained woods, they can be filled up with a grain-filler. The oil is applied with either soft rag or a piece of flannel. Each time the oil is applied the surface should be previously washed with cold water to remove any dirt or dust. Care should be taken to see that a good brand of turpentine is used to mix with the oil, as if a cheap turpentine substitute is used trouble is likely to ensue. Turpentine substitutes are now exceedingly common on the market (owing to the cost of pure turpentine being so high), and some of them contain a fair percentage of oils of the petroleum class, which are apt to dry up the linseed oil and act on the surface of the wood as a bleaching agent. The work may also turn very dull as a consequence. Several applications of hot oil should do much to restore the work to its former state. If the wood is mahogany, red oil should be used, as this will readily bring back the brightness of the colour of the wood.

Oil polish is ideal for teak which is liable, in time, to reject other finishes. A full grain finish is the most suitable.

1. Wipe over well with turpentine. This will remove the natural oil from the surface and thereby assist drying of the linseed.

2. Fill the grain with *Alabastine*. Mix a ½ teaspoonful of brown umber or powder colour with enough for the job. Pack the grain flush with a damp rag in the usual way. Remove surface filler.

3. Damp a rag in the oil and wipe over well to remove *Alabastine dust* sticking to the surface. Any surface filler overlooked may be removed with fine paper or steel wool.

4. Thereafter apply the linseed oil. This does dry slowly on teak and so, for overnight hardening, use a mixture of ½ pint linseed, one-tenth as much turpentine approximately, and then drops only of terebine. It helps if the mixture is applied warm.

Teak oil, a propriety preparation, already contains its own drying agent and gives excellent results. It can be used on any wood for which a subdued gloss is required. It takes about ten days to completely harden out.

CHAPTER XXI : TREATMENT OF OAK

OAK is a widely used furniture wood and it can be finished in many ways. Choice is largely a matter of personal fancy, but the use to which the work is to be put has also to be considered. Whatever the finish, however, remember that oak has a most attractive grain, so that the aim should be to make the most of it rather than hide it.

NATURAL WAXED OAK

Waxing is one of the most popular finishes for oak, partly because of its simplicity of application and partly because it seems specially suited to oak. This is probably because it has for centuries been the traditional method of polishing oak. The preparation of the wood is as described in Chapter II, except that many workers prefer not to use glasspaper, polishing direct on the scraped surface. If a natural tone is desired a bleached or white beeswax is used. The preparation and application of this is described in Chapter XIX. When the lightest possible shade is required use paraffin wax. This is hardly so satisfactory as beeswax, but being white has little darkening effect.

For items in everyday use subject to constant handling it is advisable to give a preliminary half-bodying with white or transparent french polish. It gives a preliminary shine, but, more important it helps to keep out dirt. Without it, it is difficult to avoid a dirty looking surface on items frequently handled.

DARK WAXED OAK

For a dark tone the wood can be stained to the required tone.

Stains to use. Any of the proprietary stains can be used according to the shade required, and two or more can be mixed together for a special effect, providing that they are of the same kind, i.e. both water or both oil stains. One of the most useful is walnut stain. It is of a rather warmer tone than most " oak " stains and is darker. It gives a rich nutty shade which can be warmed by the addition of a little mahogany stain or cooled by yellow oak stain. A point to remember is that many stains are intended for use on whitewood to make the latter resemble the familiar oak tones, and if used on real oak the effect may not be what was expected. The safest plan is to try the stain on a spare piece of the actual wood and experiment by mixing stains as required.

Walnut crystals (see page 201) are frequently used on oak, and they give a deep and rather cold brown shade, very useful for some work. It is as well to add a little ammonia to this stain as it helps to drive it well into the grain. Bichromate of potash is sometimes used (see how to make on page 201) and the slightly greenish tone it gives suits some work.

Fixing oil stains. If an oil stain is used always fix it with a couple of rubbers of french polish before applying the wax as otherwise it may lift the stain in patches. It is unnecessary over water stain, though it is common practice to build up a light shine with french polish before waxing, as it gives a foundation on which to work. However, it is not essential except as a fixative over oil stain. In the latter case allow the stain to dry completely and remove any surface grease by rubbing well with coarse rag before polishing.

Proprietary stains. The following are the main proprietary stains used on oak, given in order of depth of colour.

Yellow oak	Medium brown
Fumed oak	Brown oak
Dark oak	Black oak

also

Grey oak	Weathered oak

Wax polish. The method of making and applying wax polish for natural or dark oak is dealt with in Chapter XIX, page 89.

GREEN WAXED OAK

This with white in the grain is a finish sometimes seen. Clean up the oak and treat it with a stain made by dissolving spirit-soluble aniline green in methylated spirits. Add to half a pint of spirits as much of the spirit green as will go on a sixpence, then strengthen or dilute the stain as required. A dash of french polish will make it give a slight gloss to the work. Stain quickly, following the brush immediately with a piece of cotton waste or rag so as to get an even tone. Failure to attend to this point will result in an unsatisfactory patchiness. Although the stain dries quickly, it is best to allow, say, twenty minutes before rubbing down with No. 0 glasspaper.

The final process is to fill the grain with white wax polish and to work up a gloss by vigorous rubbing with a clean, soft duster. To make the wax polish, dissolve shredded bleached beeswax in turpentine, and add zinc white to the paste until the whole becomes quite white. Add more turpentine, as needed, to give a paste of the consistency of thick cream. Rub this well into the grain of the wood. It will stiffen after a few moments. Then wipe off the surplus with a movement along the fibres. Finally, polish up to a gloss by light, vigorous rubbing with a duster.

A proprietary wax known as *Stainax* which stains and polishes in one operation can be obtained. It is made in a variety of shades and some delightful effects can be obtained. It is rubbed on to the bare wood just like ordinary wax polish. If desired a shaded or rubbed effect can be obtained by varying the amount used, or by using a second shade in parts.

FRENCH POLISHED OAK

Stained oak. You can leave the work in its natural shade (in which case bleached shellac polish is used), or you can tone it with any of the proprietary stains (see page 95) or use vandyke crystals or bichromate of potash. An effective, deep colour is produced by the use of vandyke crystals dissolved in water with a little ammonia added to drive it into the grain. Then by using garnet french polish the rather cold tone is warmed to a rich shade. Before applying the stain go over the surface with clear warm water to raise the grain. Rub down with fine glasspaper and stain as described in Chapter IV. This damping is unnecessary when oil or spirit stain is used. Incidentally, it is usual to glasspaper oak which is to be french polished.

Filling. Oak is not usually fully filled in, in fact many workers prefer to have no filling at all, in which case the polishing follows straightway after the staining (remember to rub off the surface grease after using an oil stain). A good plan, however, is to give a semi-filling, as it effects an economy in polish and helps to build up a shine more quickly. To a pint of the polish to be used add a handful or so of french chalk. With a brush coat the work all over, stirring the mixture frequently. When dry rub down with fine glasspaper. This dries hard and gives a satin-smooth finish. Incidentally, this polish-chalk coat is useful for finishing the insides of furniture. Be careful to avoid any running down or tears. Allow twenty-four hours for the coat to harden; if it is not really hard the subsequent polishing will soften it and wash it away.

Polishing. Fadding-in, bodying, and spiriting-off now follow, as described in the chapters on general french polishing. A fair body must be built up, but it is not usual to give the high gloss associated with fine woods such as mahogany or satinwood.

NATURAL AND TANNED OAK

If white oak is worked up with white polish, using no stain or filler, a light, natural colour is produced approximating that of the plain timber when wet with water. If garnet polish is substituted, a browner, more golden tone is attained; while using button produces a more yellow colour altogether. The popular colour known as tan is attained with garnet polish. The timber may or may not be stained with walnut water stain (very weak to turn the natural whiteness of the wood) according to the particular shade required. Working right through with garnet tends to make the job rather too warmly golden, so that when the desired shade is reached it is usual to finish with white polish.

Difficulties sometimes arise, not in getting the general colour, but in matching up the timbers used. Thus red rails or legs or dark blemishes must be either bleached or, if that fails, coloured out.

Bleaching. To bleach before polishing, dissolve oxalic acid crystals in water until the latter will dissolve no more. Apply this liquid to the offending portions fairly wet. Allow a few minutes to bleach. It must then be killed by washing first in borax with a rag also fairly wet, and directly afterwards with water several times. When this washing is completed it should be allowed to dry, when the wood should be rather lighter but with no whitish deposits. When papered down smooth, it may be worked up with the polish desired.

There are also some powerful proprietary bleaches on the market and these will turn some woods almost white. For matching they must be diluted and used with caution. For fuller details see page 23.

Colouring. As an alternative, or when the bleach fails, work as follows : Put on sufficient polish to bring it to colour and no more. A good body will add difficulties that are best avoided. Procure from the oil shop or polish suppliers some yellow ochre and Chinese white, both powder colours; also litharge, orange chrome, yellow chrome, and raw umber, these being useful for toning. They are all powders sold by the pound and are cheap. Litharge is a pinkish colour somewhat like salmon. The others are obvious.

To half spirits and half polish add ochre and white, making a buff, the paleness depending on the quantity of white. This is the basic colour which must be made about the same depth of tone as the job, and, if required, can be toned down by the addition of a touch or two of one or more of the other colours until the right match is obtained. Dip the colour brush into the mixture (a No. 7 camel hair mop is excellent), squeeze out the excess, and apply quickly to the dark places. Where a rail is set back, a fraction or so from the legs for instance, work the brush from the left-hand side nearly across to the other, turn the brush into the uncoloured corner, and meet up with the first stroke. This avoids awkwardness and consequent patchiness.

Do not apply too liberally, but at the same time be sure to cover. Work confidently after the manner of painting, with the mixture as thin as possible. Use it rather as a tint than a solid paint, for it can always be gone over again, though only when the first coat is dry. The colour dries lighter, but is brought to colour again when polishing is recommenced. Whole tops are never painted out, for unsuitable timber should not be used, but mouldings, legs, rails, and streaks in the larger surfaces, all call for the colour brush occasionally.

If unsuccessful, wash off with spirits, working up a little afterwards with polish before the second attempt. Any portions not needing painting but which are lighter than required can be toned with a little colour made up of half spirits and half polish, a very small quantity of gas black and perhaps a suspicion of red polish. Just enough of these to darken the natural colour of the polish. Apply with a small piece of used wadding, e.g., an old rubber, well flattened out on some flat surface. Use just as little in the wadding as will work conveniently, and with a spot of oil on the face of same. Darken by degrees rather than suddenly, and not continuously on the same patch, or colour will be taken off as much as put on. Warm up with very weak red in the same way, as may be necessary.

Light oak. Oak that is required lighter than natural can be treated by using the white ochre mixture as before. The colour must be as thin as will conveniently cover. Brush on to the raw timber after the grain has been damped and papered down. Use in similar manner to a stain, but not wiping dry. Paper down until only sufficient colour is left to lighten the wood. No heavy, very opaque colour should be allowed to remain, though, of course, the general effect will not be so clear as the natural timber. Quickly wash in when papering is completed and the surface has been dusted off, with wadding dipped up with transparent white. Allow to dry, paper down smooth, and work up with the same polish.

LIMED OAK

The simplest way of obtaining this effect is to use one of the proprietary fillers made for the purpose. This is rubbed into the grain so that a deposit is left in the open pores, the surplus being wiped off the surface. In some cases there is a wax medium in the filler and as the rubbing is continued a shine is built up. In others the work is finished with white french polish.

As an alternative unslaked lime can be used. The process is inclined to be somewhat messy and should be done in a workshop or in the open. It is advisable to raise the grain with warm water and rub down with glasspaper as a preliminary. For *natural* limed oak take 2 lb. of unslaked lump lime, slake this in 3 quarts of water, and allow it to cool off. Mix the lime with a piece of stick until it resembles paint and apply this to the oak, rubbing it well into the pores across the grain. When the lime-paint is semi-dry take up some old rag and wipe away the surplus lime, still working in the same direction. Allow the work twenty-four to thirty-six hours to dry out, and apply a coat of white shellac polish. Allow this underlac to dry out, and cut down the surface with No. o or No. 1 glasspaper according to the roughness of the grain.

The work may now be finished in two ways. (1) Work on to the surface a few straight rubbers of white french polish, using the rubber in the direction of the grain until a dull gloss is obtained. (2) Mix together white wax with turpentine until it forms a white wax polish and add some zinc white, which will increase the white deposit which is to be left in the grain. Zinc white is in powdered form and can be obtained through any drug stores or painters' colourman.

Alternative Methods. This gives a dull shine with slight whitish film over the surface. Stain as desired and fix with two coats of french polish. Dissolve bleached beeswax in turps and add powdered zinc white to turn mixture white. Rub into grain and wipe off surplus. Leave for several hours and polish with dry rag. A little cigarette lighter petrol can be added to the mixture to speed evaporation.

The following method gives a fairly bright finish with the white flecks more subdued. Stain and body up with white polish (no filler used), and stiff or spirit out. Shake household whiting into a basin and add water to form thick paste. Rub into grain and wipe off surplus. After twenty-four hours rub off whitish film with rag or flour glasspaper. Give a rubber of white french polish using as little polish as possible. The purpose is to give a final gloss and set the filling. A saturated rubber kills the whiteness of the filling.

Yet another method involves the use of flat white paint. The oak is cleaned and glasspapered in the ordinary way and is then stained according to the general tone required. As a general rule, a medium to dark oak stain is preferable, as offering a pleasant but not too pronounced a contrast with the white in the grain. A naphtha-base stain, which has less tendency to raise the fibres of the wood, is better than a water stain.

For a first-class job, apply two thin coats of white french polish to seal the suction of the surface. Then apply the flat oil paint, of a thick consistency, all over the wood. Allow this to set from ten to fifteen minutes, but do not allow to become too tacky; then, with a piece of coarse hessian, wipe off across the direction of the grain in the same manner as excess wood-filler is removed. The effect will be to leave a white deposit in the grain cavities, but the rest of the surface will be free of paint.

Allow from six to eight hours or, better still, overnight for this to dry and harden, sand down lightly with No. 1 glasspaper used over a rubber or cork block, working with the grain, and dust off. To complete the job, apply one or two further coats of thin shellac polish; this will seal the surface and make it easier to keep clean.

In cheap work, liming is often attempted without applying the preliminary coats of shellac before the " lime " is applied. This is seldom satisfactory because, the suction not having been satisfied, the wood tends to absorb the white colouring matter all over the surface, so that, in effect the latter, becomes stained.

Although it is customary to employ a white paint, distemper, or paste, there is no reason why colours should not be used instead to fill the grain pockets. Either ready-tinted material can be used or the white base can be tinted to the required colour by stirring in the appropriate stainers, which should be ground in oil or turpentine —not added in dry powder form.

For the renovation of the limed finish see page 131. *Removal of lime is dealt with on page* 135.

WEATHERED OAK

This attractive finish for oak is usually rather difficult to obtain. A poor colour gives disappointing results, often looking the result of an accident rather than a special preparation. When well done, however, the effect is delightful, having a soft, mellow greyish tone which gives an effect of age. One feature of the process is that the medullary rays are turned a dark colour.

Dissolve 1 lb. American potash in 1 gallon of boiling water and use when cold. Dissolve 2 lb. chloride of lime in 1 gallon of warm water, allow to cool, and strain through canvas or sheep cloth. Use only the liquid and throw away the sediment. Dissolve 1 lb. pure beeswax in ½ gallon of turpentine and use after two days. Well saturate the oak with the potash solution and let it remain on the wood for fifteen minutes. This will turn it to a medium brown shade. Thoroughly wash down with cold water to free the wood from the solution, and allow to dry for twenty-four hours.

Apply the liquid from the chloride of lime, well scrubbing the wood until you see the colour changing. Allow to dry and repeat the application until the desired colour is arrived at. It may be necessary to repeat the application three times before the result is satisfactory. When dry, the whole thing will be covered with a whitish deposit which is removed in the next stage.

When dry, use No. 1 glasspaper and well brush with an ordinary scrubbing brush. Apply the dissolved beeswax freely and allow to penetrate the pores of the wood. Brush well again and finish with a piece of coarse canvas. Rubber gloves should be used with the potash. Also a grass brush is advisable; the ordinary hair or bristle brushes are of no use. With the lime it does not really matter except that when a lot has to be done gloves are advisable to protect the hands.

This process, although not permanent will last for several years, after which it tends to revert to natural oak.

A blue-grey tone is obtained with green copperas. See notes on pages 15 and 193.

Alternative method. The silvery tone which untreated oak acquires when it has been exposed to the elements for some years is probably impossible to imitate exactly by artificial means, but a reasonably good effect of weathering can be obtained as follows.

The oak should first be bleached, either with a good proprietary brand of wood bleach or with a solution of oxalic acid. This will reduce the brownish tinge of the wood. The bleaching process should be followed by thorough rinsing, to prevent any acid residue remaining in the grain and, when the surface is dry, by careful glasspapering. Next, make up a thin wash coat with either paste white lead or paste zinc oxide, bound with gold size and thinned down to almost water-like consistency with turpentine or white spirit, and apply this. It may be advisable to add a little drop of black to produce a grey shade, but this should not be overdone. It is far better to apply two or three thin coats until the right shade is obtained than to brush on one which, after it has dried, proves to be too dark and opaque.

The wash coat should be allowed overnight to dry and then given one or two thin coats of shellac. As a general rule no more than a subdued lustre is desirable for this type of finish, and wax polish or an egg-shell flat varnish should meet the case.

The lead or zinc oxide paste gives rather a dull, lifeless tone. If a more silvery effect is wanted, the following treatment should be followed. Seal the suction of the wood with shellac varnish or, alternatively, a coat of raw linseed oil. Then take aluminium powder and mix it with pale oak varnish to a semi-paste consistency. Make a clean pad of lintless rag and moisten the surface with a mixture consisting of equal parts of raw linseed oil and turpentine: dip this into the aluminium powder mixture and rub well into the grain of the wood. The oil on the pad acts as a kind of lubricant to the metallic paste: the tone of the latter can be varied to some extent by increasing or decreasing the proportion of oil. A coat of sealer, followed by wax polish or an egg-shell varnish finish is usual.

FANCY COLOURED OAK

An interesting departure from ordinary finishes on oak is that where the grain is filled with gold, silver, or fancy colours to contrast with a solid ground colour such as dark green, blue, and so on. Although the timber is coated in solid, the figure is still visible. With No. $1\frac{1}{2}$ or 1 glasspaper, cut down the work well, using a cork block to keep the surface flat. All blemishes and bruises must be stopped with shellac or hard stopping and levelled off. With a wire brush or similar tool open up the pores, working *with* the grain. This process ensures there being no bare patches on the finished article, due to some pores being too small to take up the filler.

Colouring. The job is now ready for colour, which is mixed as follows : Add a little less than one part spirits to two parts polish. To this mixture stir in enough powder colour of the desired shade to make a good opaque mixture, keeping it as thin as is consistent with this requirement. Coat in with as large a brush as is convenient, keeping the surface as free from brush marks as possible, and covering quickly. Allow to dry thoroughly and cut down with fine paper until smooth. If necessary repeat the process, when the ground should be perfectly even in tone.

Dust well off and apply a thin coat of clear polish with a new rubber, dipped up fairly wet and used lightly so as not to disturb the ground and to bring it back to colour after the papering. When dry. the grain is filled with the gold or whatever filling is desired.

Mixing the gold. The mixing of the gold is rather critical. It is mixed with turps and gold size, the latter acting as a binder. If, however, there is too much of this size it will be found to rub on with a wadding quite easily, but when the rag is used for rubbing off, the surface will be difficult to clear and rather sticky and, when dry, dull and streaky. It might be a good plan to mix the gold with the gold size into a very thick paste, thinning until workable with turps. This could be ascertained on a trial piece of timber. Only experience can judge the exact consistency.

As to the working of the mixture into the grain, use the wadding *across* the work fairly quickly and not covering too much surface at once. The wiping-off rag should be soft and free from lint and should also be used crosswise, though the last finishing touches may be *with* the grain. The resulting surface should be quite clear and free from gold everywhere but in the grain, which should show up boldly. Mouldings, carving and similar decoration may be picked out in gold paint if desired, or some contrasting colour.

A silver filling is mixed in the same manner as gold. For a white grain a liming paste may be used, or a mixture of zinc white and natural patent filler. When a fancy coloured grain is desired, add a solid colour ground in oil to the natural filler and mix thoroughly. A dry powder colour may be used, but the general effect will be somewhat duller.

Colours to use. The most usual schemes for this type of finish are green and gold, green and silver, blue and gold, blue and silver, or these colours with white, black, or grey grain. The main requirements in selecting the colour are : first, a dark tone that will throw up the grain, and secondly, thoroughly well-ground powder that is free from grit. Remember that the only need for gold size when mixing the gold is to bind the powder when in the grain, thus preventing it from being dusted out, so make certain that the minimum amount is used. Both the gold powder and the gold size can be obtained from the oilshop; the gold size, however, is sold in many varieties according to the time taken in drying. Buy that known as 8-hour, which dries at about the right speed. The gold also may be obtained in many shades, but that sold as " medium pale " is the most generally useful.

Another attractive variation is to use gold, silver, or other metallic powder, incorporated in a hard-grade paraffin wax, heated and thinned with turpentine or white spirit. This is rubbed into the grain and wiped off and finally sealed with one or more coats of bleached shellac. In this case, since the metallic powders have no staining properties, it is not essential to seal the wood before the paste is put on, but the presence of a sealer coat enables the wiping to be performed more cleanly.

FUMED OAK

Almost any tone from the natural down to almost black can be obtained by this process. It should be noted, however, that some varieties of oak take more kindly to it than others. It is therefore important that the same kind is used throughout, as otherwise the effect may be patchy. When using American oak avoid mixing white and red oak, as the latter contains less tannin and does not fume so readily. The advantage of fuming is that no liquid touches the wood so that the grain is not raised. In the preparation of the work all grease and glue must be carefully removed, as any deposit will prevent the fumes from affecting the wood and will cause patches.

The container. An airtight container for the work is needed, and this can be any form of box or cupboard, the edges of which can be

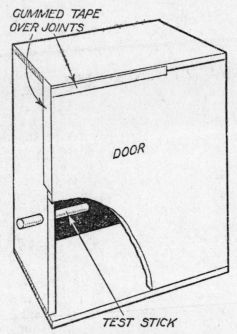

GUMMED TAPE OVER JOINTS

DOOR

TEST STICK

FIG. 38. HOME-MADE CHAMBER FOR FUMING.
Gummed tape is stuck over cracks to prevent escape of fumes. The test stick enables colour to be tested without opening the chamber.

sealed to prevent the fumes from escaping. A test stick should be fitted to enable the progress to be seen without opening the container and so allowing the fumes to get away. This can conveniently be a rounded piece of the same oak as the job inserted through a hole in the box. It can be withdrawn from time to time and the colour noted.

Testing. To test, damp the test-piece with water. This will give the approximate shade when waxed. If it is proposed to oil the work before waxing put a spot of linseed oil on the wood instead of water.

The oil gives a warmer tone to the wood. If not dark enough the process should be continued, more ammonia being added as the first becomes exhausted. Incidentally, never stand right over the box when the latter is opened as the fumes are powerful and affect both the lungs and the eyes. The time taken for the work may vary from half an hour to forty-eight hours, this depending upon the depth of colour required and the size of the container. The work should be separated as far as possible so that the fumes can reach everywhere. Overlapping must be avoided. The ammonia, ·880 (ask for " point eight-eighty "), is poured into one or two saucers placed in the container and the latter closed immediately.

Tannin powder. The process may be speeded up by first coating the work with a solution of 1 oz. tannin powder to 1 quart of water.

Pyrogallic acid. An alternative is to use $\frac{3}{4}$ oz. pyrogallic acid to a quart of water. This also speeds up the process and gives a rather redder tone than the tannin powder. A mixture of the two gives a slightly different shade than either. The acid treatment generally gives a more even tone.

Matching. If certain parts have taken the stain unevenly you can use bichromate of potash (see page 201) for matching up. A little black stain can be added if necessary. Use the bichromate with care because it can send the wood very dark, especially some varieties. Use it weak if only slight matching is required.

Finishing. You can either apply the wax polish straightway or you can wipe it over with oil first to give a warmer tone. Mix one part of linseed oil with three parts of turpentine and rub well into the surface. Wipe off all surplus and allow at least twenty-four hours to dry. Once again wipe off any traces of oil with a coarse rag (oil prevents any polish) and apply the wax polish as given on page 89. French polish can be used, but wax is the more usual finish. If it is proposed to have this finish use white french polish, or if orange or garnet polish is used allow for the darkening effect when fuming.

BURNISHED OAK

The value of this is that the wood is given a preliminary shine before the wax is applied; in fact the work can be left with no further finish, especially small items on which proportionately more time can be spent. It should be realised that the process is successful on really hard woods only—indeed, the harder the wood the better the result. Hard English oak, for instance, will take on a far better shine that Japanese oak, which is softer and more open in the grain. Soft woods cannot be successfully burnished because they give under the pressure and take on an uneven appearance.

The tools.   The process consists of going over the surface with a hard, smooth substance such as agate, bone, polished steel, or even a piece of hard, close-grained wood such as boxwood.   The object is to take out all scratches such as those left by glasspaper, and present a perfectly smooth surface.   The shape of the burnisher depends upon the form of the surface being treated.   For curved work,

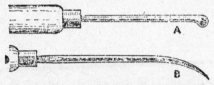

FIG. 39.   TOOLS USED FOR BURNISHING.
Any hard substance such as bone or ivory can
be used.

mouldings, and so on, the steel ball-ended tool at A, Fig. 39, is invaluable.   The curved tool B is also useful (both are normally used in leatherwork).   Sometimes the end of a tooth brush, if of the hard bone variety, can be pressed into service.   For flat surfaces the side of a bone-handled knife or some similar item can be used—it must have a wide surface, because otherwise it will dig in locally.   It always takes longer to deal with a large flat surface because a far greater surface of the tool touches the wood and it is impossible to exert the same degree of pressure.

The preliminary preparation of the work is as for any other finish. If glasspaper is used, finish off with a fine grade.   The tool should be rubbed in the direction of the grain as far as is practicable, but there are countless occasions when this cannot be done.   It does not matter a great deal providing an even sheen is built up.   After burnishing, the work should be wax polished.   It is unsuitable for work to be french polished.

OILED OAK

The process is the same for oak as for any other wood.   Any preliminary staining can be carried out or the wood can be left its natural colour.   The process is described in Chapter XX.

ANTIQUE OAK

There are really two finishes under this heading: the " rubbed " effect and the reproduction finish.   The former has only a superficial connection with antiquity, the high portions and panel centres, etc., being rubbed lighter than the rest. It is sometimes used for obviously newly made furniture and is not intended to deceive, being just a style of finish. The reproduction finish, on the other hand, is made to resemble a real antique as closely as possible.

Rubbed antique finish. Any of the usual stains can be used—Jacobean, fumed, or dark oak, according to taste. The most generally satisfactory is walnut stain. Vandyke crystals is a good alternative. Immediately after application with the brush rub the centres of panels, high parts of mouldings and carvings, etc., with a dry rag so as to remove some of the stain. Do not overdo it, because this produces a restless, uneven, and entirely unnatural effect. A slight lightening is all that is needed. If you fail to produce enough contrast in this way, rub the high lights rather more heavily with fine glasspaper when rubbing down. Now finish with either french polish or wax as described in Chapters VI and XIX respectively.

Reproduction antique oak. This is a very wide subject and some of the tricks of the maker of antiques and reproductions are known only to himself. In any case there is no " antique finish " which can be applied to all old oak work. The period to which the work is supposed to belong has to be taken into account. You can also approach the matter in one of two ways: you can give all the signs of wear—rounded corners, bruises, etc., in which case the work is intended to really look like an antique—in other words, it is a fake; or it can be given an antique finish in which the old colour is reproduced and dirt is introduced into corners and recesses, etc., but the work is not intentionally maltreated by the corners being rubbed off, scratches or bruises on the surface. In this case it is a reproduction in the truer sense of the word.

With the maltreatment of the work we do not deal here, as it scarcely comes under the heading of polishing. It is usually accomplished by the judicious use of the spokeshave, rasp, and file. An ordinary metal ring burnisher is handy for removing signs of artificial wear.

Simple finish. A straightforward finish is to stain the wood with vandyke crystals, the strength being in accordance with the desired depth of colour. A dash of ammonia will help to drive it into the grain. When dry, wet a small part with the finger to reveal the colour it will be when polished. Any correction can now be carried out. It may be that a warmer tone is required, in which case you can go over again with walnut oil stain to which a little mahogany stain is added. It all depends upon the shade required. The vandyke crystals provide the main body of colour, this being toned with the oil stain as required.

When dry, rub over with a coarse rag to remove any grease. Now shake a little fine pumice powder on to a rag and rub over the surface so that the high portions are *very slightly* lightened. Anything in the way of a sharp contrast must be avoided. Only the *slightest* lightening is wanted. Fix the oil stain with two rubbers of french polish, and polish with wax. Instead of ordinary wax polish, however, use an antique wax polish. You can buy this ready-made or you can make it with ordinary beeswax and turps to which lamp black powder is added whilst it is molten. Brush on freely so that the black wax lodges in angles and corners and in the open grain. Allow twenty-four hours for the turps to evaporate and then polish as described in Chapter XIX.

Pickling. For a still more stressed effect a pickling mixture is made up. Put some unslaked lime in a bucket and allow it to cool off. After a while the white lime will settle. Carefully pour off the water leaving the lime in the bucket, and to 2 pints of the *water* add ¼ lb. caustic soda. Finally add 3 pints of clear water. The addition of half a cup of chloride of lime will give a light, greyish tone. Alternatively, half a cup of liquid ammonia instead of the chloride of lime will give a dark shade.

If American oak is being used, it is necessary first to go over the whole surface with a mixture of tannic acid and water to help the pickle to take. The strength is somewhere in the region of a teaspoonful of tannic acid to a pint of water, but this may have to be varied in accordance with the particular wood and the shade desired. Try it out on a spare piece of the same wood. Incidentally, American oak should never be used for an English antique !

Colouring. After pickling, clean down thoroughly with two washes of clear water. Unless this is done thoroughly white patches will begin to show through. The colour at this stage will be a warm brown, and you can let it go at this or you can go over with weak vandyke crystal stain to darken slightly and make a cooler tone. Alternatively, you can use bichromate of potash. As the work is done in stages in this way it is always a good plan to do a couple of pieces of spare wood of the same kind as the job so that the effect can be tried out.

Polishing. The final stage is wax polishing, the antique wax made with beeswax, turps, and lamp-black being used. Make up the polish quite thin and apply freely, especially in angles and corners, and rubbing well into the open grain. Finish off with a thorough brushing after the turps has evaporated, and burnish with a dry, clean rubber.

CHAPTER XXII : TREATMENT OF MAHOGANY

ALTHOUGH mahogany can be finished natural colour, it is usually stained first. Most people consider that it improves the appearance, and it undoubtedly helps in toning different varieties of mahogany to a common shade. It frequently happens that mixed woods have to be used, especially when parts are veneered. It depends upon the particular wood to be used, however. Dark Spanish mahogany generally needs no stain at all. This wood is rare nowadays, however, and the light red varieties normally available are generally better for darkening. The finish is generally with french polish, though some prefer the softer gloss of wax. Oil polishing is seldom practised nowadays, but has an advantage in a table top in that it is largely free from marking by hot plates.

Preparation. The process described in Chapter II should be followed. Scraping is especially important to remove tears and plane marks because the polish built up is highly reflective, and any blemishes are at once obvious. Follow by rubbing well with glass-paper, middle 2 first, then No. 1½. For best work go over again with No. 1. Work always *with* the grain. For curly grain begin with No. 1 grade and finish with *Flour*, working with a circular movement.

Staining. The most generally successful stain for mahogany is bichromate of potash (see page 201). By using it full strength or diluting it, a wide range of tones from a dark sombre brown up to practically natural shade can be obtained. Furthermore, since its action is purely chemical, the grain is not in any way concealed. Always try out the stain on a spare piece of the same wood, and dilute or strengthen it as required.

Occasionally you may come across a piece of mahogany which will not answer to the bichromate treatment. It is rare to find this, but it does sometimes occur, and then you will have to use a direct stain. Do not use a mahogany stain alone; it will be far too red. One plan is to mix a little mahogany stain with walnut stain, the amount depending upon the shade desired.

A rather better plan is to use a medium-strength walnut water stain. Allow it to dry thoroughly and rub down with fine glass-paper. Follow then with a weak to medium mahogany oil stain. This will produce a quite good shade and can be used as an alternative to the bichromate. Exact quantities cannot be given because stains vary in tone, and it depends upon the shade required. Note, however, that oil stain should be avoided when possible on curl

109

mahogany because it is liable to render the whole lifeless. The bichromate treatment is far better for this.

Filling. Proprietary mahogany filler can be used or plaster of paris. Colour the latter with rose-pink powder, just enough to take off the extreme whiteness. Directions for its application and subsequent oiling are given in Chapter V.

Polishing. This consists of fadding, colouring, bodying, and stiffing or spiriting-off, as described in the general chapters on the subject. Remember that the colour is considerably affected by the polish used. Button polish is somewhat yellowish and gives a golden shade. Garnet gives a much warmer and deeper tone. White polish has little darkening effect, but if the whole polishing is done with it over a dark stain there is a slight tendency to give a grey film over the work. Generally the best plan is to stain somewhat light and use garnet polish, this bringing the work to the depth required. Button polish should be avoided over dark shades as it tends to give a cloudy appearance and hide the grain. If greater warmth is required red polish can be used. Details of this are given under the heading of *Colouring*, page 40.

Fumed mahogany. Fuming is occasionally used for mahogany. It turns the wood a brownish tone. The process is as described for oak. Remember, however, that some kinds of mahogany take to the process more readily, and if different kinds are used, the result may be uneven. As the wood loses much of its characteristic warm tone, many people consider fuming unsuitable for mahogany. Generally wax polish is used after fuming, this giving an eggshell sheen which agrees with the somewhat faded and sombre tone produced by fuming.

Waxed mahogany. This is much as described in Chapter XIX. Stain the work somewhat lighter than the tone required as the waxing deepens the shade. Bichromate of potash is the best stain. If you use an oil stain remember to fix it with two rubbers of white french polish after it dries, wiping off any surface grease first. No filler is needed as the wax soon fills in the grain. Use unbleached wax when making the polish, unless you wish to keep the work as light as possible. In this case use bleached wax.

Oiled mahogany. Stain the wood to the desired shade, rather lighter than the finished tone, and polish with oil as described in Chapter XX. No filler is used, the slightly open grain being characteristic of the finish. The process takes a long time and a brilliant sheen is never produced, but it is attractive for certain classes of work and is largely mark proof.

For bleaching mahogany see page 24. Note, however, that it is difficult to achieve much lightening to the Cuban variety.

CHAPTER XXIII : TREATMENT OF WALNUT

THIS wood is generally left unstained because the natural colour is quite deep. Even so, it is often necessary to apply stain to certain parts which may be lighter than the general tone of the whole. This is more the case with walnut than most woods because it is often used in veneer form. This veneer is invariably of a variety of wood different from that of the solid parts, and a difference in colour is unavoidable. A certain amount of colouring can be done in the polishing process, but staining is generally advisable.

Staining. If it is desired to make the whole thing darker, a weak walnut stain can be used; or vandyke crystals, also weak, give a good colour. Do not overdo the staining, however. To even the colour, a second application can be used, increasing the strength if necessary.

In some instances it may be desirable to bleach some parts when the finish is to be as light as possible. Oxalic acid can be used (see page 206) to lighten the wood locally, but it is a mistake to attempt to bleach a whole part. It is much better to use a more suitable piece of wood. Remember to wash away all traces of the acid after bleaching as it may otherwise attack any subsequent finish.

Staining mahogany to walnut. Owing to the shortage of walnut, mahogany is frequently used nowadays as a base for walnut veneer, and when the edges show it is necessary to take out the redness to make it tone with the walnut. As an instance, a mirror or door frame may be made of mahogany with walnut cross-veneer on the face and a walnut veneered panel. Any moulding in the solid around the edge of the frame will necessarily show in mahogany, and both this and any other exposed parts will have to be treated.

Merely to apply a dark stain will not have the desired effect; it is necessary to kill the redness with a pale blue stain. An effective stain for the purpose is green copperas. This is easily made by dissolving the crystals (obtained from the polish stores) in water, but test the liquid first on a piece of timber to ascertain the strength of the blue. This blue, if very weak, will tone with button polish to a walnut colour, but if too strong an Air Force blue will result, which will not change with the addition of polish and will spoil the job. Copperas, incidentally, goes on like water, whether strong or weak, and it is when it is dry that the blue asserts itself. A teaspoonful of crystals to a pint of water will make a fair starting-point for strength, and may be thinned or strengthened according to the shade desired.   Do not use copperas on the deep red mahoganies, which are entirely unsuitable.   After using copperas fix with a couple of coats of white french polish.

Filling.   When the wood is left in the natural colour it is advisable to give a couple of rubbers of white polish before applying any filler, to prevent any tendency for the latter to darken the colour.   Apart from this the filling is as described in Chapter V.   Either a proprietary paste filler or plaster of paris can be used.   Add vandyke brown powder colour to the latter to take off the extreme whiteness. Follow with oil as in Chapter V, and the work is ready for polishing.

Polishing.   There is no special feature about this except that when the wood is unstained white polish should be used to keep the tone as light as possible.   If a deeper tone is required and when the work is stained, either button or garnet polish should be used.   The latter especially produces a rich colour.   If the required depth is reached before the polishing is completed, finish off with white polish.   Carry out the consecutive processes of fadding, colouring, bodying, and stiffing or spiriting as described in Chapters VI—IX.

Walnut can be either waxed or oil polished, and these are much as described in the chapters on those subjects (pages 89 and 92).

Bleached walnut.   A suitable home-made bleach is ·880 ammonia diluted 10 times with water and applied in an even coat. This is followed 5 minutes later with fresh peroxide, at least 20 volumes but as strong as you can get it.   Alternatively you could use a proprietary bleaching unit.

Apply this in the same way.   Walnut is not an easy bleacher. Two applications are likely to be required.   There are several important points to note about bleaching.   Keep the solutions off the skin, etc.; use separate non-metallic containers for Nos. 1 and 2; discard any excess bleach poured out; use fibre or nylon brushes; shake No. 1 well if you buy bleach; have the surfaces freshly sanded with no marks, as these resist the bleach; allow two days between applications.   Only the surface fibres are affected and so only light papering is permissible after bleaching; when dry remove any dust or white deposit; wash well with meth. before finishing.   The result of bleaching is not apparent until after the surface is dry. For the finish use pure white polish.   Bleached finishes, or imitations, may be cleaned with a soft wash-leather and tepid water containing a teaspoonful of vinegar to the pint.

Bone and blond walnut.   There is some confusion in what is meant by these, but there is usually a yellowish tinge in them as compared with bleached walnut.   Generally the effect is obtained by the application of semi-transparent pigments to give the tone.

NOWADAYS pine is seldom used for show work. It comes in mostly for backs, unseen carcase work, and so on. For this it usually requires nothing more than stain. Any of the stains listed in Chapter III can be used, though if the wood is in bad condition it is better to use a water coat (page 17), which, being opaque, entirely conceals the wood surface.

Deal to be polished. Sometimes pine or deal has to be polished, and then the question of preliminary staining needs more consideration. These timbers, particularly deal, present something of a problem, mainly because of their unattractive grain. When either wood is obtained with a fine parallel grain there is a certain dignity, but with more common variegated, irregular figure, however, there is little beauty, and here enters the job of making them more presentable.

Staining. Water stains are best for evenness of colour, but beware of making them too strong. Deal and pine take up quite a large amount of stain and the softer parts quickly become much darker than anticipated. The harder figured portions do not attract the colour to the same extent, and remain much lighter. It is clear then that any attempt to stain the figure down to colour will only result in disaster. Set the colour by the softer timber and bring the figure down with the colour brush after fadding.

Oil stains follow the above considerations, but they are even more prone to leave the hard timber much lighter. There is also a tendency for these stains to render these softwoods " lifeless," so when great clarity is required do not use them. In any event, only a dye oil stain should be used. Any pigment stain (composed of gold size, oil-ground colour, and turps) will result in muddiness.

Filling. Deal may be worked up in the same manner as mahogany or oak, excepting the filling process, which, owing to the absence of open pores, is rendered useless. A good body may be obtained over the stained or natural timber quite easily, though it will sink rather quickly and will need several other bodies to keep a lasting shine. A quicker method is to use a size filler. Glue, gelatine, patent size, or powder size will all serve, but they must be mixed thinly. For example, glue should be strained, then thinned with warm water until all stickiness has gone. The glue still has enough body to seal

up the pores and hold up the polish.   If made too thickly, there will
be a layer of glue left on the surface.

In applying, paper the stain to make smooth, dust well off and coat
in with a large brush, working moderately wet and with the size
warm.   Allow to become thoroughly dry and then paper well down.
Obviously the size cannot be used over oil stain.

An alternative method is to use spirit varnish. Fad up the work
to a fair body, colour down, and apply the varnish with as large a
brush as is convenient, working straight and in a quick manner.
Retouching with the brush is to be avoided. For these woods no
rubbing down afterwards with spirits is necessary as the timber will
absorb quite a large amount, leaving a good working film on the surface.   For this work, brown hard and white hard varnishes may be
used, being commoner and cheaper brands and quite suitable.
However, when papering down be careful not to tear the surface,
for these two types do not set quite so hard as naphtha, crystal, and
the other more expensive varnishes.

Polishing. The only point of difference from normal hardwood polishing is that before the varnish, the fad or rubber may be
worked much wetter.   After varnish, of course, a wet rubber is of
no advantage, as there should be no sinking necessitating extra
shellac.

Colouring. Colouring is generally dealt with in Chapter VII,
but one or two points might be mentioned.   As the grain is mostly
bold, all the matching up and bringing to colour may be done with
the brush, and will be much quicker than the fad method. A tint,
however, should be used with a fad to avoid coarseness of colour.

Regarding shades mostly used, all colours, from natural through
the golden tones to cold or mildly warm browns, are popular, but
rich red colours should be avoided generally, for they are rather out
of character, resembling a poor attempt at mahogany.   Deal and
pine do not look well in the fancy colours as transparencies, but they
may be finished in solid colours, using the paint mixed as on page 100.

A preliminary groundwork is perhaps necessary and may be made
from the following : ½ oz. gelatine, 14 oz. whiting, 1 pint water or
little less.   Mix well up together and boil in saucepan of water until
the liquid is soupy. Apply while warm with a brush to the timber, quite
thickly; but first coat the wood with a coat of polish and make smooth.

Paper the filler down with a cork block and give several coats of
the coloured polish-paint, papering down well between each coat.
Polish when all is thoroughly dry in the usual manner, using transparent white polish.   It is not necessary to paper off all the filler, but
merely sufficiently to render the surface free from waviness.

Bleached and waxed pine. Yellow pine bleaches readily. The procedure is to use either a proprietary bleach or make up your own. Both are the two-solution type. Shake the No. 1 and apply. Five minutes later apply No. 2. Allow one day, then lightly paper and brush off the white deposit. Repeat if necessary and complete by wiping over with methylated spirit. There are certain important precautions. Use a fibre brush. Use non-metallic containers and do not return excess to the main containers. Bleach must be kept from the skin. It is essential to have the surface damped and, when dry, freshly sanded, because wax and fingermarks will resist the bleach. Wax already applied must be removed with turps. The bleaching action is to the surface fibres so that light papering only is permissible after bleaching. The commercial bleach is very efficient and is the one we recommend. If you wish to use a home-made bleach try ·880 ammonia diluted with 10 times as much water for No. 1. For No. 2 use hydrogen peroxide fresh and as strong as you can get it. Apply in the same way. After wiping well with meth. apply three thin quick coats of best white polish. Next day rub firmly along the grain with a pad of No. oo steel wool used dry. Remove all dust and repeat twice.

To complete the job rub well with a little silicone wax. This treatment will produce a durable wax type finish.

Scrubbed pine. Another pleasing finish is what is generally known as scrubbed pine. It is so-called because it is intended to reproduce the effect of old pinewood panelling which has been stripped of the paint or limewash which was commonly applied to it in the eighteenth century. This leaves a warm, mellow tone which, though it is difficult to describe, can be reproduced with fair accuracy by means of paint on other species of woods, providing they are pale in colour and reasonably close-grained.

The first operation is to stain the wood until it is more or less the colour of old pine. On new wood as, for instance, American white-wood, a coat of dark button polish should be sufficient: alternatively, apply a coat of oil stain of suitable shade: allow this to stand for a few minutes and then wipe off. Give plenty of time to dry and then obtain some fairly deep cream-coloured flat paint and thin this generously with white spirit. Brush this on fairly freely and then wipe off with a clean rag. The effect will be to impregnate the surface with a semi-opaque film, the presence of which is hardly discernible, but which nevertheless imparts something of the tone of stripped pine. When hard and dry, it is glass-papered and wax polish or matt or egg-shell varnish completes the effect.

Pickled pine. The chemical mainly used is nitric acid, and some

interesting effects can be obtained with it.   The effect can be varied
by the strength of the acid in water.   The result in the weaker
mixtures is to give a greyish tone to the wood, but when used in
greater strength a more reddish or yellowish tone becomes pre-
dominant.   The weak mixture might be in the region of 1–12, or
1–20, and the stronger dilution of 1–8.   The effect can again be
varied by the application of bichromate of potash after the acid has
dried out.   Yet another result is obtained by applying fairly weak
nitric acid and allowing to half dry out.   Strong nitric acid is then
dabbed on locally and you get the graded reddish tinge intermingled
with the grey.

It is necessary to get rid of the acid or perhaps neutralise it with
weak soda or borax.   Otherwise it may attack any finish subsequently
applied.

CHAPTER XXV : TREATMENT OF PLYWOOD

WHEN plywood is veneered with oak, mahogany, or whatever it may be, the veneered surface is treated as though it were normal solid wood. It is when there is no veneered surface that certain precautions have to be taken. The reason for this is that the layers of plywood are rotary-cut—that is, they are peeled circumferentially from the log. This generally results in the grain having a series of minute cracks in the surface, and this causes undue absorption of stain. The cracks may be invisible to the naked eye, but the result is that the wood turns a darker shade than solid wood. Birch, alder, and gaboon plies are all liable to turn dark in this way. Thus, after staining a solid framework to the desired shade, the stain is weakened before applying it to the plywood. This rule holds good for all stains. It is advisable to try out this weakened stain on a scrap piece of ply.

Preparing the surface. To obtain a really fine finish on plywood it is nearly always necessary to smooth it up with the steel cabinet scraper and then thoroughly glasspaper it with fine 2 and No. $1\frac{1}{2}$ grade glasspaper; for, if carefully examined in a good light or with a magnifying pocket lens, it will be seen that the knife-cut and steaming processes which it undergoes have a tendency to tear or drag the wood locally and leave it very porous. As a rule, oil and spirit stains give the most satisfactory results on birch and alder, these stains having less tendency than a water stain to raise the fibres.

Filling. For the filling-in of plywood use a moderately thick paste filler and rub it well in with a coarse rag. The heavier you can use the filler the better, provided, of course, that you can comfortably spread it.

For common work, alder or Oregon pine plywood may be stained to imitate mahogany by mixing burnt sienna in stale beer and water, equal parts. About 1 oz. of burnt sienna to a pint of the mixed liquids gives a good result. Water coatings for a cheap finish to poor plywood are given on page 17, and these must have a little concentrated size added to the colouring matter so as to bind them. Water stains or coatings used on plywood take longer to dry out than when used on solid woods.

After plywood is stained the surface should be sanded down smooth, and if this necessitates a partial removal or cutting through of the stain, the work should be carefully picked up by re-staining the offending portions with a diluted stain applied with a tuft of cotton wadding or a small soft-haired brush.

The keynote for finishing plywood, whether by polishing, spirit varnishing, or oil varnishing, is to obtain a dead flat foundation at the commencement of each process of the work. It is useless to apply extra coats of polish or varnish whilst the work is rough and fuzzy. The same processes are followed throughout as when varnishing or polishing a solid wood, except that plywood may call for more coats of brush polish between each of the rubbing-down processes. Where possible, it is good workshop practice to stain, fill-in and body-up all plywood panels and the respective edges of their frames before the work is glued together.

Plywood veneered with figured Italian walnut burrs or specially figured roey or mottled mahogany should undergo the same treatment as the solid wood.

CHAPTER XXVI : TREATMENT OF HARDBOARD

ALTHOUGH it has a compact, dense appearance, hardboard is in fact most absorbent, and to finish with polish or varnish is necessarily expensive. A single coat disappears almost at once, and a second is not much better. Of the two, varnish or lacquer is the more satisfactory as it is of a thicker nature so that the suction is more rapidly satisfied.

Depending on requirements, hardboard can either be finished as it is or it can be stained. It should be realised, however, that even without staining and using a clear varnish or polish, the colour is inevitably darkened, and this should be allowed for. If stain is used it is essential that a spare piece of hardboard is used to try out the effect, because it invariably turns out to be darker than corresponding tests made on solid wood.

The stain. An effective stain can be made from raw linseed oil coloured with burnt umber or any other suitable colour ground in oil. Add the colour to the oil gradually and try out on a test piece. A little terebine helps in drying, but is not usually necessary owing to the absorbent nature of the hardboard. Apply fairly rapidly with a rag, wiping off surplus, and finishing in one direction, generally along the length. This is of importance when a number of corresponding panels have to be finished because it is immediately noticeable if some have been wiped off in a different direction. Various proprietary oil stains can also be used.

When hardboard is used with solid wood parts in the same job, it is essential to try the effect on spare pieces of both. Just as pine absorbs stain more readily than, say, oak and consequently becomes darker, so hardboard invariably looks darker than solid wood, except when the latter is of a soft absorbent nature. Often it is necessary to dilute the stain.

Another point that arises is that certain varnishes will not dry out properly after the application of some oil stains. Sometimes the first coat appears satisfactory, but the second appears to separate and remains tacky. It is essential in such cases that a coat of sealer is applied after staining before the varnish is used. Several proprietary sealers are available. This sealing coat is not necessary when french polish is used. No filler is needed because of the close nature of hardboard, and the finish can be applied as soon as the stain (if any) has dried out.

French polish. If this is used the first two or three coats (either brushed on or put on with the rubber) can be fairly freely applied. It will sink in almost at once, and should therefore be as thick as possible. Allow about half an hour and give another coat, rubbing down flat beforehand with fine glasspaper. In this way a gradual shine is built up, but one must be prepared to use a great deal of polish and patience. The actual polishing process is the same as that already dealt with in Chapters VI–IX.

If, as the work progresses, the colour appears wrong it can be darkened or warmed by the addition of spirit-soluble stain crystals. Make up this colour polish separately, allowing the crystals to completely dissolve. Shake up thoroughly and add to the polish. Orange shellac polish is already of a yellowish brown tone, and garnet is considerably darker. Colour polish added to these gives varying tones. Bismarck brown is of a strong red colour and should be used with caution. The addition of black is often helpful.

Varnish and lacquer. These give a quicker build-up. Copal varnish or any of the proprietary materials such as clear *Valspar*, or *Universal Medium* can be used. Probably three coats will be needed, and they should be rubbed down with fine glasspaper or steel wool between the coats. Remember the note about sealing certain oil stains before using varnish.

A point in connection with hardboard which is mounted upon a framework is that it is liable to bulge at the outerside if it is finished on the one side only. This is due to the absorption of moisture from the air on the untreated side. It is therefore advisable to give the inside a sealing coat of polish or copal varnish diluted with about 10 per cent white spirit. Incidentally when varnish is used as a finish the preliminary sealing coat can be french polish, but it is impossible to use polish over varnish.

Clear cellulose applied with a brush can be used, but it is difficult on a large surface to avoid join marks owing to the rapid drying nature. Furthermore, as several coats are needed, there is the liability of the undercoat to work up when the new one is applied. Altogether it is safer to avoid it unless one has spray apparatus.

Wax can always be used as a finish, but, in common with other finishes, darkens the natural colour. It is helpful to coat with either french polish or clear varnish or lacquer before using wax as it provides a slight basic shine, and helps to keep out dirt, especially on an item constantly being handled. Rub down with fine glasspaper before using the wax.

CHAPTER XXVII: POLYURETHANE LACQUER

THIS type of finish consists of a transparent lacquer to which a catalyst or hardener is added immediately before use. If the plastic liquid only is used it merely remains wet, but drying is rapid once the catalyst has been added. It is necessary to make up enough for immediate use only because once it has set it is useless. The " mixed " life varies with different makes, but is somewhere in the region of six to twenty-four hours, though this depends upon temperature. The hotter the room the quicker the plastic sets. In some makes, however, the hardener is already incorporated, and becomes effective as the solvents begin to evaporate.

The chief advantage claimed for these is that they are heat and spirit resistant, so making them specially suitable for table tops, counters, and so on. Not all are actually burn-resistant, however, and those specially suitable for resisting spirit marking are less effective against heat marking. On this score note that, although a finish may be heat resistant in itself it cannot protect the wood beneath from scorching, so that, even though the finish may not show burn marks, the wood below may be scorched.

The wood can either be left natural or it may be stained, but a word of warning is necessary regarding some oil stains. With some a discoloration occurs, and it is therefore essential that the finish is first tried out on a spare piece of wood which has been given a coat of the same kind of stain. If it becomes discoloured it is useless to go ahead.

Water stains are quite safe, but it is advisable to go over the entire surface beforehand with warm water and allow to dry. The roughness caused by the rising of the grain is then glasspapered smooth, and when the water stain is subsequently applied the roughness is reduced to a minimum.

Some makes call for a special filler (if required), and this is invariably made by the manufacturer. This should be ascertained before using a particular make of lacquer. As a rule it is necessary to avoid plaster of paris as a filler because linseed oil is invariably used afterwards to kill the whiteness, and this may easily cause trouble. Even oily woods such as teak may prove difficult, and in such cases a degreasing agent such as *Tepol* or carbon tetrachloride should be wiped over the surface first. Some makers recommend that such woods are wiped first with their own special thinners.

In any case the surface must be free of all grease, wax, etc., and the best results are obtained directly after sanding. Mix the catalyst with the liquid plastic in the exact proportions stated and apply with the brush or by spraying. Dextrous handling is necessary when the brush is used to obtain clean join marks, especially on a large area. Work in the direction of the grain, applying a full, flowing coat. Allow to harden for several hours (temperature affects this) and rub down with a fine abrasive paper. Follow with another coat, again rubbing down. Probably three coats are needed. Depending upon the particular make the proportions of the plastic and catalyst may have to be varied in the coats, and the maker's instructions should be followed.

Various finishes may be given to polyurethane lacquers. When thoroughly hard a matt finish can be obtained by rubbing with No. oo steel wool along the grain. For a satin finish dip the steel wool into wax polish and finish with wax only applied with a polishing rag. When a bright finish is required flat the surface with grade 400 silicon carbide paper using soapy water as a lubricant. Remove the sludge with a wash leather, and polish with a rubbing compound such as the finest pumice powder. This will leave a dull gloss which is further refined by polishing with rottenstone and water or one of the rubbing compounds sold in many motor supply shops. These last named are in various grades and the finer should be used for finishing. Polyurethane lacquer is made in various grades, and for furniture the interior grade should be used.

CHAPTER XXVIII : REPOLISHING OLD FURNITURE

HERE it is assumed that we have an old piece of furniture and want to make it look as new and clean as possible. The old polish will be considered only so far as it can be utilised as an effective groundwork. The first point is the cleaning of the surface. In the case of an old job, this removes any dirt and exposes the polish so that we may judge its value. On a newer job, although the polish may not be obscured by a layer of dirt, the greasiness from handling and very probable wax polishing must be removed. Turps and linseed oil (half and half) put on with a rag and rubbed dry, followed

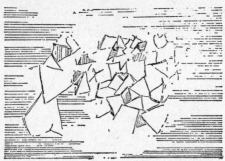

FIG. 40. EXAMPLE OF CHINESE WRITING
The film of polish has broken up with innumerable small cracks and is useless as a foundation for repolishing.

by water similarly used is as good as anything and is generally to hand.

Whether to strip. Now we can decide whether or not to strip the job. Any suspicion of what is known as " Chinese writing " is a certain case for stripping; it takes the form of innumerable cracks running in all directions as in Fig. 40. This blemish is caused by uneven drying of the various coats of lac and no matter how treated (save of course stripping) is almost bound to appear at a later date.

If the existing polish is at all powdery or perished it will be useless as a basis upon which to work and therefore must be stripped. Also, any coats of varnish colour which have been put on in an attempt at renovation must come off to allow the beauty of the timber to show. The last stripping consideration is painted work. It would appear that pieces in oak are painted over more than any other timbers, probably because the surface of oak is very often " dryer " or less polished than mahogany or walnut.

The Stripper. Regarding the stripper, do not use caustic soda and similar materials for removing the unwanted coating, for, although these alkalis may be negatived by application of vinegar, there is always the danger that some small part may remain and ruin the whole. Furthermore, they tend to darken such woods as oak and mahogany.

If darkening does not matter you can use strong liquid ammonia, scraping off the polish as the latter is softened. If possible keep the ammonia from the hands, as it can be painful to handle. Washing soda is also an effective polish stripper, but this again tends to darken the wood. It must be washed off thoroughly and any remaining traces neutralised with vinegar.

Here is another stripper :

$\frac{1}{2}$ lb. rock ammonia   1 lb. washing soda
$\frac{1}{2}$ lb. crude soft soap   1 gallon hot water.

Apply it with a scrubbing brush to which a stick has been fixed to form a handle. Wash off and neutralise with vinegar.

As all the above strippers tend to darken the wood it is better to use a proprietary stripper. There are many on the market which are free from any darkening tendency, and they are not so messy in use. Furthermore, they work much more quickly. They are, however, more expensive than the home-made variety.

How to use stripper. Coat in the work with an old brush, allow to soften, and scrape off with a paint scraper or similar tool. This will probably have to be repeated several times before the job is finally clean ; two coats of liquid before the first scraping are often necessary. It will be found that for the stripper to act really well the parts must be more or less horizontal so that the liquid can remain in an appreciable quantity on the surface. The work therefore should be stripped in sections and turned accordingly. This, of course, applies to the larger surfaces. Turned legs, etc., are frequently stripped by continually brushing them with the liquid, thus keeping the surface constantly wet.

Washing down. When clean wash with warm, slightly soapy water, following with another of water and a little vinegar. Finish off with plain water, mopping off all surplus liquid and allowing to dry. Proprietary strippers are applied just as the home-made variety, but as there is in some of them a proportion of wax which remains on the timber, the work needs washing off with turps substitute to make perfectly clean.

Bruises. Bruises often necessitate stripping. When they are prevalent they can be cleaned off with plane and scraper, so far as construction will allow, or a compromise may be made. That is to say the *very large* holes and dents may be stopped and others completely ignored. If they are not ignored and wax rubbed in, there will be nothing to show for the work but a surface which still looks bruised, and indeed unless all the shallow ones are pricked in, the wax will come out and spoil the polishing. When the main bruises are stopped the whole job may be cut down thoroughly with No. 1 or o paper, removing all pimples, runnings, and so on in the process, and leaving all nice and flat.

Varnishing. When old polish is to be covered with new shellac, however good the former may be, there is always a chance that, with the action of the spirits in the polish, the old stuff will shrivel and break up or otherwise prevent a fine surface from being attained. To avoid this give the job a coat of spirit varnish with a *rubber*. The latter is stressed because a brush coat will start the work off with a ropey and thick coat which is undesirable. Working varnish in the rubber has been dealt with in a previous chapter (page 45), and if white hard spirit varnish is used there will be no difficulty. Thin the varnish with spirits, and if the rubber feels very sticky to handle, don't worry about it, for varnish rubbers cannot be used as cleanly as polish rubbers, on account of continual re-charging and working very wet.

In coating a sunken panel, do not start the rubber quite at the ends, but leave about half an inch so that the point can make a stroke of this width to finish off each coat. About three coverings of varnish per section of surface is about right. Thus, take the four drawers of an old chest. Lay them all fronts up on the bench or floor. Coat the first all over without re-touching. Proceed with the other three in sequence, and repeat the whole process three times, not forgetting each time the drawer edges.

This varnishing thus separates the new and the old work, preventing trouble, and at the same time allows the old polish, without being worked, to set the colour and act as a groundwork. A day's drying is advisable, when a good cut down with a piece of oily No. o paper leaves a fine surface for working upon.

Polishing. The work now in connection with toning, colouring, and finishing is entirely as for a new job. If, however, the old polish is the colour required, use a pale polish so as not to change the tone. When finished any dry-looking quirks and corners can be brightened up a bit by passing a wadding dipped in a mixture of gas-black and oil into them and wiping dry with a soft cloth.

FAULTS

So far we have dealt with repolishing a moderately good polished surface, but there are occasions when, although the surface is good, there are one or two faults in or on the polish which must be put right before any attempt is made towards the new work.

White patches. This defect is caused by oil being allowed to remain under the surface of the polish. The only remedy is to set the surface upright, cover the patch affected with spirits applied with a soaked wadding, and to light the spirits left on the surface at the bottom after the wadding is out of the way. This burning with a little blue flame close to the surface will effectively prevent a recurrence of the " white " with one or more applications. This process cannot be used without re-polishing.

White heat spots. These are marks by hot plates, etc., on polished work, and may be easily removed by allowing linseed oil and turps (half and half) to remain for a short period over the affected places. Camphorated oil serves the same purpose. Either oil should be wiped off dry afterwards and the patch washed over with a little vinegar to remove all traces of oil. These methods are effective without repolishing. In a very stubborn case, however, burning with spirits must be tried.

Ink stains. These are quickly removed by covering the stain with nitric acid, and when the former turns white, wipe dry with a soft cloth.

Glass ring marks. These, caused by the bases of glasses being damp with spirits, etc., are simple to put right when the mark is only slight. A slight mark is one which, when the glass was removed, was allowed to dry naturally. This needs but a touch of glasspaper and another rubber of polish. If, however, the patch was very soft with spirits and was rubbed dry with a cloth, most of the polish would have been removed, leaving a circular hollow in the surface. This hollow, more often than not, will have lost some of its colour and need matching up again as well as fetching level. This is a job of patching and is dealt with in Chapter XXIX (page 130), but one point must be stressed, *never work the brush round the ring* : always *with* the grain. Make short, very accurate strokes, so that the coloured part is not outlined by dark spots. The painting-out discussed in repairing will apply here. When a professional has a mark of this nature to repair, he often finds it easier and quicker to remove the centre and colour the entire circle, the colouring being much better and the building level afterwards much more effective. See details on page 84.

Scratches. Those caused by pointed or sharp articles brought into contact can be either eased out with glasspaper or waxed up and polished, and coloured as soon as the wax has a coat of shellac (without oil). Another type of blemish under this heading is that of paper marks showing through a thin body. Often a job is finished and a small faulty place is cut down again and thinly stiffed. Later on the cutting-down shows through as a series of hair lines. Here is a prevention. After cutting down, gently rub the patch with spirits to darken the lines, and work up in the ordinary way. This rubbing (twice over is enough) will prevent the scratches from appearing.

Soft polish. Generally this is not realised until the job has been in use. An ornament stood on the surface leaves an outline of its shape. Sometimes it is caused by the too liberal use of linseed oil which may be trapped beneath and prevents the polish from hardening. More generally, however, it is due to faulty polish which may contain a gum which never hardens out properly. There is no cure short of stripping the surface and beginning again with a reliable polish obtained from a trade polish supply house.

White filler specks. This may appear shortly after polishing or it may be deferred. It manifests itself in the filler in the grain turning white. Bought grain-fillers usually consist of a base—silex, whitening, plaster of paris, etc.—and a colouring agent, thinning agent, and binding agent. What can happen is that most of the liquid part of the filler is absorbed into the timber leaving the pores filled with practically the solid ingredient only. This reverts to white as it dries thoroughly by which time the polish film may be on. The only remedy is to strip to the white and start again.

With proper safeguards this fault will not occur. One plan is to buy a neutral grey filler. This is brought to shade by mixing in well a suitable pigment such as umber for brown and burnt sienna for mahogany. This agent, being a powder, will not separate. A little turps may be necessary and a few drops of terebene is desirable to ensure quick oxidisation. A safer procedure, which will prevent filler bleaching, is to stain first then apply one quick coat of polish by rubber once across then once along the grain. This wash coat, as it is often called, ensures that no part of the filler will be absorbed and also makes wiping of surplus easier. The other important safeguard is to allow enough hardening time—minimum one day except for special fillers. If sealed too early the liquid parts cannot complete their particular jobs—the medium to evaporate and the binding agent to oxidise—and separation may again occur.

CHAPTER XXIX : REPOLISHING REPAIRED FURNITURE

THERE are several things to consider when an old piece is to be repaired. First, what is to be the extent of the new finishing? Is the old work to remain as far as possible, only the necessarily cleaned-off portions being repolished; or is only the new finishing to be considered of importance?

Considering the job. In the first case, if the job is of sufficient age and interest to warrant the old craftsmanship remaining, then by

FIG. 41. REPAIRED CHEST AWAITING POLISHING.
All repairs and patching are carried out first. This will leave much bare new wood which will have to be made to match the old work.

far the best way is to allow the new work to show up clearly and distinctly from the old, so that it can be understood that no attempt has been made to fake. Generally speaking, however, the old pieces are more often required for general use rather than as exhibition pieces of old craftsmanship, so perhaps it is better to make the new work tone in as near as possible to match the state of the old polish. If the old surface does not matter, then the only point is whether the work needs stripping or is good enough to remain as a groundwork.

Questions in cleaning. Take as an example an old chest of drawers. Here we have a foot to replace, rails to patch here and there, cocked beads to fit, veneer patches in drawer fronts and top. When polishing commences, there are considerable patches of raw timber from cleaning off, and to be able to stain these we must first find the colour. To do this the surface must be cleaned. If a cleaning liquid is used all over indiscriminately the liquid will probably stray on to the patch and prevent clean staining. Therefore it is best to clean a place or two away from the cleaning-off, just large enough to act as a pattern for matching the stain. Later, when all parts are stained and a coat or two of polish applied, the whole job can be cleaned all over thoroughly without fear of accident.

Cleaner. Turps and linseed oil in equal parts make a fine cleanser, removing all grease and wax. Work fairly heavily with a cloth, and dry with another when ready. Water is used next in the same way, this removing all remaining stains not touched by oil and also assisting in cleaning off oiliness.

However, having cleaned our portions for matching, we can now prepare the bare patches for stain. No. 1 or 1½ paper leaves the surrounding polish much too scratched and therefore No. 0 and " flour " are used to make smoother, and also to ease down better the step which must occur between the polished and unpolished places.

Choosing the stain. Now for staining. If very old, the stains originally used will be probably difficult to obtain and prepare, so recourse must be made in many cases to a substitute. Anything but an oil stain should be suitable (this last was not used). The effect of oil stains and water stains on timber is quite different and therefore both cannot be used together. Alkanet oil (see page 202) is not considered as an oil stain, although it serves a similar purpose.

Bichromate on oak and mahogany in varying strengths will give browns. Walnut crystals and permanganate of potash will also give browns differing slightly in tone. These stains are all cheap and therefore can be all made up for trial with little expense. A good gauge for depth of stain when no similar wood is handy is the back of the hand.

A red stain can be made by boiling 1 oz. of bismarck in 2 pints water, and adding 1 gill of vinegar when cold, thinning with water as desired. However, as red fades from the work after a time, there will be probably little call for much strong red stain, the colours mainly tending to browns of a yellowish cast.

Walnut crystals were at one time used extensively for walnut, and therefore might be a useful stain for this timber. As mentioned above, red fades, and on the more pale colours, especially on walnut, polish alone often reaches the tone.   Button polish on walnut will give a close match to faded brown walnut, which is a fine golden colour.

Applying the stain.   We will assume that the stain, allowing for subsequent toning of polish, is ready.   Apply with a rag and wipe all dry and clean.   It will be noticed that around the edge of the patch are light streaks.   These are due to the previous polish impregnating the timber and forming a kind of " size," which has prevented the stain from taking.   It is useless, therefore, to attempt to restain these streaks to colour.   If, however, the patch generally is too light, stain again, but err on the weak side, for too dark means re-cleaning off.   Paper all smooth when dry, but use care, for there are probably *enough* light places without increasing the number by uneven papering.

Filler.   For filler, plaster of paris coloured with rose-pink, dragon's blood, or some other powder colour is suitable.   Oil as usual with linseed, with or without alkanet root stain, the latter giving a reddish tone.   Rub dry and allow to stand awhile.   Now, with a colour brush, give the patch several coats of polish, allowing to dry and papering between each coat with a cork block.   This coating will gradually bring the surfaces of timber and polish nearer to being level.

Colouring.   The next job is to colour down and make all one. After papering, the patch is worked up with a rubber, but it is necessary to extend just a little way outside the area on to the old polish to bring the original colour up so that it can be seen clearly.   If the work is a pale colour, use just a little gas-black to half-and-half polish and spirits to darken the mixture.   The coldness can be taken off with a *little* red.   As the colours become browner add more black and red.

Colour down in the normal way with the colour brush, but take great care with the very light places around the edges, for these constitute what is equivalent to a joint between the old and the new work.   With the brush, tone them down first, making the brush strokes accurate and clean.   The colour should be placed just where needed and nowhere else.   Go all round, making this light area less of a distinct division.   Now while these parts are drying, work the colour as required on the portions which have taken the stain properly.   This portion should be quite easy to colour and complete without mishap.   The outer parts should be drier, ready for further darkening.   It is here that extra care must be taken to see that the brush takes colour *only* to where required.

Viewing. It sounds unnecessary to say " look at the work before putting brush to timber," but this " looking " is vital. What is meant is, do not colour one part exactly, following with the remaining parts in sequence round the edge, but rather look first for the lightest parts and decide, for each small place, just where the brush shall be placed. Having got that well in mind, do what you have decided and no more. Just because a little area next to your brush is needing colour, do not touch it before you have stood back and viewed what you have already done. This viewing will decide on the next

FIG. 42. FAULTY COLOURING.

The colouring is too dark and solid owing to the brush marks being continuous.

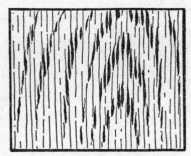

FIG. 43. CORRECT TREATMENT.

Here the brush has been taken in short strokes, thus breaking up the outline of the marks.

selection of places, so eliminating section by section the light parts surrounding.

Use of pencil brush. It now remains to take a pencil brush to the places too small for the colour brush, and your work is done as far as darkening is concerned. One word regarding the pencil brush. This has a tendency to make *lines* of colour unless care is taken, so use it either fairly dry or thin the colour down.

Perhaps you will find that you have inadvertently put some colour on the old polish and made a dark mark; indeed during early attempts at patching a regular halo of dark brush marks is made which outline the repaired places. In this case a little weak " solid " colour is handy. To half-and-half spirits and polish add a touch or two of the necessary solid colours, making a very thin, slightly lighter " paint " than the job is to be. Then with the pencil brush charged lightly, make strokes *with* the grain in such a way as to break up the outline.

It is possible, of course, to cover the whole offending patch with the light " paint," but " paint " has a nasty trick of showing up in different shades as the angle of viewing changes. That is to say, coloured from the front it may be exact, but from the side it probably takes on a much lighter cast which glares out from the rest.

Figs. 42 and 43 show what is meant. The long, dark marks in Fig. 42 are typical places where two brush strokes overlap and leave the work too dark. The general tone of the dark patches has only been lightened by breaking up into several smaller patches (Fig. 43).

If the whole recoloured patch is now given a weak tint, the job is ready for stiffing after a clean, soft rubber has first fixed the colour. If there is still an apparent ridge, a coat of spirit varnish applied carefully before stiffing and cut down when well dry will fetch all level. To make dull afterwards either rub carefully with turps and pumice powder on a wadding or a long-haired " dulling brush " and pumice.

Final touches. So much for the difficult portions. The edges of veneer patches are coloured out with thin paint as above and coloured as usual. Cocked beads are polished in a length and fitted afterwards. They are touched up a little if necessary with a small rubber.

If any veneer is in many tiny cracks, glue is needed. To get this in without stripping, lay cloths soaked in boiling water to raise the veneer and open the cracks. Repeat until sufficiently open, when put in *thin* glue. Clean off surplus and when smooth polish as usual with no oil in the first stages.

A rub with wire wool will scratch the new work if desired to nearer approach the old, and a judicious bruise or two would be helpful, but the use of a sharp tool for this work is to be avoided or cuts will be the result instead of the desired bruise.

Renovating the limed finish. After prolonged use it often happens that the lime in the pores becomes dirty, discoloured, or disappears entirely in parts. If the general condition is reasonable the lime can often be restored by rubbing in wax polish with which zinc white powder has been mixed. The powder is added whilst the wax is molten and is mixed thoroughly. Rub across the grain and wipe the surplus from the surface. The special proprietary liming compound can also be used.

When the condition is poor more drastic measures are necessary. Remove handles, etc.; protect bearing surfaces; do not reduce time intervals. If the timber is solid use warm water with some green soap dissolved in it to give a good lather. Set the surface horizontal. Use something like a large nail-brush with thin, stiff bristles. Work firmly along the grain only. Give the surface a good scrub, then clean off with a damp washleather and fresh water, leaving as dry as possible. The effect of this treatment is to remove old wax, dirt, and much of the lime in the pores, as well as much of any thin, protecting varnish film which may have been used. Each surface should be done systematically, the soapy water being changed frequently and the pieces allowed to dry out naturally for two days.

The next thing is to glasspaper the surfaces clean and get rid of most of the old lime. This is likely to be liming wax but it could be real lime or even something like paint. If the two previous operations have not removed it then the only thing left is to go over each pore systematically with something like a blunt large needle. The lay-out of the pores on plain oak is such that this can be done without undue tedium. It is not necessary to remove lime deep in the pore.

Clean off the dust and when all is ready stain the surfaces. Two teaspoonfuls of oak water stain crystals simmered for a few minutes in a pint of hot water, would give a suitable contrasting cool brown. Allow to cool, strain off, add a dash of ammonia, and weaken by test on a hidden corner to give a mid-brown. Stain quickly and evenly using a rag. Allow one day. Staining will be patchy if the previous work has not been carried out properly.

The main protection comes next. Use button polish applied by rubber only. Apply four thin coats in quick succession. Have the rubber charged just enough to lay a thin film with rubber face taut. Use no oil. Work in straight strokes along the grain, the idea being to keep the pores open as much as possible. Allow one day then flat lightly with No. ooo steel wool used along the grain only. Remove dust.

Stir the liming paste well and apply as for grain filling to pack the pores flush but with a minimum only on the surface. Allow a day then rub up with dry rags. A thin film of the paste on the surface is transparent.

If the suite is veneered it is still quite feasible to use the same procedure provided the washing is done as quickly as possible. It would be safer to use turpentine to remove wax and when dry methylated spirits or stripping agent to remove any varnish film.

Dark furniture. Although proprietary bleaches will lighten some woods, they are not effective in lightening stains. It is doubtful whether stained wood can ever be made lighter except by tool methods, such as planing or scraping. This may be impracticable on a veneered surface, and difficult on one with detail such as carving, moulding, etc. Even when the surface is scraped clean the stain may still show dark in the grain of the open woods.

CHAPTER XXX : POLISH REVIVERS AND FURNITURE CREAMS

THE main object of a reviver is to remove all traces of grease and dirt in such a way as to restore some of the lost brilliance of the polished surface.

Revivers. Water can be used to remove dust and so on, but tends to leave the surface dull. Oil takes away grease but the final traces of any oil are difficult to remove. Vinegar is useful in removing greasiness and brightening up slightly the surface. Usually a combination of these liquids is made which eliminates the bad properties of each. Thus 1 part linseed oil and 1 part vinegar is a simple reviver. The same mixture with an extra part methylated spirits is also good. The spirits may be alternatively 1 part sulphuric acid (20–1).

Reviver recipes.

1. ½ pint vinegar
   ½ pint methylated spirits
   1 oz. camphor
   1 oz. linseed oil
   ½ oz. butter of antimony.

Dissolve the camphor in the methylated spirits.

2. 4 parts raw linseed oil
   1 part terebine
   12 parts vinegar.

3. Equal parts of spirits of camphor
   Camphorated oil.

Any grease may afterwards be removed with spirits of camphor.

4. Boil 1 pint of distilled water and add to it about ¼ lb. castile soap powder. Let the soap powder dissolve completely. In a separate tin pour in 1 pint of best American turps and add to it 2 oz. of best beeswax and 2 oz. of white paraffin wax. Heat these by putting the tin in a basin of boiling water—do not heat over a flame. When the wax is completely dissolved, shoot the whole into the distilled water and allow to cool. After twenty-four hours it will be ready for use. Always stir up thoroughly first. If castile soap powder cannot be obtained use any good quality soap, shredding a small cake for the purpose.

In all the above mixtures the method of applying is the same. Use mutton cloth, which can be bought very cheaply in rolls of about 12 yards, and is the softest material to be found for such a purpose. Apply " round and round " and up and down with the cloth, finishing off and polishing with a clean, dry one.

Scratches. A useful hint for toning down scratches in the polish is to rub them with a fresh pecan nut kernel or even a brazil nut. The first of these is much richer in oil and is therefore the best. The oil which exudes when rubbing is just sufficient to take off the whiteness of the scratch.

There are also many proprietary brands of reviver on the market which are of varying usefulness.

Furniture creams or waxing pastes. When the surface is too dull to leave just " revived," the only thing to be done is to wax it with a paste or liquid wax, either proprietary or made up from the recipes given below. With a paste wax, the object is to give a thin film to the polish which, without very great effort, can be burnished up to improve the " shine." These waxes must not be confused with the hard waxes used when the work is wax finished. These are usually applied hot and burnished with brushes and heavy weighted cloths and themselves form the polish.

The following are effective home-made recipes :
6 parts carnauba wax
$3\frac{1}{2}$ parts Japan wax
$1\frac{1}{2}$ parts paraffin wax.
Melt these together and add about same quantity of turpentine. Stir and add a little french chalk and ammonia.

6 parts carnauba wax
$3\frac{1}{2}$ parts Japan wax
$1\frac{1}{2}$ parts paraffin wax
12 parts turpentine
3 parts shredded white curd soap
30 parts water.

In melting these waxes and adding turpentine, etc., care should be taken to avoid a naked flame. Heat up as far as possible in a water bath. In event of carnauba wax being difficult to obtain, substitute beeswax may be used, which is carnauba dissolved in paraffin with a colour added.

CHAPTER XXXI: GETTING RID OF THE LIMED FINISH

IN the opinion of many to-day, lime with its white deposit should never be used as a furniture finish. The essential of a good finish is to more or less seal the pores of the wood, enhance the beauty of the grain, and to form a fine film of shellac, cellulose, or wax which will give a protective covering to the surface of the timber. A deposit of lime or zinc white, even when properly bound, has always a tendency to come out of the pores when the wood contracts, and the lack of a transparent film or covering allows the work to become dirty, swarthy, and generally depressing in appearance. Much of the so-called limed oak has, after a few years' wear, found its way back to the polisher to be renovated. This renovation usually consists of stripping and re-staining the oak to a nut-brown or to a good fumed oak colour. This can be done as follows.

Stripping. When the work has been taken to pieces as far as it is possible it will require stripping to get rid of the ingrained dirt. A home-made stripper may be made as follows : 2 oz. of borax, 6 oz. rock ammonia, $\frac{1}{2}$ lb. common soft soap, and 1 lb. washing soda, which should be dissolved in 6 quarts of hot water. This may be applied with a rag mop made by tying old rag to a $\frac{5}{8}$-in. dowel rod. This stripper, if left from three to fifteen minutes, will soften any wax or old polish so that it can be scraped away with a dull cabinet scraper or painter's scraping knife. When the bulk of the wax or polish has been removed, and whilst the wood is still wet, sprinkle the surface with powdered Brooke's monkey soap and with a coarse rag proceed to wash the job.

If you wish to avoid this messy procedure you can purchase any good make of paint and varnish remover, and apply this to the work according to the instructions given on the container. If any of these solvents are used finish by washing down the work with methylated spirits.

Re-staining. When stripped and allowed two days to dry, all surfaces should be sanded down with No. 1 glasspaper. The stripping solution will have darkened the oak, and if the home-made stripper containing rock ammonia has been used it will be found that the shade of the oak is a good approximation to fumed oak. If the worker is satisfied with this shade, the job will not require staining or oiling.

135

If the work is required a couple of shades darker, wipe down the oak with a pad which contains raw linseed oil. Any surplus linseed oil should be wiped away, and if the job be then left for twelve hours it will be found that the oil has darkened and mellowed the tone of the oak. If this shade is satisfactory fill in with a fumed oak colour paste wood-filler and set aside to harden up in the pores for at least two days.

Polishing. Take a large mop gilder's brush and coat the oak in with white french polish. Again lay aside to harden off, and in due course ease down the surface and apply a second coat of white polish. This coating should be slightly thinned by adding about one-quarter of the amount of methylated spirits. When the second coat has dried, straighten out the brush marks with a few rubbers of white french polish. The rubber may be applied in straight sweeps in the direction of the grain. The work may be left at that, or it may have subsequent applications of wax furniture polish. A natural shade of wax polish is the best for the purpose. Dark orange-coloured wax polish should be avoided for a light finish.

For readers who prefer a nut-brown to a mid-Jacobean shade, the work should be stripped as previously mentioned (but not oiled) and in due course stained with an oil stain (fumed oak). Allow this to stand for twenty-four hours, and apply a brush coating of brown shellac polish. The object of this brush coating is to seal and bind the stain. Allow to stand for at least a day, after which sand down and repeat the brush coating of polish. Leave overnight, ease off any dust specks with No. o spent glasspaper and straighten off the surfaces with a few rubbers of white french polish. If the work is left at this stage it will have a semi-open-pored effect which is quite fashionable.

Those who feel disposed to body-up the job to a close-grained finish will of course have recourse to a further application of the bodying rubber, after which they may stiff off the work with a rubber of half-and-half polish and glaze. In either case, the open-pored or the bodied-up surface may from time to time be rubbed up with wax polish.

CHAPTER XXXII: FINISHING FLOORS

MOST dwelling-house floors are of softwood, and are made up of boards of white deal. The finishing of these is always a bit of a problem. It is a job about which no decorator is ever enthusiastic. White deal is a common wood, usually knotty and sappy, and it contains hard and soft patches which absorb the stain unevenly; the blue sappy portions always become darker than the heart portions of the wood. Alternate layers of wood absorb the stain unevenly and the resultant work often appears " ropey " lengthways of the grain. Furthermore, in a new house the plaster has usually been splashed about, and this causes a messy and patchy appearance.

There are various ways of finishing such a floor, of which the chief are : stain and wax polish; stain and varnish; varnish stain.

Of these the least satisfactory for a new floor is varnish stain, because the stain is contained in the varnish, and, as the varnish is worn off, the stain is worn off with it, resulting in light patches. It is, however, useful for an old floor since, being largely opaque, it covers up blemishes beneath.

Preparation. Whatever the finish, a floor must be properly prepared if the finish is to be successful. The condition of a new floor should be quite good, but it is advisable to go over it with middle 2 glasspaper held round a cork rubber, working it with the grain. If it is dirty and is marked at all it should be scrubbed with soap and water, well wiped over with clear water to remove all traces of soap, and allowed to dry. This will take twenty-four hours at least. It is then glasspapered smooth. Incidentally, it is a good plan to damp the surface in any case when a water stain is to be used. The latter is always inclined to raise the grain, and by damping and rubbing down first the worst roughness is avoided.

All nail holes should be filled in with either putty or plastic wood. The latter has the advantage that it takes stain like the surrounding wood, but it is more expensive. Putty must be coloured with brown umber powder worked well into it, the colour approximating to that of the floor after staining. The reason for this is that the stain will not take over the putty.

Staining. An effective yet cheap stain is made with vandyke crystals.

Mix the crystals with 2 pints of warm water (quantity of crystals to be in accordance with depth of colour required).

Add 1 oz. strong liquid ammonia (ask for " point eight-eighty ").
Add 2 tablespoonfuls of hot scotch glue.
This is used warm and is applied with a wide brush. Use the latter
with the grain, and deal with one board (or certainly not more than
two) at a time. In this way all joints will be avoided. Do not make
the colour too dark unless this is definitely desired, because a floor
always tends to become darker with subsequent treatment. Allow
to dry out thoroughly; this will take at least one day—probably
two.

An alternative is to use one of the colours ground in oil and thinned
with turpentine. Vandyke brown or burnt umber give good deep
browns; raw sienna is a yellowish brown; for a black finish use
brunswick black thinned with turpentine. Another dark brown stain
is made from ¼ lb. asphaltum dissolved in 1 pint turpentine with
about 1 tablespoonful of gold size added to act as a binder. All of
these oil stains cost more than that made with vandyke crystals, but
they are of special value for an old floor which may be greasy and dirty,
as water is of no value in penetrating grease. After it has dried out
(one or two days) it is advisable to rub over the surface with a coarse
rag to remove any surface oil or grease, as these may prevent the
subsequent polishing from being effective. One sometimes sees
permanganate of potash recommended as a stain. This is not satisfactory as it is fugitive and rapidly fades.

Proprietary stains can also be used. Some are ready-mixed water
stains, others oil stains, whilst others are in powder form and have to
be mixed with water or spirit according to the type. In the latter
kind make up the stain well in advance, as some ingredients dissolve
more readily than others, and, if used before completely dissolved,
the result may be a startling colour. Allow from twenty-four to
forty-eight hours to dry out, and fix with a coat of french polish
applied with a brush. This is advisable in all cases, but is essential
for a floor which has been oil stained and is to be wax polished,
because the turps in the polish will otherwise lift the stain and cause
the floor to become light in patches.

Wax polishing. Beyond the fixing with french polish no other
treatment is necessary before the wax is applied. Shred beeswax
and dissolve it in turpentine. Heating in hot water will speed up the
process. For a cheaper polish use paraffin wax instead. Make it to
the consistency of a soft paste and apply freely yet evenly with a brush
of the boot-brush type. Allow at least twenty-four hours for the
turps to evaporate—no shine is possible until this has happened.
Polish with another fairly stiff brush (a boot polisher) and finish
with a clean, dry duster. The first application will not produce much

of a shine, but continued waxing will build up a good gloss. Any of the proprietary wax polishes can be used, of course.

Varnishing. As an alternative to wax you can use varnish, this having the advantage of producing a high gloss immediately. (You may, of course, prefer the sombre eggshell gloss of wax to the bright shine of varnish.) The process after staining is rather different from that described for wax. Stain by one of the methods outlined above under *Staining*, and, in the case of an oil stain, rub off any deposit of oil or grease with a coarse rag. Make sure that the stain is dry, and, in the case of water stain, give the floor a coat of glue-size. This is to prevent the varnish from grabbing into the wood. Remember that deal is a very open, porous wood. Allow to dry out thoroughly, and rub down the surface with glasspaper to remove the roughness. Afterwards go over with a cloth to remove the dust.

There are two kinds of varnish, spirit and oil, and the chief difference between these is that the former dries rapidly and the latter slowly. From the point of view of being able to use the room soon, the spirit varnish has an undoubted advantage, but it is more difficult to use. It must be put on, worked rapidly, and left just as it is. If it is brushed too long the varnish will work up.

The best plan is to work each board at a time since the joints in the boards will largely conceal those of the varnish. Keep the edge alive as far as possible because once it becomes tacky the joints are liable to show. In the case of oil varnish, which takes a day or so to harden, the work is simplified considerably as there is plenty of time to work it. A final note is to do the work so that one finishes at the door—that is when the whole floor is being varnished. Otherwise one may be unable to escape!

Old floors. Here a great deal depends upon the condition of the floor. If the boards are very badly worn it is hopeless to expect to do much with them. Replacement is the only real solution, though if this is not to be considered a coat of paint with which varnish has been mixed will hide up a lot of blemishes. If it has been painted or varnished and this is in a bad way, it should be removed with one of the strippers sold for the purpose. Any paintshop keeps a stripper. Caustic potash will soften old paint, but it is a messy job and will probably result in the walls being splashed badly.

Even when stripped the boards are seldom left perfectly clean, and this is one of the occasions when a varnish stain is the most suitable finish, because the tendency of a varnish stain is to conceal the grain rather than show it up, and it will conceal the blemishes too. A coat of glue-size should be applied first. If an ordinary stain *is* used, a spirit or oil stain rather than one of water is advisable.

Open joints.   One trouble with an old floor is that the boards have usually shrunk, causing the joints to be open.   The remedy is to fill them in as in Fig. 44, using strips of deal of a slightly tapered section.   These are glued and hammered into the joints.   When dry they are levelled down with chisel and plane, and smoothed with glasspaper.   Deep indentations can be filled in with plastic wood. Note that a slight hollow will not hold stopping satisfactorily, and this can be made a little deeper, undercut if possible, and the surface

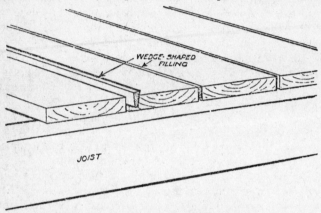

FIG. 44.   HOW TO FILL IN OPEN JOINTS.
Strips of wood of a tapered section are glued and hammered in.   They are levelled afterwards
with the plane and finished with glasspaper.

roughened by scratching.   When the edges of the boards are worn it is simpler to make a filler from old newspaper soaked in water until pulped and mixed to a workable consistency with plaster of paris, size, and about 8 per cent linseed oil.   It is rammed into the gaps and levelled as the work proceeds.   When the gap is wide it often helps to embed some thick string in the filling and force this in. If after stripping and cleaning the surface is reasonably good you can apply an oil or spirit stain and then proceed as given for a new floor.   If still bad give a coat of size and use a varnish stain.

Oak floors.   These may be in parquet form or in long boards. It is seldom that such floors are stained, because the oak is much more effective in its natural tone.   You can either apply wax polish straightway, or you can slightly tone it by wiping over with linseed oil, then waxing.   It is essential that you allow the oil to dry out completely before waxing as it will otherwise entirely prevent a shine from being built up.   Occasionally an oak floor is oiled, filled in, given a coat of spirit varnish, then wax polished.   This gives a foundation shine and continued waxing keeps it in condition.

CHAPTER XXXIII : CELLULOSE FINISHING

INTRODUCTION TO CELLULOSE POLISHES

Contributed by C. C. Stewart, Assistant Manager of Technical Development,
Cellon Limited, Kingston-upon-Thames

IN the trade, cellulose finishing has largely superseded french polishing as a means of decorating and preserving furniture. Fundamentally both french and cellulose polishing possess similarities. Both employ solutions of film-forming materials in volatile solvents, each solution drying by evaporation of the volatile portion, and neither requiring any chemical change, such as oxidation of the film, as is the case with paints and many varnishes, to produce a hard, tough surface. In both processes, too, some skilled handwork is called for, though the tendency with cellulose polishes is to minimise this. This latter fact indeed is one of the reasons why so many mass producers of furniture favour the cellulose technique.

Source of cellulose. It should be clearly understood that cellulose, as used to form the basis of a polish or lacquer, is not the cellulose of nature. It is derived therefrom certainly, but only after considerable treatment in chemical baths. The product in which the wood lacquer manufacturer is interested is that known commercially as nitrocellulose or cellulose nitrate. Raw cellulose occurs very freely in nature in the form of vegetable tissue, but one source in particular is preferred for nitrating. The flowers of the cotton plant are rich in cellulose, and after the picking process what is left adhering to the pod, termed the linters, is collected for conversion into nitrocellulose.

Though many other varieties are suitable for conversion into lacquer cellulose, a number of technical and economic considerations determine the choice of cotton linters as the main source of supply. This of course explains the use of the alternative name " nitrocotton " which is frequently given to lacquer cellulose. The linters are subjected to a cooking process in a mixture of sulphuric and nitric acids which produces impure nitrocellulose, later purified by repeated washings. Finally, the water present is replaced mechanically by alcohol to render the product safe to handle. Dry nitrocellulose is both highly imflammable and explosive and hence it is never packed without a damping agent. Alcohols are generally employed because their presence does not interfere with the composition of the resultant lacquer. Though this treatment does not render the nitrocellulose less inflammable, it eliminates the risk of explosion due to careless handling.

Conditions in the nitrating bath may readily be changed to vary the properties of the product, and many different grades are marketed. It is not intended here to delve deeply into the technicalities of nitrocellulose manufacture, for it is the job of the lacquer producer rather than the consumer to study and choose the grades most suited for conversion into furniture polishes. When discussing cellulose wood lacquers or polishes it is important to realise that there are several ways by which the user may work up to his finish. These are described later, but the point to be remembered here is that, dependent on the chosen process, so will the composition of the polish vary.

Materials used for cellulose polish. Broadly speaking, all cellulose polishes have a common root, four main classes of material being mixed to give the required results. They are : (1) the cellulose derivative, most frequently nitrocellulose, (2) a resin, of which many types are suitable, (3) a plasticiser, or mixture of plasticisers, (4) the volatile portion. According to the ultimate use of the lacquer, so will the ratios of these four types of ingredient vary one with another. Resins are used to confer increased build, lustre, toughness, and adhesion to the lacquer film, though in the lowest grade products the resin is used chiefly to lower the cost.

Plasticisers, whilst also contributing in some measure to the properties enumerated for resins, are mainly employed to cure the inherent brittleness in the nitrocellulose film. Thus they impart flexibility and the ability to withstand knocks without fracture of the film. Plasticisers should be chosen which are solvents for both the nitrocellulose and the resin constituents of the lacquer, so that in the dry film all three are homogeneously interlocked together.

The volatile portion of the lacquer has no lasting place in the final coating, and may be regarded as a necessary evil. It is necessary because, without it, it would not be possible to apply the solid constituents to the surface to be coated, and it is an evil because it is pure waste to the consumer ; no sooner has he applied the polish to his article than the volatile liquid disappears into thin air. The lacquer required to fill a gallon can is likely to contain between five and six pints of volatile liquid.

Advantages of cellulose. Many properties lacking in french polish may be found in cellulose compositions, among which two outstanding ones are heat resistance and water resistance. But this is not all ; the nitrocellulose lacquer film when correctly fortified with plasticiser and resin is of a much tougher nature than shellac, and is thus much less inclined to become brittle. Also, it is just as receptive of the energetic polishing administered by the housewife.

For the purposes of repolishing a damaged surface it must be admitted that french polish lends itself more readily. A quick rub over with the polishing pad is often sufficient to restore an otherwise deteriorated finish. This does not mean that the french polisher cannot repair a disintegrating cellulose film ; it can be done when taken in the early stage, but it is more difficult in this instance to associate the injured party with the remedy.

From the economic point of view cellulose has the advantage in that it requires far fewer man hours and a lower percentage of skilled labour.

Application methods. The methods used to apply cellulose polishes differ radically from those customary with french polish. Whereas the most commonly seen apparatus for french polishing is the piece of cloth, termed a pad, comparatively elaborate equipment is to be found in the polishing shops of to-day. Though elaborate at first glance, most of the present-day equipment is very simple to use and it takes far less time to train an operator in its use than to produce a skilled polisher.

Lacquering of wood with cellulose polishes is normally done in one of three ways—by spray, by dipping, or by brush, probably in that order of usage. The spraying technique, so universal in its application, will merit much of our attention, as it is by far the most commonly employed method of cellulose polishing. Dipping is used in a few specialised cases where the articles to be treated lend themselves by virtue of their shape to this process—typical examples being brush handles, dowels, slats, etc. Brushing is comparatively seldom used and is mainly confined to small concerns, where spray equipment is not readily available, or else for coating awkward recesses which it is not always possible to reach by spray. It does however present possibilities to the home-worker and is discussed more fully later.

CHAPTER XXXIV : CELLULOSE FINISHING—APPLICATION TECHNIQUES

VISCOSITY—SPRAY EQUIPMENT—HANDLING OF EQUIPMENT—COMMON DEFECTS—DIP APPLICATION—BRUSH APPLICATION

SPRAYING is by far the commonest method of applying cellulose polishes, and most of them are formulated by the manufacturer with this end in view. Reasonably fast-evaporating solvent mixtures are employed to speed drying time, and the thickness, or viscosity, of the solution is rigidly controlled. This latter factor is of the utmost importance to the sprayer, the limits of viscosity between which it is possible to apply an even coating being very critical. The type of plant in use and to some extent the individual spraying influence the optimum viscosity for any particular class of work ; therefore, once a set-up has been standardised, it is most important that the lacquer manufacturer maintains consistency.

There are many different types of laboratory apparatus with which to measure the viscosity of a nitrocellulose solution and different units are in use for expressing the results. One unit in frequent use is the " poise," and a lacquer for spray application has a viscosity value of approximately one poise. It is general practice to supply with the lacquer a proportionate amount of thinners, for a slight adjustment may be necessary to meet individual requirements. Also thinners are required to counterbalance loss of solvent from the lacquer caused by leaving containers uncovered. Most spray polishers who use thinners do so in a constant proportion, which is another reason why products must be consistent.

Spray equipment. The principles of lacquer spraying are exemplified in the scent spray or the fly-killer. Essentially, compressed air is harnessed to force the liquid through a fine annular orifice, thus reducing the liquid to a very fine state of atomisation. Whilst such a device is sufficient for the needs of fly-sprays, etc., certain refinements are necessary before lacquer can be applied satisfactorily and evenly. Modern spray-guns are fitted with adjustments all of which must be brought into play according to the shape and nature of the article to be coated.

The flow of lacquer to the atomisation chamber is controllable and so also is the air pressure. The shape of the spray may be altered by adjusting the position of small compressed air outlets on each side of the nozzle ; thus it can be fan-shaped to produce a flat spray across or down the article, or a round spray for fine work and touching in. Many different designs of spray equipment are obtainable nowadays and for that reason it is impossible to lay down here precise instructions—these should always be obtained from the

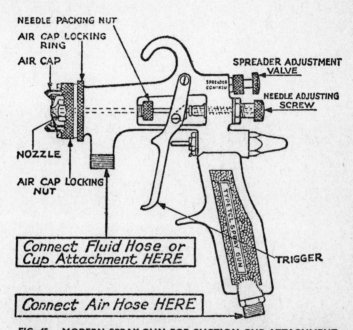

NEEDLE PACKING NUT

AIR CAP LOCKING RING

AIR CAP

SPREADER CONTROL

SPREADER ADJUSTMENT VALVE

NEEDLE ADJUSTING SCREW

TYPE TCL SPRAY GUN

NOZZLE

AIR CAP LOCKING NUT

Connect Fluid Hose or Cup Attachment HERE

Connect Air Hose HERE

TRIGGER

FIG. 45. MODERN SPRAY-GUN FOR SUCTION CUP ATTACHMENT.

This gun can have either the suction cup attachment or the fluid hose connected with a pressure-feed container. The gun is made by the Aerograph Co., Ltd., to whom we are indebted for permission to reproduce this illustration.

individual plant manufacturer—nevertheless the principles are invariably similar. Fig. 45 shows a typical gun.

For spray application of polishes certain pieces of apparatus are essential. Reduced to its simplest form, there will be needed a source of compressed air, a rubber hose for carrying the compressed air to the gun, a spray-gun, and a lacquer container. In factories it is common to possess large compressed-air generators and in this case the air must be filtered to remove the traces of oil and moisture that are usually present to some degree. Compressors capable of supplying up to 100 lb. per sq. in. are frequently used, though this is usually cut down to 40–60 lb. per sq. in. for spraying purposes. It is seldom that pressures much outside these limits are employed for application purposes. The small manufacturer may procure a portable compressor unit, driven by petrol or electricity for occasional use. The amateur may have the choice between a foot- or hand-operated outfit.

The cup gun. The principles governing the performance of guns are basically the same, a press of the trigger releasing the atomised lacquer from the nozzle. There are, however, different ways and means of feeding the lacquer to the gun. For small work a so-called " cup gun," where a cup-shaped container, varying in capacity from ¼ to 1 pint, is attached to the top of the gun body and the lacquer is passed to the atomising chamber by gravity, is frequently employed.

A variation of this has the container slung underneath, and the lacquer is then forced up and through by compressed air. It will be readily understood, however, that there is a limitation to the size of container which can be attached to the gun because of the increase in weight and subsequent tiring of the operator. Furthermore, for continuous spraying, a pint of lacquer does not last very long and much time would be wasted in constant refilling of the container.

Pressure-feed containers. Lacquer reservoirs have been devised for maintaining a continuous flow of polish to the gun, sufficient often for an entire day's work. Overhead gravity-feed tanks are still in frequent use and consist merely of a tank, the capacity of which may be varied at will, a cover with a small air ingress hole and an outlet near the base to which is connected a hose linking to the gun, the tank being fixed at a level appreciably higher than that at which spraying is carried out.

More popular now is the pressure-feed container. This is normally obtainable in sizes varying from 1 to 50 gallons, though outsize capacities may usually be procured to order. Metal containers which are capable of being made airtight are equipped with a pressure gauge, inlet and outlet attachments, a safety valve and agitating gear. This latter is not of much importance with clear lacquers, but is necessary where matting or flatting agents or coloured pigments are incorporated. There is always a tendency for these to drop down to the bottom, making the agitating gear necessary.

The air pressure in the container is usually to the order of 10 lb. per sq. in. To simplify cleaning of pressure pots, particularly when changing from one solution to another, interchangeable inner containers are often used. A fluid hose line is attached to the outlet of the pressure pot and connected to the spray-gun. An obvious

THE TWO SYSTEMS OF FEEDING LACQUER TO GUN
SHOWN DIAGRAMMATICALLY

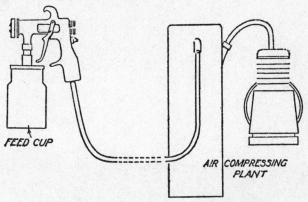

FEED CUP

AIR COMPRESSING PLANT

FIG. 46. GUN FITTED WITH SUCTION FEED CUP.

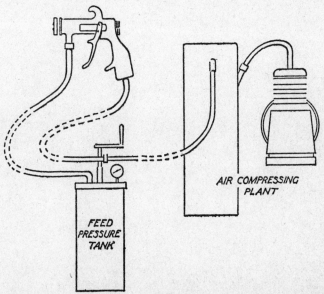

AIR COMPRESSING PLANT

FEED PRESSURE TANK

FIG. 47. GUN WITH HOSE CONNECTION TO FEED PRESSURE TANK.

These illustrations are shown diagrammatically to make clear the two methods of feeding the gun.

advantage of this method of feed is that the container may be situated wherever it is most convenient, and, by adjusting the length of the hose line, the gun may be operated over a wide area. Other advantages claimed are that a more uniform flow of lacquer to the gun is obtained and that lower air pressures are needed for spraying. Figs. 46 and 47 show in diagram the principle of the two systems.

The spraying booth. In the case of any but intermittent or out-of-door spraying considerable attention must be paid to ventilation and exhaust of fumes, and even in the case of the former it is highly desirable. There is no necessity for the operator to wear a mask so long as adequate extraction facilities are installed. As Home Office Regulations make this obligatory on all employers of spray polishers, the need for masks is seldom met. Spraying cabinets, or booths, are usually installed in which articles to be coated are placed. The cabinets are usually three sided and have a roof. Fans behind draw away excess spray and fumes and the exhaust should be evenly distributed over the whole of the interior. The front of the booth is left open to permit operations and a heavy turntable on the floor adds greatly to the ease of handling.

Fastened to the exterior of the booth are usually found pressure gauges, air purifers and attachments for holding spray-guns, airlines, etc. The roof of the booth is preferably made of glass and the booth situated in a good light so that the operator may readily examine his work. Various regulations stipulate positioning of spray booths, and factory inspectors are usually consulted beforehand.

The interiors of spray booths are painted with a compound which is easily removable with water, or by some other simple means, so as to catch excess spray and prevent it adhering to the sides. The coating should be removed at least once a week, the booths cleaned thoroughly, and a further application made. Dry spray residues are dangerous and liable to burst into flame spontaneously.

A comparatively modern innovation has been the introduction of the water-washed booth. The sides and roof are usually constructed of galvanised steel and a continuous flow of water runs down the back and sides of the booth. To the water is added a wetting agent to overcome breaks in the stream, due to surface tension, and the water is automatically filtered and pumped back into circulation. In some cases it is considered worth while to collect the filtered residues for reclaiming. Certainly the water-washed booth is very clean and labour saving in operation. Fig. 48 shows a small booth.

Cleaning. Scrupulous cleanliness of equipment is essential, as apart from the fire risk from residues dire results may obtain from contamination of the lacquers. Hence all lacquer containers, spray-guns, and fluid hose lines should be regularly washed with proprietary cellulose cleaners, obtainable from the manufacturers, particularly when changing from one lacquer to another. Insufficient attention to these details has resulted in many failures being wrongly attributed to the polish. Further, the fine orifices and moving parts of the gun are readily choked by dried or semi-dried lacquer deposits. It is advisable to strip down a spray-gun

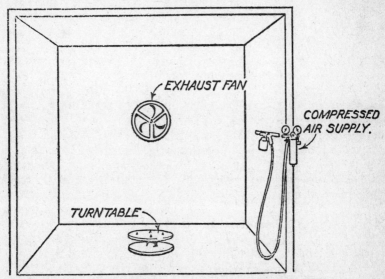

FIG. 48. DIAGRAM SHOWING SIMPLE SPRAYING BOOTH.
Note the fan to withdraw fumes.   The turntable is a convenience for revolving work to enable sides and back to be reached easily without unnecessary handling of the work.

completely at the end of the day's work and to leave the parts soaking in cleaners overnight.

Using the gun.   The art of spraying is not learnt in a day, but practice teaches more than all the books written on the subject. The first mistake made by most novices is to flood the article with lacquer, leading to immediate running of the coating. It is caused by too heavy a hand on the trigger. The next attempt may produce a dry, almost granular coating, the result of insufficient pressure. Soon, however, the correct pull will become apparent.

The distance of the gun from the work and the angle at which the spray is presented to the work are both important. An angle of approximately 45 degrees and a distance of 9–12 in. from the job suit most purposes, but this varies with the size and shape of the work. The gun must be kept continuously on the move whilst spraying, any hesitation, even but a momentary one, will cause an immediate build-up of lacquer. On a flat surface it is preferable to start at the top with a horizontal motion, working in as near straight lines as possible and overlapping about half way each stroke with the next. When this has been mastered and an even flowing coating produced, the next stage is to learn to cut off the lacquer supply from the gun at the end of each stroke, which means just short of the edge of the work. The gun should be moved in a straight line parallel with the work. The temptation is to " arc " the gun, and this results in the centre part receiving a more concentrated deposit. This is made clear in Figs. 49 and 50.

Most spray-guns possess two pressures on the trigger : the first releasing air only and the second air and lacquer together. The supply of air and lacquer are controllable independently and experience soon shows the best adjustments for a particular job. Most guns too are supplied with several interchangeable nozzles of varying size, and again the one most suited to coat a particular size or shape has to be learnt by experience. The release of the lacquer from the gun is actually controlled by a needle operating on a spring attached to the trigger ; some gun manufacturers supply different diameter needles to match their nozzle sizes.

It will be gathered from all this that spray lacquering is highly specialised, but the home worker would find a much simplified plant suited his purposes. Many of the requirements mentioned are primarily intended to economise material, labour, and time in large-production factories. The man who wishes to experiment at home is hardly concerned with these considerations. There is no doubt that the day will soon be here when portable spray plants are within the reach of all. To-day some vacuum cleaners are so fitted that pressure in place of vacuum may be generated, and harnessed to apply paint, by reversing the motor. The simplest possible construction of gun is used and nobody should experience any difficulty in its use.

Defects in sprayed surfaces. We must now consider briefly some defects which may occur. It is generally possible to eliminate these by methods mentioned here ; but if they are persistent and the consumer feels certain that every reasonable precaution has been taken, he should immediately contact the lacquer manufacturer and request the visit of a technical representative to investigate the matter. The effects of too heavy or too light a squeeze on the gun trigger have already been mentioned, and flooding of the surface, leading to sagging and running of the film, is almost invariably due to bad spraying.

Air and lacquer supplies to the gun should be adjusted, and by varying the pressure on the trigger it should not be a difficult matter to correct this fault.

Too light a squeeze was blamed for a dry-sprayed effect, but it is not the only possible cause of a rough or severely orange-peeled surface. Insufficient thinners, too high a spraying pressure, and too

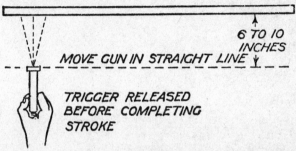

FIG. 49. HOW THE GUN SHOULD BE KEPT PARALLEL WITH WORK.

FIG. 50. TEMPTATION TO USE GUN IN AN ARC.

These two diagrams make clear the necessity of keeping the gun parallel with the work in a straight line. Otherwise there will be an uneven building up of lacquer on the surface.

great a distance between gun and object all tend to produce a similar effect ; consequently attempts at correction should take into account all these factors.

Cissing. It is sometimes noticed that an otherwise perfect surface is marred by a few small round depressions, which may or may not be whitish in appearance. This effect is known as " cissing " and is almost certainly due to traces of water or oil, or both, in the air line. Frequent clearing of the air system and the installation of traps and filters are the remedies.

Chilling. A much more disfiguring fault associated with contamination by water is known as " chilling" or, sometimes, " blushing," but this is brought about in quite a different manner. Lacquer films dry by evaporation of the volatile constituents, which have different degrees of volatility. When a solvent evaporates it lowers the temperature of the surrounding air to a degree according to the rate of evaporation ; thus a rapidly volatilising solvent will cause a greater reduction in the surrounding air temperature than one which is slower. The surrounding air has a moisture content, or relative humidity, and that moisture content may be such that, whilst it is held in suspension at normal room temperature, any reduction in temperature will lower the dew-point sufficiently to cause deposition of water.

This is precisely how chilling is caused, for when water is deposited on the surface of a wet lacquer film it precipitates out of solution the nitrocellulose and other solid constituents, giving rise in extreme cases to a completely opaque, white surface. There are two ways of overcoming this trouble, the more important of which is to ensure that application is not carried out under conditions of extreme humidity—most finishing shops are designed so that the relative humidity does not exceed 70 per cent.—and the other involves the slowing down of the rate of evaporation of the solvents. Most lacquer manufacturers market so-called " anti-chill " thinners, for use in extreme cases, which are really mixtures of low-volatility solvents and the addition of 5–10 per cent. to the lacquer depresses the rate of evaporation considerably.

An opaque, white affect in a clear lacquer film may be caused by the use of wrong thinners, i.e. thinners that are not designed for and are 1ot compatible with the lacquer. In most cases this would be evident during the mixing process, when thickening and precipitation within the lacquer would take place, but sometimes the initial mixing may appear satisfactory and incompatibility shows itself only on drying. The importance of using only the maker's thinners for any lacquer cannot be stressed too highly. Too frequently one sees lacquer stores containing several different makes of lacquer, and one brand of thinners used indiscriminately with all. It is asking for trouble, and when trouble arrives it is most difficult to decide where the fault lies.

Soft surface. Continued softness of a lacquered surface is almost certainly due to applying too much in one operation, or building up too many coats in too short a time, thus trapping a considerable amount of solvent. It is preferable to apply thin, even coats of spray polish, allowing one hour between coats to facilitate evaporation of the solvents.   It may also occasionally be due to excessive wetting up of the film during the pulling-over operation (see next chapter).

Blooming.   A further surface defect is " blooming."   It is sometimes observed on articles of furniture, usually when installed in the home.   A deposit like the bloom on a grape settles all over the surface.   It is easily removable when the article is polished, but constantly recurs.   This is a characteristic of the lacquer and the differing types of resins which are incorporated, and it is therefore controllable mainly by the lacquer manufacturer.   There is little

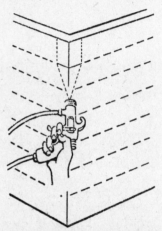

FIG. 51.   FINISHING A CORNER.
After working sideways over the ad-joining sides, the corner is finished vertically.   When a gun with feed cup is used, it should be kept upright.

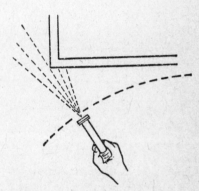

FIG. 52.   FAULTY CORNER FINISH
Note how the spray is partly overshot, re-sulting in faulty deposit around the corner. In any case avoid arcing.

doubt, however, that damp conditions aggravate the trouble, and the finisher may play his part in overcoming it by lowering the humidity of his polishing shop down to the minimum.

DIP APPLICATION

The dip application of cellulose polishes will not occupy much of our time for it is applicable only in certain cases where the shape of the article is suitable.   For the mass finishing of similar articles such as brush handles, or dowels, etc., dipping is the most economical. Large tanks often containing as much as 200 gallons of lacquer are employed, and immersion and withdrawal of the articles from the tank is mechanically controlled.   The articles may be lowered and raised from the tank, or they may remain static and the tank be moved up and down hydraulically.

The actual withdrawal time of the articles from the lacquer bath may be adjusted, a common rate being 2 in. per minute. Complete smoothness of operation is essential as any unevenness is shown up in different thickness of lacquer deposit. Very viscous lacquers are used, the solvent mixture of which has to be carefully balanced with a view to its use. Considerable evaporation may take place from the surface of the tanks, and whilst these should be kept covered as much as possible, occasional topping up with thinners and thorough stirring must be carried out at times. It is important, however, to disturb the lacquer as little as possible for, owing to its viscous nature, any bubbles formed will take a long while to disperse —and the bubbles if transferred to the article will remain in the finish.

BRUSH APPLICATION

The brush provides the readiest means of application at the disposal of the amateur at home. With a little care and the realisation that he is dealing with something very different from household paint or varnish, very passable results may be obtained.

Brushes. The type of brush to be recommended is one of camel hair, and a range of shapes and sizes should be available, the flat type being suitable for most purposes. Owing to the fact that the solvents and diluents used in cellulose lacquers may attack rubber, the bristles or hairs of the brush should not be set in this medium, but ordinary glue is quite suitable. Full, flowing coats should be applied with as little brushwork as possible, as owing to the rapid drying it will be found impossible to brush it out and lay it off as one would an oil varnish. Again, one coat will appreciably soften the preceding one, however old, which is a further reason why brush work should be cut to the minimum.

Brush processes. In general, the processes laid out in the next chapter, though primarily intended for spray technique, may be adopted for brush application, and for that reason we do not give separate ones here. A lengthening of the time intervals between individual operations would be of advantage to the brush hand and would lessen the tendency for one lacquer coat to be picked up by the next, otherwise these processes may be followed through, reading " brush " for " spray."

Most lacquer manufacturers market special cellulose thinners for brushing purposes, which are composed of volatiles of slower evaporating rate than normal. These tend, of course, to keep the surface open a little longer and it is a good idea to moisten the brush in these thinners periodically to ease application. The lacquers sold for brushing purposes themselves have slower solvent mixtures than the equivalent spraying types, but are otherwise constructed similarly. Cleaners again are an essential part of the polisher's equipment, and brushes, etc., should be scrupulously cleaned when finished with, as the bristles will soon become extremely hard.

Drying. In concluding this chapter on application some mention must be made of drying conditions. However the lacquer is applied, by spray, dip, or brush, the coated article should be left to dry in a dust-free atmosphere. Absence of draughts is essential, though a gentle circulation of warm, dry air is of considerable advantage to rapid elimination of solvent and vapours. Small articles or components may be racked in drying cupboards, whilst large articles should be so placed to allow free circulation of air round all lacquered surfaces. In some factories to-day forced drying conditions are installed, and the solvent is driven from the lacquer film at temperatures up to 140° F. It is important to eliminate the solvents rapidly and thoroughly not only for speed of production but also to ensure stability of the finish and to guard against marking during packing and transporting.

CHAPTER XXXV : CELLULOSE FINISHING—
FINISHING PROCESSES AND SOME RECIPES

FURNITURE producers have, according to the quality and nature of their goods, evolved several different finishing systems. The process that is popular for radio cabinets is not necessarily suited to the production of bedroom suites or brush handles, so we shall have to examine some alternative methods. As the spraying technique has become so universally adopted we restrict the present description of processes to those which involve spray application of the cellulose polish. Four types of finish are commonly found : the pull-over finish, the burnished finish, straight-from-the-spray, and the dull finish.

Staining and filling. The initial stages of staining and filling are similar however the lacquer is to be worked, and depend mainly upon the kind of wood used and the ultimate shade required. These operations do not differ much from those customary with french polishing ; and more than one type of base stain is available. Spirit stains, whilst yielding bright colours and being very fast drying, have largely gone out of fashion because of the comparative fugitiveness of the dyestuffs. Oil and naphtha stains are popular because they are easy to apply, give a fairly uniform coloration, and are of good permanence. They are quick drying and no skill is required in their use.

Water stains are generally the most fast to light, and the skilled stainer can obtain almost any depth of colour with an even tone by means of their use. The two main disadvantages usually associated with them are comparatively slow drying and a tendency to raise the grain. Some stain manufacturers have, however, overcome the latter defect by making suitable additions to the water which eliminate the raising of the grain. This suggests that water stains will become increasingly popular in the future, as no laborious sandpapering will be necessary after the staining.

Application of stain. Before staining, the wood should be well papered to produce a smooth surface. The stain is usually applied by rag, though sometimes by brush and occasionally by spray, and is rubbed over the surface in the direction of the grain. A well-wetted rag gives the best results, the excess being wiped off with a second clean rag. The stained timber should be given ample time to dry before any further operation takes place.   See further notes in Chapter IV on Staining, page 19.

Filling the grain.   On walnut and mahogany it is usual to fill the grain.   Paste fillers are obtainable in a variety of shades, and one possessing a similar tone to the base stain should be chosen.   Here again application is usually by rag, and the thick paste is worked with a circular motion into the pores and grain of the wood, the excess being wiped clean.

In some cases the use of a stain filler replaces the preliminary base staining, the filler then being applied to the bare wood, but it does not seem possible to get the same clarity and brilliance of colour with a filler alone as it does with a stain.   The filler is usually based on an oil varnish and is therefore quite slow drying.   Most manu-facturers recommend an overnight drying period before proceeding to the next stage, though some now market so-called " synthetic fillers " which harden very much more rapidly and may be over-sprayed with cellulose within an hour or two.   Oak is seldom filled, and the filling process may be either omitted or substituted by a wash filler of thin consistency, which gives a partially filled effect.

Sealing the grain.   It is from the filler stage onwards that the differences in method become evident.   Generally, some sort of sealer coat is employed to seal the stained and filled timber and to provide a smooth surface for subsequent operations.   Frequently a fad of french polish is used which produces a thin skin to act as a buffer between the cellulose lacquer solvents and the filler, and which, after light sandpapering with a fine-grade paper, gives an even surface without any " nibs " showing through.

Also frequently employed is a cellulose-based material known as a grain sealer.   This is something of a misnomer, because its sealing properties are no different from those of any normal cellulose lacquer, but there is generally incorporated a flatting agent.   A cellulose polish by itself will not paper readily, causing clogging of the paper and much waste in effort and materials.   A flatting agent is therefore added to the polish which produces a sharpness of cut when papered, usually associated with the formation of a whitish, powdery deposit which serves to indicate where flatting or papering has taken place.   A perfectly smooth surface is thus produced on which it is possible to build up the subsequent finish.

Note that the french polish sealer must not be used for surfaces which are to be treated with a heat-resistant cellulose.   The reason for this will become apparent later.

Matching.   The next important operation is that known as matching.   It will be appreciated that, particularly when dealing with veneer sections, even after the preliminary base staining, a difference in depth of colour is often apparent from one end of a panel to another. It is necessary, then, to even up, so far as is possible, the general effect. Matching by spray is much practised these days and involves the use of a stain of similar tone to the base colour. This must possess a small amount of a binder dissolved in solvents which possess sufficient attack on a sealer or lacquer coat to anchor the stain as soon as applied.

A fine gun-nozzle and low air pressure are generally employed for the matching or shading process. The operator soon learns to pick out the areas which require shading and thus an even coloration is produced. It is always much easier to match on to a glossy surface, for the sheen shows up the base staining much better than a matt finish. On the other hand it is necessary to protect the matching stain with at least one coat of lacquer before the article of furniture is put into use. A papered sealer produces a matt surface which is not ideal for matching over, but if only one further coat of lacquer is to be applied, it has to be done then or never. If the process allows of two coats after the sealer stage, then the matching operation is best carried out between the lacquer coats. Where no sealing coat at all is used, and there are some cellulose polishers who prefer not to use one, matching takes place over the first lacquer coat.

Though all these comments are intended to apply specifically to spray matching, they are generally true of other methods of colouring, such as by brush or cloth pad. Whatever the method the lacquer coat to follow and fix the matching stain may be applied almost immediately afterwards.

Spraying the lacquer. In accordance with the quality of the finish there may be only one or two coats of lacquer, and the particular lacquer used depends upon the finish. It is advisable here to turn to page 162, where the stages in various finishes are described, and the materials listed. It depends upon whether a bright or matt finish is needed, the quality of the finish, and whether it has to be heat resistant. If there are to be two coats, there should be an interval of at least an hour between them, and the last coat should be left to dry overnight before any further process is attempted.

Pulling-over. The commonest method of finishing off a spray polished article of furniture is that known as " pulling over." A pull-over, or levelling solution, is a mixture of volatile liquids having but a mild solvent action on nitrocellulose. A pad is made from cotton waste, damped with the pull-over and covered with a fine-grained, soft wash-leather. This pad is worked over the sprayed surface with a circular movement as in Fig. 53, in a similar fashion to the french polisher's pad, until all trace of " orange-peel " and other irregularities have been removed.

The final movements of the pad should always be in the direction of the grain (Fig. 54) ; and a last smooth over with a rather moister pad produces an even, brilliant finish. With a correctly formulated pull-over solution it is unnecessary to use any oil to prevent the pad

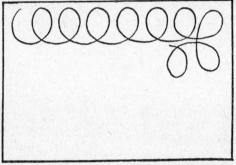

FIG. 53. CIRCULAR MOVEMENT OF PAD WHEN
PULLING OVER

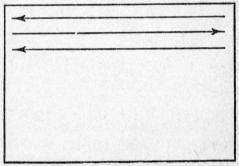

FIG. 54. STRAIGHT MOVEMENT WHEN FINISH-
ING OFF.

sticking. So long as it is not allowed to remain stationary on the lacquer and is kept working, there need be no fear of the pad dragging away the lacquer. Not only does pulling-over eliminate orange-peel and yield a level film of lacquer, but also it has the effect of forcing part of the lacquer into the open parts of the grain and thus, when used in conjunction with a scheme employing a paste filler, of producing a choked finish.

This is the simplest and quickest means of surfacing a lacquer and is used almost entirely for obtaining bright finishes on suites of furniture, whether they be constructed of oak, walnut, mahogany, or some less usual timber.   Two or three sprayed coats of a good quality and appropriately formulated lacquer over the filler, dependent on whether or not a sealer coat is employed, are sufficient to produce a first-rate finish when pulled-over.   Cheaper finishes are obtained by cutting down the number of lacquer coats and by using an inferior quality lacquer.

Burnished finish.   Whilst the pull-over finish is satisfactory for most articles of furniture, particularly where large areas are encountered, another method of obtaining a bright finish is often employed for specialised articles, typical examples being pianos and radio cabinets.   The pull-over pad, though producing an even brilliance, does, upon close examination of the finish, show a slightly striated surface.   This is because it is almost impossible to obtain a completely smooth wash-leather.   A rub over with a polishing cream, or "reviver," as it is sometimes termed, tends to eliminate these marks.

For radio cabinets, and some smaller articles, however, a mirror-like smoothness and sheen has become the fashion.   To achieve this, the final lacquer coat is cut down with fine, wet, abrasive paper and then burnished, sometimes by hand and sometimes by machine. A considerably harder lacquer is called for in this process than that used for pulling-over.   Walnut and mahogany are the most popular timbers for this class of finish and three or four lacquer coats are usually sprayed over the filler, matching taking place as usual between coats.   The final coat should have at least twenty-four hours' drying period before cutting down, and more if possible.

The burnishing operation, which succeeds the cutting down, is performed in two stages.   First a medium-grade cutting compound, tripoli powder in oil or some similar mixture, is rubbed in the direction of the grain, commencing with fair pressure and subsequently easing off.   After that a polishing cream is used on a soft cloth in a circular motion until the surface is perfectly clean.   A finish like a sheet of glass is the result.

Sinking.   It is sometimes observed that, although the initial finish is excellent, after a day or two the glass-like finish becomes impaired and minute depressions occur, corresponding to the open portions of the grain.   This effect, known as "sinking," is caused by the evaporation of traces of solvent, which have remained in the lacquer film until this stage, causing the film to shrink and shape itself to the contours of the wood.   This, then, is the reason for leaving the lacquer coat as long as possible before burnishing, so as to provide every opportunity for this residual solvent, or at any rate the major portion of it, to evaporate before the friction polishing fills in the grain.

Dulled finishes. It was mentioned earlier that straight-from-the-spray finishes are sometimes produced. There is little to be said about these for producing a bright finish, as they are seldom used except for very cheap ware. It is when we are dealing with off-gloss, satin, eggshell, and matt finishes, however, that they become of importance. Any off-gloss effects may be achieved by hand or by spray. In the former case an existing bright finish may be rubbed over with the finest grade of wire wool and followed by a light waxing. The extra handwork here involved is, however, too much for many furniture manufacturers and it is certainly a much speedier process to dull by spray.

Dulling by spray. Dulling by spray may be done either by misting on a matting solution, usually thin and with little binder present, over a bright finish, or by substituting for the bright lacquer a full coat of a material which has been specially formulated to give the desired sheen. This latter type of lacquer is formulated in a similar way to the conventional types described earlier, but they contain an addition of a matting agent, in quantity according to the degree of sheen required. These matting agents may be in the shape of either very finely dispersed and transparent powders, or synthetic resins which, because they are chosen so as to be only partly compatible with the nitrocellulose, produce an off-gloss effect.

When using an eggshell, satin, or matt lacquer this material takes the place of the last clear lacquer coat in a scheme such as that suggested for furniture suites or for radio cabinets, and the finish is left entirely as obtained from the gun. Apart from the very tasteful effects which can be produced with an eggshell finish, definite utility features are present ; for many imperfections in the timber, which would be exaggerated by a bright finish, are rendered inconspicuous by an off-gloss sheen.

Heat-resistant lacquers. Many specialised requirements are catered for by the lacquer manufacturer, among which heat-resistant and spirit-resistant finishes are important. The production of these extra characteristics does not demand any real departure from the conventional processes, but requires lacquers specially formulated to these ends. This provides further proof of the need for co-operative interchange of information between lacquer consumers and producers. Heat-resistant lacquers generally contain a lower percentage of solid matter than normal types, the reduction being effected at the expense of the resin.

One important thing to be remembered when producing a heat-resistant finish is that no french polish or other composition containing shellac should be allowed to enter the scheme. Even a thin

TYPES OF FINISHES AND THE PROCESSES INVOLVED

Class of Work	Base Staining	Filling	First Lacquer Coat	Colour Matching	Finishing Lacquer Coats
Best quality bright finish, suitable for walnut or mahogany bedroom suites.	Rag apply naphtha or oil-base stain, wipe clean, and dry for 2 hours.	Rag apply paste filler, wipe clean, and dry overnight.	Thin fad of french polish to seal filler, dry for 1 hour and paper lightly.	Touch in with matching stain, by spray or brush where necessary to even shade.	Two sprayed coats best-quality non-bloom pull-over-type lacquer, 1 hour drying between coats, final coat dried overnight. Lightly paper, pull-over and revive after 5 hours with polishing cream on soft cloth.
Second quality bright finish, suitable for oak suites.	—	Rag apply stained wash filler, wipe clean, and dry overnight.	One sprayed coat of cellulose grain sealer, papered after 1 hour.	Touch in with matching stain by spray or brush.	One sprayed coat high-solids pull-over lacquer. Pull-over after 7 hours.
Best quality eggshell finish for oak, walnut or mahogany.	Rag apply naphtha or oil-base stain, wipe clean, and dry for 2 hours.	Rag apply paste filler, wipe clean, and dry overnight.	One sprayed coat of cellulose grain sealer, papered after 1 hour.	Touch in with matching stain by spray or brush.	One sprayed coat best-quality non-bloom lacquer. Pull-over after 7 hours. Dry overnight. One sprayed coat eggshell lacquer, finish left from spray.
Cheap matt finish, suitable for a variety of jobs and timbers.	—	Rag apply stained wash filler, wipe clean, and dry overnight.	One sprayed coat of cellulose grain sealer, papered after 1 hour.	Touch in with matching stain by spray or brush.	One sprayed coat matt lacquer left from spray.

	Staining	Filling	Sealing	Touching in	Finishing
Heat and wear resistant, natural colour, satin finish for oak dining-tables, trays, office furniture, etc. Also suitable for preserving identity of pale sycamore, maple.	—	—	One sprayed coat of water-white hard cellulose lacquer. Dry for 1 hour.	—	One or two sprayed coats, 1 hour between coats, of water-white hard cellulose lacquer. Dry final coat for 4 hours, rub over with finest wire-wool and lightly wax.
Cheap bright finish for chairs, babies' cots, etc.	Dip into naphtha or oil-base stain, wipe clean with rag. Dry overnight.	—	—	—	One or two sprayed coats of cheap, high-solids lacquer, 1 hour between coats and final coat left from spray or pulled over after 5 hours.
Best quality finish, bright or off-gloss, particularly suitable for walnut and mahogany radio cabinets and occasional furniture.	Rag apply naphtha or oil-base stain, wipe clean, and dry for 2 hours.	Rag apply paste filler and wipe clean. If oil-base type used dry overnight, but best results with synthetic type. Allow to dry for 1 hour.	One sprayed coat cellulose sealer, papered after 1 hour; or one coat of best-quality non-bloom burnishing lacquer, dried 1 hour.	Touch in with matching stain by spray or brush where necessary to even shade.	Two or three sprayed coats best-quality non-bloom burnishing lacquer, allowing 1 hour between coats. After 24 hours' drying final coat should be wet flatted with fine paper and, after further overnight drying, burnished with cutting compound and polishing cream. If required, finish may be dulled by spray misting solution to desired sheen.

N.B.—Times mentioned in the above table normally represent the minimum periods of time which should elapse between operations. Exceeding these figures should not prove detrimental.

skin of french polish, protected by three or four coats of heat-resistant cellulose lacquer, will betray its presence by a crop of blisters if a hot container is laid on the surface.

To sum up these notes on production processes, we give on pages 162 and 163 some specimen finishing schedules on the more usual types of work which are likely to be encountered. It will be realised that most polishing foremen have their own pet processes, but these schemes will be found quite practicable and will produce good results.

MODERN DEVELOPMENTS IN CELLULOSE LACQUER TECHNIQUE

In the early days of cellulose polishing, one of the main drawbacks to the process was the comparatively low weight of solids it was possible to apply in one operation. This brings us to the question of viscosity. For practical purposes this word may be regarded as a measure of fluidity; and a high viscosity grade of nitrocellulose is one which, for an equal concentration, will give a stiffer consistency solution than a lower viscosity grade.

Low viscosity lacquers. One of the recent outstanding developments in the cellulose field was the introduction of extra low viscosity types; and the increased solid content thus obtainable in solution served for a while to satisfy the demand for more and more concentrated polishes. The advantages to the furniture manufacturer were obvious ; fewer coats were necessary to achieve the required build, with a subsequent reduction in time and labour costs. The durability of a coating made up from an extra low viscosity grade nitrocotton, however, is never so good as that of an equivalent formulation based on a higher grade. Consequently the finish will not retain its high polish for so long.

Hot spraying. A more recent development is the advent of hot spraying. Under normal spraying conditions it is not possible to spray above a certain viscosity. Conversely, if it is required to apply a lacquer having a viscosity higher than that which can be sprayed, it is necessary to add thinners, the function of the thinners being to reduce the viscosity. The adding of volatile constituents automatically reduces the solid content of the lacquer, and so a vicious circle exists.

An alternative method of reducing the viscosity of a lacquer is to elevate its temperature, the most marked reductions taking place between 60° C. and 80° C. The lacquer is stored in a cool container under slight pressure, whilst a circulating air pump forces the lacquer through heated coils. From there the lacquer passes through a fluid hose line, up to the gun, and a further fluid hose returns the excess to the coils. Thus the lacquer is constantly circulating through the system, and after the plant has been running for 15–30 minutes a steady temperature is reached. The heated lacquer is sprayed normally.

The advantages of this process are marked. It is now possible to spray-apply a cellulose polish many times thicker than the conventional solution, and containing a considerable increase in solid content, without the necessity of adding volatile solvents. Thus one sprayed application will produce a much heavier deposit than is possible with a cold sprayed lacquer. Further, it is possible to apply a greater volume on to vertical surfaces without risk of forming runs, curtaining, etc., because of the much higher initial viscosity and the fact that the lacquer is quite cold when it reaches the surface to be polished. It is generally estimated that the number of coats necessary to produce an equivalent finish, by means of the hot spray technique, when compared with a heavy-bodied cold spray application, is one-half.

The developments so far discussed have largely been the outcome of research work carried out by cellulose lacquer manufacturers The furniture-maker can play his part too. There has in the past been a lamentable craze for besmearing timber with the darkest and heaviest stains obtainable and finishing off with a " jammy " gloss surface which is neither flattering to nor characteristic of wood. Wood should reveal its natural beauty, and the finish, whilst serving as a protection to the surface, should emphasise it. Such a finishing scheme presents advantages to both furniture producer and buyer. The simplicity of the finishing operations and the small total time required to produce a natural finish both make for economy, and the durability and good wearing qualities which go with a thin, satin surface will benefit the purchaser.

Having selected the timber to be as nearly uniform as possible and carefully sanded the surface, the polisher has but to spray on two coats of a thin, tough, water-white cellulose solution. The coats may be applied allowing an interval of half-an-hour between, and in a further two hours the finish is hard enough for handling, stacking or packing operations. A rub down with fine steel wool and a light waxing produce a finish which is proverbially smooth to the touch, which will withstand incessant hard wear without marking, and which is almost infinitely resistant to water, spirits, heat and discolouration ; all this coupled with an appearance which is pleasing and which typifies good taste.

CHAPTER XXXVI : VARNISHING—KINDS OF VARNISH

THE chief value of varnish is the high degree of protection it gives to the wood to which it is applied, combined with brilliancy of appearance. It has greater resistance to wear and the effect of weather than polish, and this makes it more suitable for work which is subjected to heavy usage or which is exposed to all weathers. Various grades are manufactured to suit the purpose for which it is required.

Modern varnish is manufactured on a large scale, and unfortunately a good deal is not of a quality that carries recommendation with it. Thoroughly good varnish properly applied (and there is much art in this) becomes indeed a lasting preservative, besides adding enormously to the beauty of the article thus treated, especially in the case of finely wrought woods.

Properly speaking, varnish may technically be described as a solution of any resinous material in a solvent, alcohol and oils being the usual ones employed. It is important that the solution should be thin and fluid, and it ought to be easily capable of being spread evenly over any surface; while, by the use of colouring substances such as, say, gamboge, turmeric, saffron, dragon's blood, etc., beautiful tints of yellow, brown, and red, etc., can be given, so as to render the varnish highly decorative.

But when we consider that the staple materials used, such as gum copal and other well-known varnish gums, vary in price by pounds sterling per cwt., that the quality of the linseed oils used is of very special importance—for on that depends much of the beauty of the resultant varnish—and that the methods of making differ greatly, it is clear that the choice of a good varnish is not easy. Varnishes for paintings, high-class cabinet work, and for fittings generally all differ greatly, and many valuable productions that have cost invention, skill, and labour are ruined because of the use of an unsuitable varnish. A good varnish will lie on the surface thin, be perfectly transparent, and of a diamond hardness, capable of being readily cleaned and of resisting the effects of time indefinitely. To obtain the best results it is necessary to use the best materials, and to know the suitability of the varnish to the article to be varnished, as well as the various influences affecting these.

The materials used in the making of varnishes are various gums, resins, etc., dissolved in linseed, cotton-seed, or nut oils, spirits of turpentine, methylated spirit, or wood naphtha, either by a cold process or the application of heat. The quality, durability, and beauty of the higher-class varnishes are dependent upon the care used both in the selection of materials and their skilful manipulation in the process of manufacture. Many of the most popular varnishes are kept for longer or shorter periods to mature before being sent out to customers, and all varnish manufacturers of note keep a register of the date when boiled, bulked, and bottled—the date always appearing on the label, as the age adds to its value.

The best quality varnish is made from the finest selected fossil resin and the purest refined Baltic linseed oil, at a carefully regulated and steady heat over sandbath-protected furnaces to prevent its firing, and is used for high-class decorations, carriage, and other work, when cost is not the first consideration. It is a slow dryer, but is of great lustre and durability. It should be applied in a room of uniform temperature, from which all draughts are rigidly excluded.

A very high-class varnish is made from selected gum copal, with a small addition of gum damar (to give elasticity), oil, and turpentine. It is used on good-class work, is suitable for decorators, etc., and is equally applicable for inside or outside work.

The various lower-class varnishes are made from the same kinds of gums, oils, etc., of lower grades and darker shades, with the addition of common resin, cotton, rape, fish, and other oils, and the cheaper spirits, such as coal-tar spirit, mineral naphtha (rectified petroleum), and benzoline as adulterants. These are bought mostly by people whose chief object is to get the maximum quantity at a minimum cost. Their qualities, like everything else of the cheap kind, are moderately poor.

CLASSES OF VARNISH

Varnishes may be divided into three classes—water, spirit, and oil, according to the vehicle employed in the process of making. Water varnishes are gums, etc., dissolved in water. Spirit varnishes are gums or resins dissolved in spirits. Oil varnishes are gums or resins dissolved in oils.

Water varnishes are composed of gum-arabic or isinglass dissolved in water, and are mostly used for the protection of paper. There are also shellac water varnishes. Shellac is not soluble in water, therefore borax or other ingredients are added to make these varnishes.

Spirit varnishes include the french polishes, white and brown hard spirit varnish, japanner's varnish, paper varnish (for use on wall papers), patent knotting, and flatting varnish—a varnish that dries without gloss. All quick-drying varnishes—from french polish to floor stains—are, more or less, spirit, and are made (or should be) by dissolving shellac, sandarac, or other brittle gum in turpentine or methylated spirit. Spirit varnish is used principally upon furniture, floors, and for other domestic purposes. A finer class is also used (on account of the hardness of its surface) for pianos and office and other heavy furniture requiring much handling. There is also a spirit varnish used for wallpapers, prints, maps, etc.—all of which require to be sized before applying the varnish, which should be made with the softer gums and turpentines by the application of heat.

Spirit varnishes are of three kinds, viz. : bleached hard, a colourless varnish; white hard, white in colour and not so transparent as the bleached variety; and brown hard, a dark brown varnish for use on dark-coloured woods. All these contain methylated spirit as a solvent, and are of a quick-drying, lustrous nature. Ether varnish, as its name implies, contains ether instead of spirit, and, consequently, dries quicker than methylated varnish. Naphtha varnish is another very quick-drying varnish, wood naphtha being used as the vehicle for dissolving the gums. It is more commonly used on builders' work, such as fronts of shops, hand-rails, etc. Varnishes can also be obtained coloured, or can be coloured by the addition of liquid spirit stains.

Oil varnishes may be divided into white oil varnishes, pale oil varnishes, medium oil varnishes, dark oil varnishes, and mastic varnish. This last is mostly used for paintings and pictures of value. Amongst the white oil varnishes may be mentioned white marble varnish, coburg, french oil, etc., these being used for the best kind of internal work. The pale oil varnishes include maple varnish, pale copal, and pale carriage varnish. The medium oil varnishes may be known by the names of carriage, pale oak, etc., and are made suitable for either indoor or external work. The dark oil varnishes are generally known by the names of church oak, hard oak, etc., and these also are manufactured for both inside and outside work.

Oil varnishes dry not by evaporation, like spirit varnishes, but by oxidation; that is, the oil in the varnish absorbs oxygen from the air and solidifies the oil with the gum, thereby forming a skin of a preservative character. A certain amount of evaporation does take place, however, as some proportion of spirit (generally turpentine) is usually added to the oil varnishes to make them more easily workable. But the best class of varnishes contain very little of this spirit element, and are consequently slow-drying varnishes.

Natural varnishes. In addition to the above there are also what might be termed natural varnishes, as india-rubber solution, lacquers, etc. Lacquers and spirit varnishes dry and harden by the evaporation of the volatile spirit, thus leaving the gum or resin as a thin shell over the surface of the work.

Varnishes may be subdivided into hard and elastic varnishes. Of course there is no strict line between the two qualities, for there is hardly a varnish of the hard type which does not possess a certain amount of elasticity; and there is not an elastic varnish which does not possess the quality of hardness, even though it may be comparatively infinitesimal. Then between the two extremes we get varnishes possessing varying degrees of hardness and elasticity, until we arrive at some which it would be a difficult matter to determine to which class they really belong.

Generally speaking, the spirit varnishes belong to the hard class, as do also the majority of the dark oil varnishes such as church oak, dark oak, hard oak, etc. The paler the oil varnishes the more elastic they are as a rule. These latter are usually made from gum copal, which is a clear and very elastic gum.

The hard varnishes are made either from resins or from gums which are more resinous in their nature. These will not stand hard wear, and should not be used where subject to sunlight or the outside air.

It is not safe to use a hard varnish either under or over an elastic one. Hard varnishes do not give much " key " for the subsequent coats, and therefore the latter will not have the hold upon the ground that they really should have. If, on the other hand, a hard varnish is placed directly upon an elastic one, it will inevitably crack and crawl, owing to the elastic varnish underneath " pulling " in various directions.

The elastic varnishes are particularly suitable for outside wear, being yielding enough to contract and expand with the changes of temperature to which they are subjected. They should therefore be used on all articles or interior surfaces which are near the window or the door. Readers may have noticed varnish round the inside of windows very badly cracked, while the rest of the varnish in the room is in good condition. This is because a hard varnish has been used, and has suffered where it is in contact with the sunlight.

When there is any doubt as to the comparative hardness of two varnishes which have to be used one under the other, it is a fairly safe plan to add a small percentage of turpentine to the under one, or, as an alternative, to rub it out very sparingly and allow it to harden thoroughly for at least a week before finishing. When uncertain as to the nature of the varnishes about to be used, apply the following test: procure two pieces of tin, and give a coat of each varnish to them; allow them to harden for a day or two, and then scratch with the thumb-nail to see which is harder, or bend the tin to see which is more elastic.

Church varnish. When choosing a varnish for church seats, it should be remembered that it not only has to be handled very much, but that it also has to undergo the stewing of the heated and moist atmosphere charged with the breath of crowded congregations. For an oil varnish to stand this, it should be of a very hard drying quality. Most of the varnishes provided for church seats have been manufactured to suit the damp and cold climate of a country where the clamminess of a hot summer's night is comparatively unknown. These varnishes do not always dry hard enough for church seats elsewhere. If the seats are new, it is well to avoid oil varnish or to use only the best hard-drying carriage varnish. A better plan is to polish them or use spirit varnish. The heat of the hands or the heat of a crowded room will tend to make even the hardest oil varnish sticky.

To prepare properly seats for re-varnishing, where the old varnish has become black with handling and fluffy from stickiness, the old stuff should be removed with a paint remover or with a solution of caustic soda, and the whole begun afresh. It is little use putting on a good hard-drying varnish on the top of one that remains sticky. The old must be removed or made to dry. Sometimes the varnish underneath may be made to dry by rubbing it down with turpentine. A coat of hard-drying carriage varnish may then be applied.

If spirit varnish is put on the top of a soft oil varnish it is sure to crack, and the same effect is likely to take place if a hard-drying varnish is put over a sticky surface. The best way is to clean the whole of the old stuff off and begin afresh, taking care that the seats are dry and clean before applying the first coat.

Rubbing varnish. This is a hard-setting varnish which can be burnished to a high finish by the application of a fine grade abrasive. Soft or elastic varnishes are useless for the purpose. Its application is described on page 179.

CHAPTER XXXVII : VARNISHING—BRUSHES : PREPARATION

APART from the selection of the right kind of varnish, there are other factors to be considered if success in varnishing is to be attained. The conditions necessary to ensure satisfactory work are numerous, and one of the most important conditions is cleanliness. It matters not how particular you may have been in choosing the right varnish for the job, or what care you may have exercised in bringing the work up thus far; unless the rule with regard to cleanliness has been scrupulously observed the result is certain to be disappointing.

New wood. Varnishing cannot take place upon *any* kind of ground. We will take, for instance, new wood. Here the main consideration is the number of coats of varnish that the work is to receive. If the job will allow of any number of coats being applied provided that the result is good, then we might with advantage dispense with any kind of preparation. But if the work is to receive only a limited number of coats—say two, or perhaps three—then we must apply some method of stopping undue suction of the wood in places and make it more even, otherwise the work will appear when finished bright in some places and dull in others. This unevenness of gloss is caused through the unequal absorption of the varnish by the new wood. It therefore follows that the wood must receive a coat of some preparation to prevent this.

For this purpose glue size may be used. It should be applied before varnishing, and care exercised to see that no superfluous size is left on the edges or in quirks or mouldings. Too much size will damage the varnish and affect the gloss. The preservation of the wood is best ensured by giving it a coat of varnish on the unprepared surface; then a coat of isinglass size is applied and the varnishing is again proceeded with.

Painted work. In varnishing on painted work some little knowledge of painting is essential. To produce the best results the last coat of paint should be what is termed in the trade " flat "; that is, it should be dead—without gloss. Paint is mixed with linseed oil and with turpentine to make it workable. The more oil there is put into the paint the greater will be the gloss when dry. The more turpentine is added the flatter the paint becomes. Therefore to get the last coat of paint dead, it should be mixed almost entirely with turpentine.

If a greater proportion of oil has been mixed with the paint than should have been the case, the oiliness may be removed by washing the work down with fuller's earth and water.   Dissolve about 1 oz. of fuller's earth in a pint of water, and sponge the work over with this, drying off well afterwards.   In all ordinary paint a certain proportion of what is called " driers " is added to the pigments to make them dry more quickly than they otherwise would.   There are various forms of driers, but most of them are injurious to varnish. As turpentine is a drying liquid, no driers need be added to the last coat of paint, and thus another danger will be averted.

Red lead should not be used under varnish, neither should barytes, whiting, or vandyke brown.   These are sometimes used under varnish, either through ignorance or because of necessity. They can, however, be guarded against by those who need a specially good job.   Soap and soda are sometimes used to kill grease on work which needs varnishing, but this, unless well rinsed off with clean water, is a dangerous practice.   Woodwork which has been newly grained should not be varnished for some days—that is, if it has been grained in oil.   If it has been grained in water it may be varnished as soon as it is dry enough.

Re-varnishing.   In re-varnishing, the old varnish work must be thoroughly washed, particular care being taken to see that no dirt is left in corners or crevices.   In this washing no soda should be used, or it may soften up the surface of the work and spoil the whole.   Use ordinary bar soap or a small quantity of dry soap in hot water, but not too hot or it will soften up the varnish.   Do not use flannel cloths to wash with, as the work is then left practically covered with bits from the flannel, and these show up much larger when varnished than they really are.   Use only cotton cloths, such as cheese cloths or mutton cloths, which have been well washed; those of an open texture are the best for the purpose.   After a good washing with the soap and water do not forget to rinse down thoroughly with clean cold water.   It is not a wise plan to varnish over gilding, as the gold, being a metal, does not need the protection of the varnish, and the latter is sure to darken (sometimes blacken) the colour of the gold.

BRUSHES

The tools used in varnishing are not many.   First of all we will take the brushes, as being the most important of the tools required by the varnisher.   There are the larger brushes and the smaller ones, for broad work and narrower work respectively. They do not differ greatly from paint brushes, though they are made from the finest bristles, firmer and straighter than those used in any but the best paint brushes. They vary from the latter in appearance in that they are generally bevelled, in consequence of their never being used upon rough preparatory work to break them into shape. Varnish brushes are also specially cemented to withstand the action of spirits; they are not always made to resist water, as they are not supposed to be put into water.

In Fig. 55 A is the usual pattern of large varnish brush. D is a

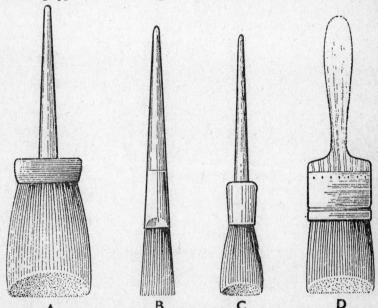

FIG. 55. TYPES OF BRUSHES USED IN VARNISHING.
A. Large varnish brush.   B and C. Smaller brushes.   D. Modern type of large brush.

varnish brush of more recent innovation, and one designed for highly finished woodwork and for enamels. This belongs to the flat type, of which there are many variations; but these brushes do not last so long as the other type on general work. They are, however, in a better form for leaving a high finish than the one shown at A. The smaller brushes are shown at B and C. These are for use on moulds, ornamental parts, narrow bands, and all small work. Some are bevelled like the larger brush.   Both kinds are illustrated.

Keeping brushes. Paint brushes are kept in water. Varnish brushes must be kept either in linseed oil or in varnish.   It is, however, recommended that for best work the brushes should be suspended in varnish. They should be kept in a clean vessel used only for that purpose, and be so suspended that the bristles are entirely covered, yet not over the head of the brush. An excellent plan is to procure a piece of stout wire, bore a small hole through the head of the brushes, push the wire through the hole, and rest each end on the edge of the jar or vessel containing the varnish. Fig. 56 will give some idea of what is meant. The vessel should be covered in, so as to be as airtight as possible, or the varnish inside will become thick. The cover will also keep out dust and dirt, which, if it managed to get on to the bristles of the brushes, would ruin the next job that they were used upon. Some workers keep their varnish brushes in oil, but as a certain amount of this is bound to be retained in the brush and mixed with the varnish in which the brush is next put, it is not a practice to be recommended. A spoonful of this oil would damage a canful of varnish.

Rinsing. Before putting brushes into the varnish to be used, they should be rinsed out in a little clean turpentine. Twirl the brush round to shake the turpentine back into the can again. To do this properly, place the handle of the brush between both palms, and spin the brush round quickly by working each hand alternately backwards and forwards. The head of the brush should be in the can or jar whilst doing this. When finished with put it carefully away with all the precautions advised.

FIG. 56.   KEEPING BRUSHES
They are suspended in varnish with the tips away from the bottom.

Novices wash their brushes out in soap and hot water when they have finished with them for the day. This is a bad practice, however, for it is not only a very dirty job but injures the brushes. Whenever they do want washing, wash them in turpentine only. Do not on any account use a dirty brush, as that would spoil everything.

New brushes. For best work do not use a new brush. In this there are always loose hairs which would cause much trouble. A new brush, too, is always full of dust, which takes some time to get thoroughly rid of. It is not a bad plan to use new varnish brushes in paint for a few times and then to thoroughly clean them out and put them into varnish.

Vessels. The ordinary paint can is the kind of vessel most used in the trade, but there are others called patent varnish cans. The vessel which is most handy and cheapest is the ordinary earthenware pot with a side handle. Owing to smooth inner surface and freedom from quirks caused by the joining in iron pots, it can be much more effectively cleaned than the latter kind. When such pots are not to be had, a small thin-lipped jelly mug forms an excellent substitute.

CHAPTER XXXVIII : VARNISHING—APPLYING OIL VARNISH

IT is a curious fact that, generally speaking, varnishing is better done on a wet day than in warm, dry weather. On a fine morning it is usually found that objects are wet with dew, or if not very wet there is a perceptible dampness which is fatal to varnishing. On a wet day it will be noticed that there is very little or no dew deposited where the rain does not reach. This is due to the fact of the falling rain having kept the temperature uniform, and it is only when the air is quickly lowered in temperature that this moist deposit takes place. Hence it turns out that a rainy day is really the safest, so long as the work is under cover and properly ventilated.

Bloom. The early morning is the best time of day for varnishing, because one of the chief troubles inseparable from varnishing is " bloom "—a peculiar milky appearance caused chiefly by moisture collecting on the surface when the varnish is nearly dry, and remaining afterwards imprisoned in the varnish. This kind of bloom can be avoided by finishing varnishing of exposed parts early in the day, and so giving the varnish a chance to get sufficiently dry on the surface to throw off any moisture that may settle upon bright surfaces in the cool of the evening, especially after a warm day. The moisture settles on such surfaces in the same way that the dew falls on the cool grass. The same thing applies if it is in a warm house exposed to cold air from the outside—perhaps by merely having a window left open and so admitting a chilly draught.

It is desirable that a uniform temperature be kept in the room until the varnish is dry, because if it be too low fogging and blooming may result, while if it is too high the varnish loses in body and becomes less elastic, besides setting too quickly to allow of proper working on large surfaces. Whether the temperature be high, medium, or low, uniformity should at any rate be aimed at, for even a damp but uniform atmosphere is not after all usually detrimental to successful varnishing, whereas a sudden dampness or chilliness occurring before the work has dried may be.

Dust. As a further aid to success there may be mentioned the need for a dustless atmosphere, although it might be said that such a condition never exists. However, precautions can be taken, and these may consist of having the floor washed, moving about with caution, and also having some clean newspaper tucked in at the bottom of the door so as to prevent the entrance of more dust. As atmospheric dust is continually falling to the floor, part of it to be raised again by currents of air or the movements of the feet, a good plan is to damp the floor with water, particularly around that portion on which the feet will stand when doing a piece of work.

Previous to the application of varnish, all the work should be thoroughly dusted. This, though a simple operation, is of the utmost importance, for upon it depends to a great extent the cleanliness of the finished work. For the best results two dusters are necessary—one for the preliminary, the other for the final dusting. As the first dust-down is liable to make the brush dirty with dust particles, more especially when dusting objects very near the floor, it is advisable to have a second one, not only to ensure the complete removal of any trace of dust but also to prevent dirtying the work, which is particularly necessary when dusting white or very delicately tinted work for varnishing. Needless to say, both dust brushes must be well washed in soap and water and thoroughly dried before commencing the operation, and after it has been finished sufficient time should elapse to allow any dust to settle previous to varnishing.

Dipping the brush. The first essential is to take the varnish bottle into the room where the work is to be done, for by doing this small quantities of varnish may be taken out at a time instead of having, say, a potful to begin with, which is almost sure to become dirty before it is emptied. Sufficient varnish should be put into the pot so that the brush-tips do not touch the bottom, yet care must be taken to put in more than will suffice for a certain part of the work.

When lifting the varnish from the pot another precaution is necessary. This consists of carefully dipping the brush into the varnish, giving it a twirl so as to hold the material properly—not slapping it against the pot side, which simply causes dust, but lifting it straight on to the work. The brush should not be taken out of the pot dripping with varnish and messing the floor all over, but is so manipulated that the varnish is held in until it is put on to the work.

Applying the varnish. The varnish should at once be spread with an up-and-down stroke, then crossed with a very slight pressure, and finally finished off downwards or upwards—in the one direction at any rate, and preferably the latter.

Before giving the finishing strokes, the brush should be scraped free of varnish against the edge of the pot, so that no surplus material may ooze from it when placed on the work, and so that the toe may be brought to a fine point more suited to finishing with. As varnish in itself flows to a level surface, the main point is to see that it is equally spread, for, as runs are caused by more varnish being put on one place than another, it follows that equal spreading is a preventive of running. Generally varnish should not be crossed more than once, or twice at the most, and the less crossed the better. The heavier the coat the more brushing will the varnish stand, but for a perfect flow quick finishing is essential.

The quantity put on should vary with the number of the coats. Thus a first coat on bare wood may be full, as much as will be absorbed; other undercoatings on similar work, or on paint, should only be medium in quantity, so as to allow of proper hardening and easy glasspapering; while the last coat in every case of brush-finishing should be applied full and flowing. At the same time, too much should not be put on at the last coating, for, besides increasing the risk of runs, a loss of lustre may eventually occur through imperfect drying of the varnish. Half an hour after work which contains mouldings has been done, the mouldings should be examined, and any surplus varnish wiped out with a small tool or fitch. This is always necessary when a flowing coat has been applied, and especially with a slow-setting varnish.

Felting down. When two or three coats of varnish are to be given, the first coats should be rubbed down smooth before the subsequent coat is put on. This may be done with powdered pumice stone, using either oil or water as a lubricant. Sometimes a shoe-brush is employed, which should be a fairly stiff bristle brush of good quality. With a painter's tool apply raw linseed oil over the varnished surface. Take up a quantity of the pumice powder on the shoe-brush and apply liberally and with plenty of friction, more oil being added if necessary. If the varnish is too hard for the pumice to cut, add a small quantity of flour emery. As the surface becomes dulled use less oil, and finish off with a drier brush and plenty of clean, soft rag, in order to leave the surface free from grease. Excess of oil or a greasy appearance may be corrected by wiping over with benzoline.

The felting method of dulling varnished work is by using a piece of felt, or, better still, a solid felt rubber, which may be purchased ready-made. The grinding agent is pumice-stone powder of varying degrees of fineness. For the most highly finished work it is well to grind the pumice stone to avoid all extraneous grit matter which may have found its way into the powder. Stir a pound in a large basin of water, allow the coarser particles to settle, and then pour off the top water into a second basin; the finest of the powder will be in this water, and will, in due time, settle at the bottom.

For working, first damp the work with a sponge, using just enough good yellow soap to prevent cissing. Then soak the felt in water and sprinkle a little pumice on its face; gently rub with a light circular motion, taking large sweeps similar to the method of working french polish, and going systematically and regularly over the whole surface many times. The rubbing should be continued until a uniform dullness is obtained, showing no light streaks or scratches.

CHAPTER XXXIX : RUBBING VARNISH

THIS is a hard varnish which can be friction-polished to a high gloss. A fine abrasive is used in the polishing and a fair amount of hard work is involved but the results are excellent. The materials needed are a quantity of rubbing varnish—half a pint will be sufficient for about one square yard of polished surface for a two-coat finish, some rottenstone for the burnishing, 320 and 400 grade wet or dry paper for the flatting, and liquid car polish, preferably one that is not too fierce in action.

Preparation of wood. Clean up in the manner usual for polishing and stain with any but a water stain; naphtha base stains are excellent. Open grain woods may require to be filled with a patent filler or the polisher may prefer to make his own with whiting and gold-size, stained with black japan to the approximate shade of the work. This is made to a thick consistency and applied with a heavy or coarse rag, first with and then across the grain. Leave to dry and paper away the surplus.

Varnishing. The rubbing varnish must be applied in a warm, clean room and with a good clean brush—this is most important as grit in the varnish brush can only lead to a poor finish. Grit *in* the brush is very different from dust *on* the surface of the varnish, as dust may be easily flatted off whereas grit will only be removed by breaking the varnish film.   Use the varnish from a clean cup or jar and not from any old tin; it is not necessary to thin the varnish with any turps or thinners.   The first coat should be well brushed out to allow it to dry hard and the work must now be left for at least sixteen hours, longer if possible.   When next the work is picked up another coat may be applied directly on the first coat without any further ado; no flatting between coats is necessary.

This time leave the work for at least twenty-four hours to harden thoroughly.   The varnish, incidentally, is dry to touch at about six hours but needs to get thoroughly hard right through the film.

Flatting.   The next step is to carefully flat the whole of the varnished surface with 320 paper, using soap to avoid scratching. The inside of top rails, though varnished, would not require getting up to such an extent as the legs and top.   Flatting operations are carried out using a sponge and clean water.   Scrupulous care is needed to avoid transferring grit that may be picked up on the paper to the varnished surface.   Should a piece of paper be dropped on to the floor do not use it again but put another piece into service. Use only moderate pressure so as to avoid generating heat and thus softening up the varnish, and do not overflat near sharp corners as, if the surface is rubbed through, the water may swell the fibres of the wood and impair the finish.   Thoroughly wash off and dry with a leather and again set the work on one side for a few hours.

Examine the job to see if the surface has sweated or gone back to its original shine; this sometimes happens when the flatting is done without the necessary hardening period being allowed.   Should this be the case, re-flat, this time using the 400 paper (and soap as a lubricant, of course).

Burnishing.   Rottenstone may be obtained from a drysalter or oilshop.   Take a piece of muslin or other fine cloth folded to a pad, damp it well and rub it on a piece of rottenstone until enough of the brown sludge seems to be on the pad.   Using even strokes and a moderate pressure burnish the flatted surface until a shine appears. Repeat until a satisfactory finish is achieved.   There will be a haze on the finish, however, that the next operation will remove.

Polishing.   The liquid car polish will now be used to polish away the haze and bring up the finish to a mirror-like surface.   Use a separate pad of muslin for applying the polish and use the polish sparingly, rubbing vigorously but not with much pressure.   Leave to dry before polishing off with a clean cloth.

Super-finish.   From the second coat of varnish proceed with the flatting with the same care and thoroughness as before, but, without setting the work aside for a period, apply a third coat of varnish rather more full than the first but not so heavy as the second may have been.   Leave for a hardening period of anything from twenty-four to forty-eight hours.

When hard dry this first coat of varnish must be flatted carefully using 400 paper and soap.   Extreme care is necessary to avoid picking up grit; a scratch or two now would be ruinous.   Allow a sweating period before burnishing back to a shine with rottenstone.

It is interesting to note that the finish will stand heat.   Thus a table top may with safety have cups placed upon it, although it would only be fair to avoid doing this for the first week or so.

CHAPTER XL : VARNISHING—APPLYING SPIRIT VARNISH

THE subject of spirit varnishing is of perhaps more importance to the general reader than oil varnishing.   Spirit varnish is easier to make than oil varnish, and in some respects it is easier to apply, particularly on small surfaces, though it has its own special difficulties.   It is a varnish that admirably lends itself to the amateurish efforts of the beginner; but it is also a varnish capable of producing a very high-class finish if placed in practised hands.   Its manner of application is very different from that of oil varnish, for whilst the latter is slow-drying, spirit varnish is very quick-drying. Owing to the fact that it dries so quickly, caused by the spirits evaporating, it is not suitable for large, plain surfaces.

The object in varnishing is not only to produce a gloss, but also to produce an absolutely smooth surface.   This object is not attained when the joinings overlap each other and create ridges.   There is, however, at least one advantage that spirit varnish possesses over oil varnish, and this lies in the comparatively easy way in which the varnish can be rubbed down smooth.   A small quantity of naphtha or methylated spirit on a wad of cotton wadding will soon remove any ridges or uneven places on the surface of the varnish, provided it has not been allowed to get too hard and dry.

The successful spirit varnisher should have a knowledge of french polishing.   Unlike oil varnish, spirit varnish does not flow level after leaving the brush, and here lies the chief difficulty in applying it. Each successive coat should be levelled with either very fine glass-paper or the polish rubber, and success will be more certain if, before any varnish is applied, the pores of the wood are sealed with either size or french polish. This will prevent the unequal absorption of the varnish. If polish is used instead of size the grain will not rise as much as when a water solution such as size is applied over it.

Brushes for applying spirit varnish should preferably be small ones. Those known in the trade as camel hair are suitable. Brushes bound in tin should be avoided, as the shellac in the varnish will corrode the tin. The latter will then react upon the varnish and turn it dark-coloured. The vessel used to hold the varnish should be an earthenware or glass jar, and absolutely clean.

Applying. As regards the mode of application much depends upon the nature of the articles being varnished. The inexperienced almost invariably apply too much varnish, with the inevitable result that the work cracks. It should be laid on in the same direction as the grain of the wood, as evenly and regularly as possible. The manner of applying resembles that of staining, particularly the water and spirit stains, and we cannot do better than direct the reader's attention to the chapter dealing with the application of stains (page 18). In panelled work the panels should be done first, then the stiles, and finally the mouldings. (See Fig. 9, page 22.)

The varnish should be rubbed down between every coat, so as to keep the work smooth as it proceeds. Care should be exercised in the rubbing, lest the edges or prominent members of mouldings be rubbed too much. This will make the subsequent coats sink in at such places and render the finished surface uneven in gloss. The last application of varnish will be better if at the close of the rubbing-down process (which should be done with about half spirits and half polish) a few drops of glaze are added to the rubber.

For small fretted articles spirit varnish is much to be preferred to oil varnish, owing to its thinner body and intense hardness and quickness in drying. All edges should be done first, and end-grain should have one or two extra coats to bring such parts up to the level of the rest of the work. It may be mentioned here that in either polishing or varnishing thin fretwork, both sides of the wood should be coated, as this not only shows a better finish, but acts as a preservative and also prevents the wood from warping.

Varnishing floor margins. A job which often falls to the lot of the practical man is the margin on the floor of a sitting-room between the edge of the carpet square and the skirting board, and a few hints on its treatment will be of service. After well scrubbing, size the parts to be stained with glue-size as used by painters. This is to stop suction, or prevent the excess absorption of the stain.

When dry, rub lightly with No. 1 glasspaper and dust well off. The stain is made by mixing the required colour pigment in equal quantities of varnish, linseed oil and turpentine; strain before use. When this coat is dry and quite hard (better for standing a day or two), go over again with fine glasspaper, stop up all nail holes and joints with stained putty, and wipe over with a damp wash-leather before varnishing.

If a more durable job is desired, two coats of varnish should be given, adding a small quantity of turps to the first, which should be well brushed out; the final coat of varnish should be generously used and well worked in all directions. Use a good *hard*-drying varnish, such as church oak or floor varnish.

Outdoor varnished work. During the last few years wheelwrights, coach and railway carriage builders, and other vehicle makers have with advantage bodied up much of their work, such as panels, etc., with french polish. After this treatment they are coated with the best pale carriage varnish, owing to the fact that ordinary polish will not stand the weather. Many shop fronts are now treated in this manner. The timber is filled in, bodied up, coloured, and fastened, after which a good outside varnish is used to finish up the work. This prevents the unsightly bare patches so often seen on outside work when only polish has been used.

Flatting varnish. This is a varnish that really belongs to the class of spirit varnishes, and is one that dries quickly, but without gloss. It produces what is termed a flat or matt finish, which gives a very rich appearance to some woods, particularly the darker varieties. Flatting varnish may be made by adding white wax to ordinary copal varnish, and thinning out with turpentine. Both the varnish and the wax should be heated for this purpose, and also the turpentine should be warmed a little before adding to the varnish. Heating the several ingredients assists in the amalgamation.

This varnish is applied in the same manner as ordinary spirit varnish, as it dries quickly. It is, however, usually done upon a full-gloss oil varnish, and thus requires expert handling in order to avoid bright flashes or patches, caused by not properly covering up the glossy surface underneath. Should the edges of the varnish be allowed to set before joining up, such parts will look partially bright when dry. The varnish is a thin one, and is consequently easily applied. With practice it may be laid upon the work with the speed it requires.

COMMON FAULTS—GENERAL HINTS ON VARNISHING

BLOOM. Perhaps the most prevalent of defects in varnishing is what has already been termed "bloom" (page 176). The varnish takes on a whitish film or sort of mist, which may come and go or may remain permanent. The defect is more common among the better class of varnishes than among the cheaper ones. The smooth, glossy surface offered to the air by good varnish induces the condensation upon it of the moisture in the atmosphere. If this takes place before the varnish is thoroughly hard, bloom is certain to result. It is, however, sometimes caused by water in the varnish—that is, moisture in the gum from which it is made, and which has not been properly eliminated. Vapour arising from a damp floor is also liable to cause blooming. Varnish which has been left uncorked for some time or which has been stored in some damp place will also bloom.

To avoid blooming, the work must be freely ventilated (but without draughts), so as to hasten the drying as far as possible. An even temperature should also, if at all possible, be kept in the room where the varnishing is taking place. Blooming due to moisture or frost may be removed by warmth, washing and brisk rubbing with warm water, or rubbing with a wad and olive oil. It is sometimes cured by rubbing with oil and vinegar, afterwards wiping quite dry. But when it is due to the varnish itself, it can seldom be entirely eradicated without re-varnishing. In some cases it may be necessary to clean the varnish right off before re-varnishing, and this might be done with ammonia.

Dead or sleepy patches. These terms imply that the varnish is lacking its full lustre in certain places. The causes may be unseasoned timber, soft undercoats, or through the ground being very porous and abnormal suction taking place. An unequal distribution of the varnish will cause the same defects, for where it is barely applied there will naturally be less gloss than where it is freely applied. Another good coat of varnish is necessary as a remedy.

Blistering. The varnish rising in places like blisters is caused by heat playing on the surface and softening the undercoats; or, when moisture is imprisoned underneath the varnish, the heat on the surface causes the water to form into vapour, and this, expanding, lifts the varnish. To remedy, clean off and re-varnish.

Cracking. This is produced by using a hard varnish over an elastic one, or by coating over paint which is only partly dry. The soft undercoats expand and contract with the varying temperatures, and so pull apart in places the upper hard varnish, which does not respond to the same influences. Diluting the varnish with too much turpentine will also cause cracking. If not too badly cracked, it may be remedied by rubbing down and giving another coat of varnish. Cracking often occurs on varnished bakers' vans, owing to hot bread being placed inside the van.

Pinholing and cissing. These are caused by a recession of the varnish from a given point, usually a grease spot or a minute hole. This must be provided against by thoroughly rubbing down and wash-leathering before varnishing.

Pock marks or pitting. These are marks or indentations which do not extend to the ground (as in cissing), but are in the varnish itself. They are caused by the presence of steam or smoke or hot moist air in the room when the varnish is applied. They may also be caused by turps in the varnish brush. These marks can only be removed by rubbing down and re-varnishing.

Flaking and peeling. This consists in portions of the varnish separating from the ground. These faults are not very frequent, but when they do occur it is very probable that they are caused by a lack of cohesion between the different coats of varnish, or between the varnish and ground, or by the undercoats being greasy, or by drying too hard. Or they may be caused by moisture in the wood, by poor vehicles, or by bad pigments.

Grittiness. This is sometimes caused in the varnish by its being stored in a cold, damp atmosphere, by frost upon the cans during transit, or by chill to the varnish. Sometimes the fault lies in using a varnish of a too new manufacture. Dirty brushes and dirty methods of working are all too prevalent causes of grittiness.

Specks. These are formed in varnish by similar conditions. No cure is possible other than grinding down and re-varnishing.

Perishing, or gradual loss of lustre. These troubles are invariably caused by too frequent washing with hot water, or from the influence of damp, ammonia, coal gas, salt sea air, or limestone.

Wrinkles or crinking. This defect occurs from too heavy a coat of varnish, or when it has not been sufficiently brushed out.

Creeping. This is a similar defect, the result of similar causes. It is also caused by the presence of oily patches on the ground work, or by varnishing in too low a temperature. As the result is an uneven surface, the varnish should be cleaned off, after being rubbed down smooth with pumice stone and water.

Streakiness in the varnish may be caused by the imperfect mixing of driers, oil, or turpentine with the varnish. When it appears on unpainted wood, it may be due to uneven planing or filling-up. Very often an extra coat of varnish will put the thing right.

Varnish not drying. Much of the cheap, poor quality varnish possesses this particular defect. In the use of good varnishes it will very rarely occur, unless there has been some fault in the preparation of the surface or in the manner of applying. Varnish will not dry on a greasy surface. When it is desired to varnish some old work which is probably greasy, an application of weak lime laid over the greasy parts, allowed to dry, and then brushed off will kill the grease. A solution of common washing soda or benzoline will also suffice. Neglect of these precautions (the use of a brush that is not perfectly clean, or of a brush that has been suspended in oil and the oil not eradicated, the use of varnish that has been left uncorked or otherwise exposed to atmospheric influences for a long period) will prevent oil varnish from drying properly.

Varnish that remains quite wet on the article in hand should be cleaned off with turpentine and cotton rag. On no account should flannel or other woollen cloths be used for this purpose. If the varnish is merely tacky—that is, sticky to the touch, but not properly wet—then a coat of terebine (liquid drier) should be given to the work, and afterwards another coat of varnish.

Ropey surface. Much apparently unexplainable trouble arises from the fact that varnish is thoughtlessly exposed to different temperatures before use. Varnish is certain to turn out " ropey " and " curdling " when it has been standing for some time in a cold, damp place and has been brought straight into a warm room and used. On the other hand, it will look poor and thin if brought out of a hot, stuffy place and used straightaway on a cold job, such as outside on a cold or damp day.

Finger-marks may sometimes be removed from varnished work by saturating a piece of chamois leather with sweet oil and applying it gently to them.

Dull varnished surfaces can often be brightened by washing with clean cold water or a mixture of equal parts of vinegar, turpentine, and raw linseed oil, and finally polishing with a piece of chamois leather or soft flannel. Another mixture consists of 1 gill of spirits, 1 pint of raw linseed oil, 1 gill of vinegar, and 1 oz. of butter of antimony. This must be applied very quickly. A vigorous rubbing with a wash-leather is, however, a more desirable means of heightening the lustre of varnish than the use of the above mixtures, as there is then no fear of any ill after-effects, such as the cracking of the varnish, which may occur as a result of a too liberal use of these mixtures or by employing inferior materials.

Testing varnishes. Varnishes may be tested by spreading them upon a piece of plate glass, and by using them upon a flat, white painted ground or a white piece of wood well sized to prevent absorption. The former method is the test for hardness, drying and tenacity; the latter for colour, fineness, body, and flow. One of the good qualities of varnish is that it should dry throughout, and not merely skin over hard on the surface. This may be tested by using the varnish as if it were gold size, putting it on rather freely, and as soon as tacky gilding it. If it is a varnish that dries superficially first, it will cause the gold to wrinkle in a few hours, and the greater this wrinkling the more faulty the varnish is in this respect. This is, however, by no means the most important point to consider in a good varnish, as some of the best have this fault, especially finishing varnishes. A method of testing the elasticity of a varnish is to apply two coats of it on a piece of tin, and when dry to bend the tin; or coat a sheet of parchment paper or linen, and after it has properly dried try its flexibility or tendency to chip off by crumpling the material between the hands.

General hints. In applying varnish to the work the following points must be attended to. Flow on a good body of varnish, and do not rub it out barely; rather put on as much as you can without allowing it to run.

Uniformity. Be careful to lay it equally over the whole surface, not thinner in one part than another. Do not allow it to accumulate in corners, crevices, quirks, or mouldings, and all such places where it will gather and wrinkle, even if it does not flow out over the adjoining piece of plain surface and produce unsightly runs. Do not work it about unnecessarily; it must not be crossed and re-crossed, but judgment must be used to place it exactly where required straightway, without any unnecessary after-spreading.

Undercoats. When giving undercoats of varnish which are to be rubbed down, it is best to use less than for a finishing coat, as if the coat be a thick heavy one it will take too long to harden sufficiently to rub down with safety and certainty. The edges of the wet varnish must not be allowed to set before attempting to join on with another patch, but must be kept well alive. A perfect job of varnishing cannot be produced with less than three coats, of which the first must be well felted down with pumice stone.

Double-coating. In ordinary practice it is sometimes useful to double-coat work instead of felting down and re-varnishing. A very fine gloss can be got in this way. Give the work a medium coat of varnish, and when this is tacky (not dry) repeat a coat of the same varnish, working very lightly and rapidly, taking care not to work up the undercoating. Great care and skill are required to do this perfectly, as the less hard the undercoat is the finer will the gloss and finish be. No preparation of any kind must be used between the two coats.

Straining. Oil varnish ought not to require straining, but if by reason of accidental agitation or other cause it does require it, the straining is best accomplished by lightly plugging a wide-nosed funnel with about an inch and a half of cotton wadding, and tying a bit of coarse muslin over the nozzle to keep it in ; the varnish is then allowed to trickle through of its own weight. A fine cambric or linen handkerchief makes a fairly good strainer.

CHAPTER XLII : LACQUER WORK

CHINESE lacquer work is, as its name implies, an oriental art, and authentically is applied only to furniture of a particular period and style. Chippendale pieces, for example, offer excellent scope for its application. When, however, the ornament or decoration is omitted, the basis of the art can be used with excellent results on any furniture—especially modern pieces.

FIG. 57. BLACK LACQUERED BUREAU ON STAND.

Furniture treated in this way may be made up from any wood—whitewood being as good as any for the purpose. A variety of odd timber in the same job makes no difference.

Materials. For materials the following are required :

Flat white lead undercoating, turpentine, linseed oil, whiting, jelly size, white polish, pumice powder, one or two flat paint brushes —not more than 2 in., a camel hair mop, and some middle 2 glasspaper. Should there be knots in the wood, a little knotting will be wanted also. All can be obtained from a good-class colourman.

Cleaning up. First, clean up the work with glasspaper, and, should any knots be visible, paint these over with knotting. The quantities of materials used must be governed by the job in hand : in any case, purchase only a small amount of each; it will go a long way.

Undercoating. Commence with a 1-lb. tin of flat white lead undercoating. Stir up this with a stick, digging it well up from the bottom until it is thoroughly mixed, then pour it into a paint kettle or similar vessel. Add to this turpentine and linseed oil in equal parts until it is very thin. This preparation *must* be thin, and not applied in any solid manner as in painting. It must be used as a priming, and should therefore soak into the wood rather than lie on the surface.

Paint it over the entire woodwork, inside as well if this is open to observation. Do not be afraid of brush marks, but put plenty on, in any direction, so long as it is evenly distributed. The work must now be left until quite dry—at least twelve hours.

Groundwork. Now the whiting must be slacked by breaking up the lumps in a receptacle and covering with water. It should be left overnight. When the job is *quite* dry, proceed with the manufacture of the groundwork preparation, which is called gesso. First, strain off the water from the whiting, and gradually warm it up on a *low* gas. Stir at intervals to prevent caking or burning. While this is warming up put some size in another receptacle—a steamer on the lines of a glue pot is best. Use a little less size than the amount of whiting used and melt it down; then, stirring all the time, add about a dessertspoonful of *boiling* linseed oil and a couple of brushfuls of hot glue. When well mixed, continue stirring, and add by degrees the whiting. On no account allow it to boil. This preparation is the groundwork of the lacquer.

To make gesso for all raised ornament seen on Chinese lacquer work, the same process is observed, with the addition of a little resin in the linseed oil—the resin hardens it, while the oil keeps it from becoming brittle. When the gesso is cold, it will be set in a very stiff paste, therefore it must be used when warm.

With a large brush paint it over the entire job. Put on plenty. Do not work the stuff out, but just lay it on thick in every direction—never mind the brush marks, only be sure to cover all the work. When this is dry (which will be from two to six hours) another application is necessary. The gesso will have to be warmed up first. Do not make it *too* hot—*never let it boil*—just allow it to steam and run easily.

When the second coat is dry, paper it down with some middle 2 paper wrapped around a block, and finish off with a finer paper. The result should be a perfect surface, as smooth and burnished as a piece of glass—if not the work must receive another coat and be papered down until the surface is perfect.

Colouring. Of the colours in Chinese lacquer work, black, red, and green are the most used. Any other colours may be used, however, for a job on modern lines. Whatever the colour procure it ground in turps. A ½-lb. tin is about right for any ordinary job.

Put a quantity of the colour in a paint kettle or similar vessel and well mix with equal parts of turpentine and Japan gold size. See that it is quite fluid and in no wise thick. Paint or rather flow it with the brush over the work; do not scrub or use undue pressure—just flow it on. The brush marks will run in together, forming a perfectly ribless surface, and when dry will have a matt or dull appearance without any suggestion of shine.

When dry go over the whole job with a camel hair mop dipped in white polish. Put the polish on quickly and evenly and avoid going over a place twice, because the polish dries almost at once, and in doubling back on it, it may be dragged up, leaving an ugly mark. Allow from half to one hour to harden.

Get a can of water and some pumice powder—separately, not mixed. Dip a good-sized piece of rag in the water to make it quite wet, and dab it in the pumice powder. Work it in a circular motion all over the job, using a little pressure. At intervals use more water and pumice.

This is the final groundwork process and makes a perfect surface by grinding and burnishing away any grit, dust or irregularities, etc. Clean up with a soft dry cloth. There should now be a wonderfully smooth and burnished surface as flawless and perfect as a piece of glass, without the slightest suggestion of stickiness so often noticeable in painted pieces.

If you do not intend to pick out the mouldings in a colour or in gold or silver, the job is finished as a plain piece and has only to be french polished.

CHAPTER XLIII: POLYESTER LACQUERS

THE term *polyester* refers to resins which were originally used only in the plastics industry but which have recently been modified for use as woodfinishing lacquers. For this reason these are often described as " plastic " lacquers; also, because they are cured or hardened by the addition of a catalyst, are sometimes described as *catalyst* finishes.

It has long been the aim of the research chemist to produce a wood finish, one coat of which would give an adequate film and which would have all the qualities desired such as good ageing, clarity, hardness, high resistance to abrasion, heat, solvents, etc. Polyester lacquers are the nearest approach so far attained to this ideal.

It must be made clear from the outset that the various lacquers of this type, although basically the same, are prepared in different ways, and it is therefore absolutely essential to follow the maker's instructions precisely. However, many of them consist of resin dissolved in styrene, this being hardened by premixing a given proportion of the catalyst—sometimes known as the *initiator*. For cold curing it is usually also necessary to add another hardener known as the *accelerator*.

The resultant mix may, for all practical purposes, be considered as 100% solids because evaporation of the solvent styrene is almost negligible. This does, in fact, combine chemically with the polyester resin to form a solid film. Further, since the film hardens solely by chemical action, it is safe to apply fairly thick coats. These will indeed harden just as quickly as thin coats.

In the original product the proportion of catalyst and accelerator to be added to the polyester/styrene mixture was in the order of 2%, which made preparation difficult because thorough and precise mixing was necessary or the film would not harden. Various systems are now in use to simplify things. In one system the bulk of the catalyst is increased considerably by adding styrene so that the resin/catalyst ratio for premixing is in the region of 3 : 1 which can be done much more accurately. At the same time the accelerator is mixed with the resin at the factory. This may be done because the accelerator has no effect on the resin/styrene solution except in the presence of the catalyst. In production work another solution is to use a two-component spray-gun which mixes the ingredients correctly in the spray cone.   In still another product the hardening agent is incorporated in the material by the manufacturer and does not become active until the lacquer is applied to the surface.

Polyester lacquers may be applied by brush, spray, and, in at least one case, by fad.   The final surface needs to be flatted and burnished or matted as required.   It cannot be pulled-over.   Most films are dust free in a few minutes and may be worked on with abrasives after the full curing time.   Full hardness is not attained for several days.   Flat with 350 silicon carbide and soapy water, followed by No. 400.   After wash-leathering finish with a polishing compound to a clear bright surface.   The lacquer is best applied to horizontal surfaces.   Consider that when most finishes are applied there is rapid solvent evaporation and consequent rapid increase in viscosity which tends to prevent the formation of sags and runs.   However, as explained, there is negligible solvent loss in polyesters which makes it rather more difficult than usual to obtain uniform films on vertical surfaces.   On the other hand the fact that there is so little solvent loss practically eliminates sinkage so that grain filling, even on open pored woods, is unnecessary.   Fillers, if they are used, must be of special formulation.

Either water stains or special stains for polyesters may be used. Other stains, especially oil stains, are liable to affect film adhesion. It has to be remembered that although the film is highly heat resistant the styrene in which the resin is dissolved is highly inflammable. It has also an unpleasant smell and is slightly toxic, so that good ventilation is desirable.

The cured polyester film will not respond to the usual stripping agents.   If the film has to be repaired it must be scraped or buffed away.   It is important to keep the catalyst and accelerator off the skin.   Any spots should be washed away immediately.   It is necessary also not to mix the catalyst and accelerator alone by mistake as the mixture would be liable to explosion.   After the ingredients have been mixed or prepared to instructions it must be used within a given time—its pot-life—which may vary from $\frac{1}{2}$ to 24 hours. Also if the main material is not used within a certain time—usually from about 3 to 12 months, its shelf-life—it may become unusable.

CHAPTER XLIV: AGENTS USED IN WOOD FINISHING

P = poisonous.   H = harmful to touch.

Acetic acid 6%. Used in some furniture revivers and for removing ink stains.

Alkanet root. Used chiefly for making red oil (page 202). The roots are 4–6 in. long and anything up to ½ in. thick.

American potash is used for the weathering of oak (page 99). It turns the wood a deep brown, causing the figure to become almost black. Subsequent treatment with chloride of lime turns it grey. P.H.

Ammonia. Used chiefly for fuming oak (page 101), but is also useful for adding to water stain as it helps to drive the latter into the grain (page 201). Obtain ·880 (ask for " point eight-eighty " ammonia) and keep well corked as it speedily loses its strength when exposed to the air. P.H. Rock ammonia is used for some polish strippers (page 206).

Aniline dyes are obtainable in many colours and soluble in water, spirits, or oil. P, usually. The kind required should be stated when ordering. The prices of the different colours vary. Shades of chief value to the polisher are :

  black, blue, crimson, magenta, orange, red, yellow,
  bismarck brown, vandyke brown, green, maroon, purple.

The dyes are used for making stains (page 15) and for tinting polish (page 199). Colours can be blended with each other, but the three kinds water, spirit, and oil cannot be mixed together.

Asphaltum is used chiefly for making a dark brown stain (see Jacobean stain, page 202). It is of dark brown colour and looks like broken pieces of pitch. Soluble in turpentine.

Benzoin or gum benzoin. A resin used for making glaze (page 199). It is in the form of small blocks or pieces and looks like a mass of dried twigs compressed together in which are white specks. The more of the latter the better the quality.

Benzoline. Sometimes used to remove excessive oil in varnishing (page 186). P.

Berlin black. See drop black.

Bichromate of potash. Purchased in crystals of a deep orange shade. Used chiefly for making stain for mahogany (page 201). Can also be used for oak. P.

Bismarck brown. An aniline dye of fiery red colour. If used too strong it has a greenish hue. It is very strong and should be used cautiously. A little goes a long way. P.

Borax. Used in some strippers (page 135) ; also for water varnishes (page 167).

Brown umber. A brown pigment which can be worked up in water or turpentine. Mixed with water and bound with glue-size it makes a cheap water coating for inexpensive furniture backs (page 203).

Brunswick black. A thick black liquid drying with a shine. Used in woodwork for floor stains, for which purpose it is thinned out (page 203).

Burnt umber. Similar to brown umber but of deeper tone.

Butter of antimony. A dark brown liquid which has a slight hardening effect on polish. Used in making furniture revivers (page 200). P. H.

Camphor. Used in some furniture revivers (page 200). P.

Camphorated oil. A mixture of four parts olive oil and one part camphor. Used for the removal of heat and water marks on a polished surface (page 125). P.

Carbon tetrachloride. Used chiefly for degreasing. Chief use in woodwork is on greasy woods before gluing. P. H.

Carborundum powder. An abrasive obtainable in various grades. The fine grade is used in making the black coating for blackboards to give a bite to the chalk (page 204).

Caustic potash. Used as a stripper for polish, paint, etc. (page 205). It tends to darken some woods and should be used with care. P. H.

Cellulose nitrate or nitrocellulose, the main chemical material used in making cellulose polishes. It is mostly derived from the cotton plant.

China clay. Used for making paste wood filler (page 30).

Chloride of lime. Imparts a greyish tone to oak. Is used in the weathered finish (page 99).

Copal. A gum used in the manufacture of varnishes which have an oil basis (page 167). It comes from Africa and has the appearance of a pale, yellowish resin, though some varieties are darker.

Copperas. There are three kinds ;

  Green copperas (sulphate of iron) P.
  Blue copperas (copper sulphate) P.
  White copperas (sulphate of zinc) P.

Of these the first is the most useful to the polisher. The crystals are dissolved in water which assumes a muddy greenish colour. Its effect on the wood is chemical. It is used to kill the redness of mahogany when the latter has to imitate walnut (page 111). It can also be used on oak to give a blue-grey tone The strength depends upon the effect required and the wood on which it is used. It can vary from a slight grey tone to an Air Force blue. It should be tried out on the same wood as that used in the job in hand.

Blue copperas with the addition of liquid ammonia can also be used, but generally is not as effective as green copperas. Both should be sealed with white polish before filling with plaster and water.

Copper sulphate.   See copperas.

Crocus powder.   A fine abrasive used for dusting over a polished surface to dull it.

Dragon's blood.   A red agent for colouring polishes.   It has been largely superseded by aniline dyes.

Drop black.   Obtained in the form of a thick paste which is thinned with turps.   It is used sometimes in ebonising and in the preparation of blackboards (page 203).   Dries without shine.

Emery powder.   An abrasive sometimes used in the preparation of blackboards.   It gives a bite to the chalk.   Also used for rubbing down varnished work (page 178).

Eosin powder.   A red powder used in water stains to warm the tone.   See also aniline dyes.

Flake white.   A white powder sometimes mixed with white polish for lightening the tone of the wood.   P.

French chalk.   A finely powdered white powder used in making the half-filling for oak to be french polished (page 204).   It is really a form of talc, an acid magnesium metasilicate.   It is of a slippery nature, hence its use for dance floors.   An entirely different substance from vienna chalk.

Fuller's earth.   Used in varnishing for removing oiliness (page 172).

Gas-black.   A preparation made by suspending a sheet of tin over a fish-tail gas burner.   Used chiefly in ebonising (Chapter XIV).

Glue-size.   Sometimes used as a partial filling for deal before the application of polish (page 113).   Also used in the preparation of water coatings, in which it acts as a binder (page 203).

Gold size.   A quick-drying varnish normally used for the application of gold leaf and gold paint.   It is also a useful binder for colours ground in turps.   Sometimes used in making paste fillers (page 204).

Gum benzoin.   See benzoin.

Hydrogen peroxide.   Used for bleaching.   100 vol. is generally used diluted with 2 parts water.   Some chemists supply not less than 2 gallons.   P.

Hyposulphite of soda.   This is the chemical used in photography.   It is sometimes useful for removing iodine stains (page 84).

Lamp-black. A black powder colour used for water coating (page 17). Also in ebonising and for black wax polishes (page 200).

Lime. Unslaked lime is used for the limed oak finish (page 98). Also used in the antique oak finish (page 105). P. H. if hands damp.

Linseed oil is derived from the seed of the flax plant and can be obtained either raw or boiled. It takes up oxygen on exposure to the air and is thus a *drying* oil. Boiling makes the oil dry more rapidly.

Raw oil is used in french polishing for killing the whiteness of filler, in lubricating the rubber, and for making red oil. It is also used in oil polishing and in the manufacture of putty. Paint makers use the raw oil for light shades and boiled oil for darker tones.

Raw linseed oil is somewhat viscid, fairly clear, and is brownish yellow in colour. It is used for lubricating the rubber in polishing.

Boiled linseed oil is of a reddish brown tinge, and is rather more viscid than the raw.

Linters. Portion of the cotton plant left sticking to the pod after the picking process. Used for conversion into nitrocellulose.

Litharge. A pinkish powder used in colouring (page 97). P.

Logwood. The heartwood of a tree found in Central America, which, when cut into chips, is soaked and boiled in water. It is used as a basis for stains, but discretion must be used since its shade varies in accordance with other substances with which it comes into contact. It may vary from red, straw colour, purple, to black.

Mastic. A resinous gum, pale yellow in colour when fresh and inclining to darken when kept. It is used in varnish making.

Methylated finish. See methylated spirits. P.

Methylated spirits. This is used mostly for making french polish and stains. It is ordinary alcohol with wood spirit, etc., added to make it undrinkable, in which form it is sold free of duty. There are several kinds of mixtures permitted by the Customs and Excise to be produced for various purposes, and they are all subject to regulations. French polish manufacturers use industrial methylated spirits, known as " I.M.S.," but this is not obtainable by the general public. P.

That sold in oil shops is coloured and is made further unpalatable by the addition of wood spirit, mineral spirit, pyridine, and methyl violet dye. French polish can be made with this successfully because the colouring effect is small and soon fades. A better method, however, is to use "methylated finish." This is colourless, but contains three ounces of resin per gallon. This resin may be common rosin (this is the more usual as it is a cheaper substance), or it may be white lac. For the purpose of polish making " methylated spirit white lac " is more suitable, and can generally be obtained if specified.

Mineral oil. See white mineral oil.

Naphtha. Used sometimes in spirit varnishing to remove ridges (page 181). P.

Nitric acid. A chemical sometimes used in the manufacture of stains, and also used to remove ink stains. It is also used in the pickling process on pine. P.

Nitrocellulose. (See cellulose nitrate.)

Oxalic acid. Used chiefly for bleaching wood and for removing stains. It is made and used as described on page 206. As bought it is in the form of small crystals. Being a poison, care should be taken not to leave it about, and to avoid contact with the fingers. If it cannot be avoided, wash well after using. P.

Ox gall. Used in the acid finish for french polish (page 56).

Paraffin, medicinal. Used as a lubricant for the polishing rubber on light woods.

Pearl ash. Sometimes used for stripping off old polish, varnish, etc.

Permanganate of potash. Obtained in the form of fine crystals. It is sometimes used for making a stain, producing a deep, rich brown, but it is not really satisfactory as the colour is fugitive. Strong solution P.

Plaster of paris. Used chiefly as a filler before french polishing. The " superfine " grade obtainable at most oil shops should be used. It must be kept in a dry place.

Plasticiser. Used in cellulose polish to cure the brittleness of the nitrocellulose film.

Poppy oil. Preferred by some workers as a lubricant for the polishing rubber.

Potash. See under American, caustic, bichromate, etc.

Powder colours. These are used chiefly for tinting plaster of paris when making wood filler (page 27), though they are also handy for water coating (page 17). Useful colours are vandyke brown, brown umber, burnt umber, raw sienna, yellow ochre, venetian red, red ochre, lamp-black, flake white.

Precipitated chalk. Sometimes used in the acid finish as a substitute for vienna chalk when the latter is unobtainable.

Pull-over. A levelling solution used in the cellulose finish, producing an even and bright lustre.

Pumice powder. A white powder obtainable in various grades. It is useful as a fine abrasive and is sometimes used in the polishing and varnishing processes for taking out the roughness of a surface. The usual plan in polishing is to use it in a pounce bag, this being dabbed on to the work, leaving a fine deposit of powder which is taken up by the polishing rubber. The finest grade should be used.

Pyrogallic acid. Sometimes used in the fuming process, in which it produces a warm tone (page 16).

Reckitt's blue. Used in the ebonising process to make black polish a deeper and more intense black (page 77).

Red oil. See alkanet root.

Red sanders. The heartwood of an Indian tree. Small splinterings are used for dyeing the spirits used in making french polish, producing a blood-red shade (page 33).

Resin used in cellulose polish to give toughness, lustre, and increased adhesion.

Rose pink. A powder colour used for tinting plaster-of-paris filling (page 204).

Rosin. Added to wax polish to give a harder finish (page 89).

Rottenstone. A fine abrasive (finer than pumice powder) and sometimes used in the pounce bag (see pumice powder). Also known as Tripoli powder.

Russian tallow. Occasionally used as a filler (page 204), but it never hardens properly. Often used in polishing coffins.

Sandarac. A pale yellow resin used in making spirit varnish.

Shellac. This is the basis of all french polishes. Most of it comes from the Calcutta and Mirzapur districts and is derived from the exudation of the lac insect. It varies in colour considerably. White shellac is merely an orange shellac bleached with chemicals to lighten it, and " pulled out " in a similar method to that used by the toffee maker, and looks rather like sticks or knots of thick white toffee. It should be kept under water or stored in damp sawdust as it quickly becomes denatured if exposed to the air. The other shellacs are in the form of thin flakes. The following are the shellacs normally obtainable, given in the order of their colour :

White, orange, button, garnet.

The button shellac has the reputation for being rather harder than the others, but is inclined to make a somewhat muddy polish.

Silex. A powder substance used in making paste filler (page 204).

Soda. Ordinary washing soda is useful for removing grease from a surface. It must not be used strong or it will strip off polish, and all traces must be washed off with clear water.

Sodium perborate. Sometimes used in the bleaching process.

Spirits of camphor. Used in some furniture revivers (page 133). P.

Sulphate of copper. See copperas.

Sulphate of iron. See copperas.

Sulphate of zinc. See copperas.

Sulphuric acid. Used for the acid finish in french polishing (page 55). P. H.

Tannic acid. Used sometimes in the fuming of oak (page 16).

Terebine. A drying agent sometimes used in correcting faults in varnished work (page 186). P.

Toppings. The clear liquid suspended above the stock solution of white french polish. It is strained off the polish and sometimes used as a finishing glaze. It cannot be bought ready-made.

Tripoli powder. A fine abrasive used for dulling the extreme gloss of french polished and cellulosed work (pages 87 and 160). See also rottenstone.

Turpentine. Used for making many oil stains and in making wax polish. Many substitutes are on the market owing to the high cost of pure turps, and some contain oils of the petroleum class which may act as a bleaching agent. Pure American turpentine is the best.

Vandyke brown. A brown powder used for making stains, and for water coating. It will not mix directly with water. Add it to ammonia to form a paste and mix this with warm water and glue-size. A better stain is made with vandyke crystals (*q.v.*).

Vandyke crystals. Obtainable in crystals and used for making a deep brown stain (page 201). Sometimes known as walnut crystals.

Venetian red. Used for mixing with plaster-of-paris filler to tint to a reddish tone.

Vienna chalk. A form of precipitated chalk. It is a white and soft variety of slaked lime containing magnesia. It is used in conjunction with sulphuric acid in the acid finish for french polish (page 55). As a substitute use ordinary precipitated chalk.

Vinegar. Frequently used in furniture revivers (page 200). It helps to remove grease, oil, etc.

Walnut crystals. See vandyke crystals.

Wax. Used in wax polishing. The chief kinds are : beeswax—bleached and unbleached ; Japan wax ; ozokerite wax ; paraffin wax ; and carnauba wax.

Beeswax. The unbleached wax is of a yellow to brown colour suitable for dark woods. For light woods the bleached wax should be used. Beeswax is the basis of most wax polishes.

Japan wax. Sometimes mixed with beeswax in making wax polishes.

Ozokerite wax. A natural earth wax also used with beeswax.

Paraffin wax. A petroleum product of a whitish colour, used for light wax polishes.

Carnauba wax. A vegetable product used for making wax polish harder. In purified form it is of a pale yellowish shade. Polish made entirely with carnauba wax gives a very hard finish, but with repeated coats is inclined to flake. It is more satisfactory used with softer waxes.

For details of making and using wax polishes see page 200. Wax is also used in making stopping (page 204).

White mineral oil. Used as a lubricant for the rubber when french polishing (page 34).

White spirit (turps substitute). Used in making some oil stains, and for cleaning. Should be as free from grease as possible. Test by soaking blotting paper and leave to dry. Good quality will dry out without residue. Greasy turps will leave a greasy deposit.

Whiting. Used in making putty (page 205) and for some wood fillers (page 205).

Yellow ochre. A powder colour used in colouring wood fillers and for water coating (page 17).

Zinc white. A powder used in liming (see page 99). Ask for zinc white " dry."

CHAPTER XLV : RECIPES

FRENCH POLISHES

WHITE **polish.** Dissolve 7–8 oz. bleached shellac in a pint of methylated spirits. Crush the shellac and dry it before a fire before using. The shellac is best kept in damp sawdust, hence the necessity for drying.

Transparent polish. Dissolve 7–8 oz. bleached and dewaxed shellac in a pint of methylated spirits.

Orange (or brown) polish. Dissolve 6–7 oz. orange shellac in a pint of methylated spirits.

Button polish. Dissolve 6 oz. button shellac in a pint of methylated spirits.

Garnet polish. Dissolve 6 oz. garnet shellac in a pint of methylated spirits.

Black polish. Dissolve ½ oz. spirit black aniline dye in 1 pint white french polish (see above). Strain through two thicknesses of muslin. For a richer black add a piece of Reckitt's blue about the size of a filbert nut.

Red polish. Dissolve ¼ oz. spirit bismarck brown aniline dye in 1½ pints orange polish (see above). Strain through muslin. Alternatively steep 2 oz. red sanders in 1 pint orange polish (see above). Strain through muslin.

Coloured polishes. Dissolve any of the spirit aniline dyes— yellow, brown, scarlet, mauve, green, blue, etc., in french polish. For yellow, mauve, green, and blue use white polish. Orange polish is generally used for brown and scarlet, though white can be used.

Quantity of dye is $\frac{1}{4}$ oz. to $\frac{1}{2}$ oz., according to required tone. **Do not use strong.** Strain through muslin.

Brush polish. Dissolve 4 oz. orange shellac and 2 ozs. gum sandarac in a pint of methylated spirits. A tablespoonful of crushed resin can be added to make a varnish for toys.

Glaze. Dissolve 5–6 oz. crushed benzoin in 1 pint methylated spirits. Allow to stand a few days and strain through muslin.

WAX POLISHES

Normal polish. Shred yellow or brown beeswax and dissolve in pure American turpentine. Speed up process by heating the container in a basin of hot water. Consistency should be that of a thin paste. A small amount of carnauba wax can be added to harden the polish, but this is not essential. For notes on dissolving carnauba wax see page 90.

Light polish. As normal polish (above), but use bleached wax.

Extra light polish. Shred five parts paraffin wax and one part carnauba wax and dissolve in pure American turpentine.

Antique polish. To the normal polish (page 199) add lamp-black powder, stirring in whilst polish is still molten. Mix thoroughly.

White polish. To light wax polish add zinc white powder until it becomes white. This polish is used chiefly to form a white deposit in the open grain of the wood.

Petrol (lighter) is sometimes added to wax polish to speed up evaporation.

POLISH REVIVERS

1.
1 part raw linseed oil
1 part vinegar.

2.
1 part raw linseed oil
1 part vinegar
1 part methylated spirits.

3.
$\frac{1}{2}$ pint vinegar
$\frac{1}{2}$ pint methylated spirits
1 oz. camphor (dissolved in the spirits)
1 oz. raw linseed oil
$\frac{1}{2}$ oz. butter of antimony.

4.
4 parts raw linseed oil
1 part terebine
12 parts vinegar.

5.
Boil 1 pint of distilled water and add to it about $\frac{1}{4}$ lb. castile soap powder. Let the soap powder dissolve completely. In a separate tin pour in 1 pint of best American turps and add to it 2 oz. of best beeswax and 2 oz. of white paraffin wax. Heat these by putting the tin in a basin of boiling water—do not heat over a flame.

When the wax is completely dissolved, shoot the whole into the distilled water and allow to cool. After twenty-four hours it will be ready for use. Always stir up thoroughly first. If castile soap powder cannot be obtained shred a cake of any good quality soap.

FURNITURE POLISHES OR CREAMS

1.

6 parts carnauba wax
$3\frac{1}{2}$ parts Japan wax
$1\frac{1}{2}$ parts paraffin wax.

Melt waxes together, stir well and add about same quantity of turps. Continue stirring and add a little french chalk and ammonia.

2.

6 parts carnauba wax
$3\frac{1}{2}$ parts Japan wax
$1\frac{1}{2}$ parts paraffin wax
12 parts turpentine (pure American)
3 parts white curd soap, shredded.
30 parts water.

STAINS

Walnut water stain. Suitable for oak and for walnut if well diluted. Can also be used on mahogany for the more sombre tones if diluted. Dissolve vandyke crystals in warm water. If there is any sediment strain through muslin. The amount of crystals can be varied to suit the depth of colour required. The addition of about a tablespoonful of ·880 ammonia will make the stain more penetrating and of slightly darker colour.

Bichromate stain. The most universal stain for use on mahogany, on which it gives a deep, cold brown. Used on oak it produces a slightly greenish brown tone. It is effective on any wood containing tannin. Dissolve bichromate crystals in water to make a concentrated solution, i.e. one in which the water will absorb no more. This is full strength and can be diluted as required. It is of a rich orange tint which, however, bears no resemblance to the deep brown shade it produces in the wood. It is useless for deal, pine, or American whitewood, on which it has no effect.

Ammonia. This, used in liquid form, will darken oak and mahogany somewhat, giving a rather cold tint. Use ·880 ("point eight-eighty") and avoid standing over the work, as the fumes are strong. Only a slight darkening is produced, a far more effective way of using ammonia being fuming (page 15). Chestnut takes on a good colour when treated with ammonia. Avoid handling ammonia with the fingers as it can be painful.

Aniline dyes. These should be used with care because the colours are violent, and many of them entirely unorthodox for woodwork. They can be obtained soluble in water, oil, or methylated spirits. Make up a fairly strong solution, and when entirely dissolved strain through muslin to get rid of the sediment. Bottle and dilute as required. A spoonful of glue added to water stain will act as a binder. For spirit stain add the same amount of french polish. Oil stain is mixed with turps, and a little gold size added.

Varying shades can be produced by mixing colours, but make up the individual stains first and mix the liquids as needed. It is easier to judge the tone in this way. The shades of value are:

black, blue, crimson, magenta, orange, red, yellow, bismarck brown, vandyke brown, green, maroon, and purple.

It is obviously impossible to mix spirit-soluble anilines with those intended for water. State which is needed when purchasing.

Jacobean stain. One of the most satisfactory is walnut water stain (above). Another can be made with aniline water or spirit vandyke brown. The addition of a little bismarck brown or black will make the tone warmer or colder as required. See notes under Aniline dyes.

Asphaltum also gives a good rich brown stain. The asphaltum, which looks like pieces of broken pitch, is dissolved in turpentine, the vessel being heated in hot water, glue-kettle fashion. When fully dissolved strain through muslin and add a tablespoonful of gold size to each pint of stain to act as a binder. This can be used on deal, American whitewood, or satin walnut, on which it produces a rich walnut shade.

Red oil. Although not strictly a stain this is used for warming the colour of pale mahogany. Alkanet root is used, this being in the form of short sticks which are bruised with the hammer. About ¼ lb. of these are steeped in a pint of raw linseed oil and allowed to remain for two or three days. Stir occasionally and strain through muslin. A little turpentine (one tablespoonful to a pint of oil) can be added to increase its spreading power. It is used chiefly on mahogany, though pale walnut can be improved by its use. It is applied before polishing. Try its effect first, however, for the redness can be easily overdone. It can of course be diluted with oil. Today oil-soluble red aniline dye is usually used.

Ebony stain. Aniline spirit black dissolved in methylated spirits with a spoonful of french polish added makes a good deep black. Alternatively, use aniline water black with a spoonful of glue added to act as a binder. See notes for preparation under aniline dyes. Another stain is drop-black, ground in turpentine and mixed with turps, with about ½ oz. gold size to each pint added as a binder.

Mahogany stain. For darkening real mahogany use bichromate of potash (see bichromate stain). A cheap stain for deal to resemble mahogany is made with 1 oz. burnt sienna ground in water, ¼ pint stale beer, and ½ pint warm water. Add a tablespoonful of hot glue to act as a binder. Use warm. This can be used on satin walnut which is to resemble mahogany. It may be desirable to fad in with red polish to warm the tone.

Floor stain. For a new floor vandyke crystals can be used (see walnut water stain). Alternatively, use aniline water colour. The vandyke brown colour is effective for an oak or walnut shade, or a little bismarck brown can be added for a warmer mahogany shade. See notes on mixing, under Aniline dyes.

For an old floor which is likely to be greasy an oil or spirit stain is more effective. Thin down some burnt umber ground in oil with raw linseed oil and turpentine and add a little liquid drier. For a mahogany tone substitute venetian red ground in oil for the burnt umber. If the floor is to be waxed it is essential that it is fixed first with a coat of either shellac polish or varnish.

Brunswick black thinned with turpentine makes an effective floor stain, giving anything from a light to a deep brown according to the amount of turps added. For a dark shade a second coat can be added after the first has dried. Fix with french polish brushed on, or with varnish if the floor is to be waxed.

Asphaltum can be used—see notes under Jacobean stain. Even with the addition of the gold-size binder the stain may be inclined to lift if polished vigorously with a turpentine wax polish. It should therefore be fixed with a coat of shellac polish.

Aniline spirit colour can also be used. It should have a little french polish added to bind it. For preparation see Aniline dyes.

Mahogany-walnut stain. For toning mahogany to resemble walnut, green copperas can be used. Dissolve the crystals in water, this producing a pale blue shade. Apply weak, testing on a spare piece of wood. If used too strong the wood will have a bluish tint. For further notes, see page 111.

Colour coating. This is not staining, strictly speaking, but may be dealt with here conveniently. It consists of mixing powder colours with water and binding with glue-size. It thus forms a sort of water paint which is handy for covering backs and similar parts when a cheap wood has been used. All blemishes in the wood are thus concealed. Take any of these dry powder colours—burnt umber and vandyke brown are dark browns, raw sienna is yellow, red ochre is a reddish brown, etc.—and mix with water. The powders are not really absorbed by the water, and if used without a binder will brush off as the water dries out. Use warm water and stir well, adding about ½ lb. size to each quart of water. The amount of colour can be decided by the effect required. Stir the mixture every time the brush is dipped in. Apply warm. Note that this coating is a cheap finish only and is generally used to cover up poor material. It should never be used for work to be polished.

Blackboard coating.

1. Give coat of paint priming. When dry rub down and give coat of special blackboard composition made for the purpose. The following can be used at a pinch though they are not so satisfactory.

2. Give coat of black priming paint. Rub down when dry and give a second coat to which has been added some fine pumice powder—about 2 tablespoonfuls to the pint.

3. Stain with water or spirit ebony stain. You can make this with water or spirit aniline black, or you can use lamp-black bound with glue-size. Allow to dry, rub down evenly, and give a second coat if it appears too pale. Thin out some drop-black with turps so that it works freely without being too pale. To a pint of this add a dessertspoonful of gold size, and stir in two tablespoonfuls of finely ground carborundum powder. Apply with a brush and give a second coat twelve hours after the first. The carborundum powder gives a bite to the chalk and is bound by the gold size.

4. Stain the board as given above. Mix 2 oz. fine pumice powder, 2 oz. fine carborundum powder, $\frac{1}{4}$ lb. rottenstone, $\frac{1}{4}$ lb. lamp black, and mix with methylated spirits to form a thick paste free from lumps. Thin this down with a quart of thin french polish (5 oz. shellac to a quart of spirits), stirring thoroughly meanwhile. Strain and apply with a wide brush. When dry give a second coat. If it appears too glossy felt it down with a little pumice and water.

FILLERS

Plaster. Superfine plaster with powder colour added to suit wood : rose pink for mahogany ; vandyke brown for walnut or oak, etc. Apply as described in Chapter V.

Russian tallow. Used as it is and rubbed into the grain, or with whiting or plaster of paris added. This filler never hardens thoroughly and should not be used for good work, but is useful for temporary work such as coffin polishing.

Half-filler for oak. Add handful of french chalk to a pint of french polish. Apply with brush (page 29).

Size filler. Often used for deal. Ordinary glue-size thinned until it no longer feels sticky between the fingers (page 113).

Paste filler. 1 pint boiled linseed oil, $\frac{1}{4}$ pint gold size or brown japan, $\frac{1}{4}$ gill turpentine.

Mix the above together and add china clay or silex little by little until a stiff paste is obtained.   Allow to stand twenty-four hours and thin with turps as required.

Another recipe :

Add to whiting enough powder colour to suit wood—rose pink for mahogany or brown umber for walnut or oak.   Mix well.   Add turpentine to bring to a paste and add about a tablespoonful of gold size to each 1 lb. of whiting mixture.

STOPPING

Cabinet stopping or beaumontage.   Mix equal quantities of beeswax and crushed rosin, add a few flakes of shellac, and melt in a tin.   Stir thoroughly and add powder colour in accordance with wood to be stopped—vandyke brown for walnut and dark oak and red ochre or venetian red for mahogany.   Colour the stopping to match the *stained* tone of the wood.   For light woods finished natural colour no powder colour is needed.   Take care not to burn the wax.   It can be kept in the tin and the latter heated whenever it is used, the molten stopping being applied with a little pointed stick. Alternatively, it can be poured into the corner of a tin box lid, where it will set like a rough stick of sealing wax.   To use this a hot pointed iron is held over the hole and the stopping pressed against it, when it will run down into the hole.   See page 10 for notes on its use.

Plain wax suitably coloured is sometimes used, but it is not so hard as beaumontage.   Sealing wax is an alternative, but although this is hard, it is also brittle.

Polisher's putty.   Mix dried whiting with french polish—white polish when the wood is light.   Put a little drop of polish into the hole, let it set, and press in the stopping.   Allow it to stand proud of the surface.   It will set hard in about half an hour.   Level with glasspaper.   Unless the polish is used first the stopping will not stick.   This stopping will take spirit stain like the surrounding wood.

Plaster stopping.   Suitable for cheap deal work.   Mix plaster of paris with glue and press into the hole.   Allow to set, and level with glasspaper.   This stopping will absorb water stain readily.

Putty.   This is generally used for painted work, though it is occasionally used for wood to be polished.   In the latter case the putty should be coloured with powder colour kneaded into it, vandyke brown or burnt umber for walnut or dark oak, venetian red or red ochre for mahogany.   Putty is made with crushed dried whiting and boiled linseed oil.   Raw oil can be used, but the putty takes longer to set.

STRIPPERS

When it does not matter if the wood becomes darkened by the process, one of the following strippers can be used. In every case all traces of the stripper should be thoroughly washed away with two rinses of clear water, as otherwise any subsequent finish may be attacked. When it is important that the wood is not darkened use a proprietary stripper which is known to be free from any darkening tendency.

Washing soda dissolved in hot water and used fairly strong makes a good polish stripper. Leave on the surface for a while and remove the polish as it softens with either a scraper or a brush.

Caustic potash is a still stronger stripper, used in the same way.

Liquid ammonia (·880) also softens the polish, enabling it to be pushed off with a putty knife or scrubbed off with a brush.

Here is another effective stripper :

$\frac{1}{2}$ lb. rock ammonia, $\frac{1}{2}$ lb. crude soft soap, 1 lb. washing soda, 1 gallon hot water.

Apply with a brush tied to a stick to form a handle, and feed it with pumice powder. Do not handle these strippers, especially those containing ammonia and caustic potash.

BLEACHES

Dissolve oxalic acid in hot water to make a concentrated solution, that is, one in which the water will absorb no more acid. Try 2 oz. in half a pint of water. This can be diluted if required. Wash well down with borax—1 oz. to the $\frac{1}{2}$ gal. water— afterwards, and later with clear water, as any trace of acid may attack any subsequent finish. Oxalic acid is a poison and should be kept from the fingers.

There are several powerful proprietary bleaches which are useful for some work. Used in concentrated form they will take the natural colour out of the wood, turning it almost white. They are thus useful for the treatment of woods before polishing to obtain a bleached effect. They require to be used with care in the correction of dark patches, because although the darkness may be lightened, the tone may be different, so that a patchy effect is produced. The instructions supplied with the product should be followed. Fuller details are given on page 23.

INDEX

INDEX

INDEX

INDEX